W9-ADD-582

Twayne's United States Authors Series

EDITOR OF THIS VOLUME

Warren French

Indiana University

Arthur Miller

Revised Edition

TUSAS 115

PS
3525
.I5156
Z77
1980

ARTHUR MILLER

By LEONARD MOSS

State University College
Geneseo, New York

REVISED EDITION

TWAYNE PUBLISHERS
A DIVISION OF G. K. HALL & CO., BOSTON

Salem Academy and College
Gramley Library
Winston-Salem, N.C. 27108

Copyright © 1980 by G. K. Hall & Co.

Published in 1980 by Twayne Publishers,
A Division of G. K. Hall & Co.
All Rights Reserved

Printed on permanent/durable acid-free paper and bound
in the United States of America

First Printing

Frontispiece photograph of Arthur Miller by Inge Morath.

Photographs of author's interview with Arthur Miller by Toby Gutwill.

Library of Congress Cataloging in Publication Data

Moss, Leonard, 1931–
Arthur Miller.

(Twayne's United States authors series; 115)
Bibliography: p. 144–79
Includes index.
1. Miller, Arthur, 1915–
—Criticism and interpretation.
I. Title.
PS3525.I5156Z77   1980   812′.5′2   79-25071
ISBN 0-8057-7311-8

Dedicated
to the Memory of my Mother
Pauline Miriam Gutwill

Contents

About the Author

Leonard Moss attended three state universities—Oklahoma, Indiana, and California at Berkeley—then went on to teach at another—New York. He has been with SUNY for twenty years, first at Binghamton, now at the College in Geneseo, where he is a professor of comparative literature.

His interest in Arthur Miller goes back to graduate school; he wrote his master's thesis on Miller and Maxwell Anderson at Indiana University in 1954. Twenty-five years later, in connection with this edition of his book, he conducted a long interview with the playwright (included here as an appendix). The encounter, if belated, was wholly satisfying and gave a further dimension to his understanding and appreciation of America's preeminent living dramatist.

Professor Moss's interest in Miller fits in with another subject that goes back to his graduate school concerns—the theory and practice of tragedy. He wrote his dissertation in that area, and later published articles on four major theorists on tragedy, Plato, Aristotle, Hegel, and Nietzsche. Besides Miller, he has written on Aeschylus, Sophocles, Seneca, Milton, and Kafka. Recently he completed an essay on a rhetorical concept in *King Lear*, and if he lives long enough he hopes to realize a lifelong goal—a critique of tragedy.

Preface

After such knowledge, what forgiveness? Think now
History has many cunning passages, contrived corridors
And issues, deceives with whispering ambitions,
Guides us by vanities.

—T. S. Eliot, "Gerontion"

Almost everyone believes that Arthur Miller deserves the title of
"social dramatist"; apparently the only question is whether to call
him a Marxist or a humanist. The first label has had a certain
currency: some critics believe his work presents a socialist
commentary on the economic structure of the United States. "It
would be going beyond the evidence to suggest that he adheres to
any 'line,' whether political or ideological," Tom Driver declares;
"nevertheless, he bears a quasi-Marxist stamp and most of his plays
tend to become mere partisan social critique."[1] William Wiegand
sees Miller as a borrower of Odets's "Marxist" themes—as a
preacher who sermonizes on the pathetic martyrdom of an
oppressed middle class.[2] And Eleanor Clark arrives at this conclusion concerning *Death of a Salesman*: "It is, of course, the
capitalistic system that has done Willy in; the scene in which he is
brutally fired after some forty [*sic*] years with the firm comes
straight from the party line literature of the 'thirties, and the idea
emerges lucidly enough through all the confused motivations of
the play that it is our particular form of money economy that has
bred the absurdly false ideals of both father and sons."[3]

Even when readers and spectators do not go so far as to find
Miller a socialist reformer bent on condemning the faults of
capitalism, they usually take his plays to be pointed critiques of
contemporary values. They feel that his purpose is to render
humane judgment. "The merit in Miller's treatment of his material
lies in a certain clean, moralistic rationalism," writes Harold
Clurman; "his talent is for a kind of humanistic jurisprudence."[4]
Paul West argues that Miller's warning against dedication to

material success supports "Christian existentialism."[5] "He does blame the 'System,'" Henry Popkin claims, through "a liberal parable of hidden evil and social responsibility."[6]

It is quite understandable that Miller should be regarded as a writer with a message, whether affirmative or negative, humane or socialistic. His early socialist associations and his hearing before the House Committee on Un-American Activities in 1956 were widely publicized. In many essays he has affirmed his belief that tragedy "brings us knowledge . . . pertaining to the right way of living in the world."[7] During the Depression—he recalls in an article entitled "The Shadows of the Gods"—he had been impressed by "the powers of economic crisis and political imperatives which had twisted, torn, eroded, and marked everything and everyone I laid eyes on. . . . So that by force of circumstance I came early and unawares to be fascinated by sheer process itself. How things connected. How the native personality of a man was changed by his world, and the harder question, how he could in turn change his world. . . . You can't understand anything unless you understand its relation to its context."[8]

Above all, his plays appear to be vehicles for argumentation. Put in non-Marxian terms, their argument might be summarized as follows: to achieve dignity, to develop their talents, and to avoid self-defeat, individuals must acknowledge and adjust to their limitations rather than obsessively pursue egoistic ambitions. "You can know there's a universe of people outside and you're responsible to it," Chris Keller instructs his father in *All My Sons*.[9] Other lines and situations in the plays can be cited to support a radical social thesis. "Half the Goddam country is gotta go if I go!" Joe Keller shouts in an attempt to justify dishonest business dealings; and in *Death of a Salesman* Biff calls "all wrong" Willy Loman's desire "to come out number-one man."

Is Miller not pointing an accusing finger at a culture that encourages "wrong" values? Is he not campaigning against an uncharitable social order that deprives honest workers of constructive labor, then discards those who are no longer useful (*Focus, Death of a Salesman, A Memory of Two Mondays, The Misfits*)— an order that condones profit criminally gained (*All My Sons*), fosters belief in the inferiority of minority races (*Focus*), and suppresses liberty in the name of a sacred cause (*The Crucible*)? Is he not attacking, in short, a system that is geared to exploit the common man? There are some particularly impatient words spoken by a character in an early unpublished play, *They Too Arise*: "the day is coming Dad when the people are going to take back what's been stolen from them. . . . I'm a Communist because I want the people to take the power that comes with ownership away from the little class of capitalists who have it now."[10] Miller *must* be haranguing his audience on the evils of our "machine civilization" (his term) and on the virtues of communal cooperation.

The purpose of this study is to view Miller in a different light. His plays do register indignant protests against injustice; they do suggest a humanistic thesis on mutual responsibility. In his best writing, however, that thesis is implied in the psychological consequences of fanatic self-assertion, not prescribed in "moralistic" pronouncements on "the right way of living." Miller's forte is to visualize the causal complexities and the intensity of deeply personal motives: his moral insight focuses most clearly upon subjective process. The playwright has well summarized his subject, his ethical bias, and his theatrical perspective in a comment on *After the Fall*: "this play is not 'about' something; hopefully, it is something. And primarily it is a way of looking at man and his human nature as the only source of the violence which has come closer and closer to destroying the race. It is a view which does not look toward social or political ideas as the creators of violence, but into the nature of the human being himself."[11]

As an analysis of a playwright's distinctive "way of looking," this discussion centers its attention upon Miller's technical resources— dialogue styles, narrative conventions, symbolic devices, and structural principles—and undertakes to judge the success with which progressions of personality, theme, and tension have been executed and interrelated. Almost every technical shortcoming can be attributed to a self-conscious attempt by Miller to augment his work's "social" or philosophical significance. When he tries to formulate objective truths about man's place in the "outside world," his language becomes superficial, his structure disorganized. Ironically, when he explores his characters' inward "nature" he comes closest to fulfilling his ambition to write coherent social drama. The plays and essays testify to a persistent artistic dilemma; Arthur Miller's effort to unify social and psychological perspectives has been the source of his accomplishments and his failures as a dramatist.

Preface to the Revised Edition

Although his recent theatrical output has not been prolific, Miller continues to retain his place as America's most notable living playwright. For this edition I have made minor revisions in my original text (1967), added a chapter on *The Price* and *The Creation of the World*, and updated the Chronology, the biographical chapter, the Selected Bibliography, and the Notes and References. I have also included the text of a conversation I had with Miller in the summer of 1979, in which he outlined his present perspective on drama and society. The conversation and his latest plays confirm my interpretation of that perspective.

LEONARD MOSS

State University College
Geneseo, New York

Acknowledgments

I wish to thank Mr. Arthur Miller for his courtesy in responding to my inquiries; the Academic Center Library of the University of Texas for information on its collection of Miller's manuscripts; and the editors of *Modern Drama* and *Educational Theatre Journal* for publishing parts of this book in those journals. In addition, I am grateful to Professors Sheldon Grebstein and John Hagopian for their valuable suggestions, to Professor Carrol Coates, Miss Janet Brown, and Mrs. Francis Hanks for their assistance, and to Professor Sylvia Bowman for her patience and good counsel.

Permission to quote at length from material protected by copyright has been granted by Harcourt, Brace and World, publisher of *Focus* (originally published by Reynal and Hitchcock, 1945), and by Viking Press, publisher of the *Collected Plays* (1957), *The Misfits* (1961), *After the Fall* (1964), *Incident at Vichy* (1965), *The Price* (1968), and *The Creation of the World and Other Business* (1973).

Chronology

1915   Arthur Miller born October 17 in Manhattan, to Isadore and Augusta Miller.

1929   Father's financial position undermined during the Depression; family moves to Brooklyn, New York.

1932   Graduates high school in Brooklyn; works in automobile parts warehouse.

1934   Enrolls in journalism at the University of Michigan.

1936- Receives Hopwood Awards in Drama, University of Michi-
1937   gan, for *No Villain* (1936) and *Honors at Dawn* (1937), and Theatre Guild Bureau of New Plays Award for *They Too Arise*.

1938   Receives Bachelor of Arts, University of Michigan.

1938- Works at various jobs; writes scripts for Federal Theatre
1943   Project, Columbia Workshop (CBS), and Cavalcade of America (NBC).

1940   Marries Mary Grace Slattery.

1944   Tours army camps collecting background material for screenplay, *The Story of GI Joe*; publishes journal of tour, *Situation Normal. The Man Who Had All the Luck* published and produced; receives Theatre Guild National Award.

1945   *Focus* (novel) published.

1947   *All My Sons* produced and published; receives New York Drama Critics Circle Award.

1949   *Death of a Salesman* produced and published; receives Pulitzer Prize and other awards.

1950   Adaptation of Ibsen's *An Enemy of the People* produced.

1953   *The Crucible* produced and published; receives Antoinette Perry Award.

1954   Denied passport to visit Brussels by State Department.

1955   *A View from the Bridge* and *A Memory of Two Mondays* (one-act plays) produced and published in New York.

Possible Communist associations investigated by New York City Youth Board. Divorces Mary Grace Slattery.

1956 *A View from the Bridge* (two-act version) produced in London. Testifies before House Committee on Un-American Activities but refuses to identify persons seen at meetings organized by Communists. Awarded honorary degree at the University of Michigan. Marries Marilyn Monroe.

1957 Found in contempt of Congress after trial. *Collected Plays* published.

1958 Contempt of Congress conviction reversed by United States Court of Appeals. Elected to the National Institute of Arts and Letters.

1959 Awarded Gold Medal for Drama, National Institute of Arts and Letters.

1961 *The Misfits* (screenplay) produced and published. Divorces Marilyn Monroe.

1962 Marries Ingeborg Morath.

1964 *After the Fall* and *Incident at Vichy* produced by the Lincoln Center Repertory Theater.

1965 Elected president of P.E.N., international literary organization (term expired 1969).

1967 *I Don't Need You Any More* (short stories) published.

1968 *The Price* produced and published. Serves as delegate to Democratic National Convention.

1969 *In Russia* (travel journal) published.

1972 *The Creation of the World and Other Business* produced. Serves as delegate to Democratic National Convention.

1974 *Up from Paradise* (musical version of *The Creation of the World*) produced in Ann Arbor, Michigan.

1977 *In the Country* (journal) published. *The Archbishop's Ceiling* produced in Washington, D.C.

1978 *The Theater Essays of Arthur Miller* published.

1979 *Chinese Encounters* (journal) published.

CHAPTER 1

The Man

THOUGH intrigued by "interior psychological questions," Arthur Miller has tried in his plays to create a "sense of dealing with an existing objective fact."[1] One way he does this is to draw upon history or autobiography for his plots and characters. With the possible exception of *Focus*, his only novel, and *The Creation of the World and Other Business*, all his writing alludes in some manner to actual persons and events. Usually such references are unobtrusive; sometimes as in *The Crucible* and in *After the Fall*, they are quite prominent. A good deal of this allusion is autobiographical. For example, Chris Keller's speeches on social "relatedness," in *All My Sons*, echo a discovery Miller published in his report on returning veterans, *Situation Normal*:

> No man has ever felt identity with a group more deeply and intimately than a soldier in battle. But . . . the usual veteran returning to his city or town on the usual day finds no common goal at all. He finds every group in town excluding the proximate group. . . . Now he must live unto himself, for his own selfish welfare.
>
> *(Situation Normal)*[2]

> Everything was being destroyed [in the war], see, but it seemed to me that one new thing was made. A kind of—responsibility. Man for man. . . . And then I came home and it was incredible. I—there was no meaning in it here; the whole thing to them was a kind of a—bus accident. I went to work with Dad, and that rat-race again.
>
> *(All My Sons)*

Miller's characters reflect his history as well as his convictions. *After the Fall* evokes most of the important figures in the playwright's private life.[3] The Jewish family of *They Too Arise*—a small-scale coat manufacturer, his wife, father-in-law, two sons, and daughter—duplicates Miller's family. The younger son, rem-

1

iniscent of Arthur Miller as a youth, does not care for the business world and its savage practices, attends college in Michigan, "wants to be a writer," and leans toward a socialistic solution to the economic problems of the 1930s. Miller's Austrian-born father was serious in his business dealings but jocular at home, just as Abe Simon in *They Too Arise,* Joe Keller in *All My Sons,* Charley in *Death of a Salesman,* and the fathers in *After the Fall* and "I Don't Need You Any More" (a short story). Like Joe Keller, Miller's father teased the neighborhod youngsters and persuaded them to "stand guard and watch the block."[4]

Willy Loman—if he is not "a god in decay"[5]—may resemble any one or a combination of the many salesmen Miller knew well: his father's employees sold coats; his brother, carpets; his first wife's father, insurance; and countless relatives, almost everything.[6] Bert in *A Memory of Two Mondays* is obviously an autobiographical figure: Miller left the same job (clerk in an automobile parts warehouse) in the same city (New York) at about the same time (1933), after saving enough money to start college. Bert was born in 1915, the year of Miller's birth; also born that year, judging from evidence in the plays, were Chris Keller (*All My Sons*), Biff Loman (*Death of a Salesman*), Eddie Carbone (*A View from the Bridge*), and possibly David Frieber (*The Man Who Had All the Luck*) and Quentin (*After the Fall*).[7] Finally, it seems probable that Miller modeled the charming heroine of *The Misfits* after the celebrated actress to whom he was married at the time he wrote the screenplay. The two features he particularly admired in Marilyn Monroe are noticeably visible in Roslyn—"spontaneous joy" and "quick sympathy."[8]

One should be discreet, however, in proposing connections between an author's life and his narratives. "Once the author's identity is 'discovered,'" Miller warns, "a certain counterfeit of knowingness spreads through the reader's soul, quite as though he had managed to see through an attempt to trick him into believing that the work at hand was art rather than a disguised biography."[9] Certainly, biographical identification alone cannot illuminate art. But, because Miller's reference to personal experience is so extensive, it may be helpful to know a few "objective facts."

I *"Brooklyn Boy Makes Good"*

The dramatist was born in Manhattan on October 17, 1915, to Isadore and Augusta Miller, a conventional, well-to-do Jewish couple. Young Arthur was as intense an athlete and as weak a scholar as Biff Loman. Decidedly nonintellectual, he spent his boyhood playing football and baseball, skating, swimming, dating, failing algebra three times, reading adventure stories, and "just plain fooling around." "Until the age of seventeen I can safely say that I never read a book weightier than *Tom Swift*, and *Rover Boys*, and only verged on literature with some of Dickens. . . . I passed through the public school system unscathed."[10] "If I had any ideology at all it was what I had learned from Hearst newspapers."[11] His sister remembers that he became "very handy with tools. He built the back porch on our house, and some of the roses he planted in the back yard are still blooming."[12] In brief, as Miller phrases it, "I was a very physical kid."[13]

Indulgence in physical activity assumed a more practical nature after 1928—Miller has called his thirteenth year a turning point— when economic conditions forced his father to give up the coat business and to move the family to a small frame house in Brooklyn (a house said to be the model for the Brooklyn home in *Death of a Salesman*).[14] By the mid-1940s, Arthur Miller had worked as a delivery boy for a bakery; as a dishwasher and waiter; as a singer at a local radio station; as a warehouse clerk, night editor of a university newspaper, mouse attendant in a laboratory, truck driver, tanker seaman, factory laborer, and shipfitter's helper; and as a writer of over thirty radio plays and movie scenarios. All this experience left him with great respect for hard work: "I did not believe . . . that you could tell about a man without telling about the world he was living in, what he did for a living, what he was like not only at home or in bed but on the job."[15] Several of his characters, indeed, consider manual skill to be all-important. "Nothing is mine but what I'm good enough to make!" David Frieber shouts in *The Man Who Had All the Luck*; and in *Death of a Salesman*, Biff Loman remarks about his father—who, like Miller, loved gardening, carpentry, and athletics—"there's more of him in that front stoop than in all the sales he ever made."[16]

After graduating from high school during the Depression, Miller saved thirteen of the fifteen dollars he earned weekly in an auto-parts warehouse for his college tuition. He occasionally read a good book: "on the subway to and from work I began reading. . . . A book that changed my life was *The Brothers Karamazov* which I picked up, I don't know how or why, and all at once believed I was born to be a writer.[17] Although certainly no avid reader as a young

man, he was impressed, eventually, by Shakespeare, Bertolt
Brecht, George Bernard Shaw, Eugene O'Neill, Jean Giraudoux,
Jean Anouilh, Sidney Howard, and others. He attributes his chief
literary obligation to Henrik Ibsen; until the time he began *All My
Sons* in 1945, he states, "only once in my life had I been truly
engrossed in a production—when Ruth Gordon played in the Jed
Harris production of 'A Doll's House'" (*C.P.*, 16).[18]

In 1934 Miller convinced the admissions officer at the University
of Michigan that his poor high-school grades did not represent his
abilities accurately, and he enrolled in journalism "because I heard
they gave writing prizes there."[19] The university was a formative
influence. Students from various parts of the United States and
from other countries familiarized him with their regional styles. He
observed, for instance, the Midwestern small-town manner de-
picted in *The Man Who Had All the Luck* and in *All My Sons.*
Everyone was involved with the social causes of the period: "the
place was full of speeches, meetings and leaflets. It was jumping
with Issues. . . . It was, in short, the testing ground for all my
prejudices, my beliefs and my ignorance, and it helped to lay out
the boundaries of my life."[20]

Eighteen months after entering the university, he began to write
plays—winning the Avery Hopwood Award with his first effort,
No Villain, a piece written in four days. "Since I had seen only two
plays—and those in my childhood from which I remembered
nothing—and had read about three others," he recalls, "I could
only decide to end the acts by asking a friend how long an act took.
I adopted his estimate and won the award."[21] Winning the prize
"made me confident I could go ahead from there. It left me with
the belief that the ability to write plays is born into one, and that it is
a kind of sport of the mind."[22]

Granted the Bachelor of Arts in 1938, he returned to New York,
worked briefly with the Federal Theatre Project, "and in two
months was on relief." Later he married Mary Grace Slattery, to
whom he had become engaged while at Michigan; he "settled
down to a plain life in Brooklyn remote from Bohemia and
fashionable intellectual circles."[23] His wife, Maurice Zolotow
claims, "was political, literary, intense in the style of the 1930's, and
she was an intellectual—it was she who was the family intellectual."[24]

In this period Miller wrote plays for radio programs such as the
Columbia Workshop (CBS) and Cavalcade of America (NBC),

receiving about one hundred dollars for each script. The restrictions imposed by the networks and advertising agencies aroused an antipathy toward commercial control of the arts. "About radio, quote this if you like," he protested in a 1947 preface to a radio play, *The Story of Gus*: "No medium of expression can fulfill itself if its forms and its content are prescribed beforehand. There is so much you can't say on the radio that for a serious writer it presents a blank wall. . . . Radio today is in the hands of people most of whom have no taste, no will, no nothing but the primitive ability to spot a script that does not conform to the format"[25] (*The Story of Gus,* incidentally, was not produced; it did not conform to the format.) Miller later delivered similar criticisms of motion pictures, the Broadway theater, and television: "the most important thing for a playwright . . . is connection, belonging to a theatre. In our theatre he is completely disconnected. It is one reason why playwrights go to Hollywood."[26] "I don't think they want to get mixed up with anybody of any independence," he said concerning television producers in 1962. "I don't believe television is a separately afflicted medium. Commercialization of all media is now a fact."[27]

Kept from military service by an old injury, Miller visited army camps during the war to collect material for a movie, *The Story of GI Joe,* based on Ernie Pyle's book, *Here Is Your War.* He published the journal of his tour, *Situation Normal,* in 1944. That year his first Broadway production, *The Man Who Had All the Luck,* appeared, and this work was followed in 1945 by a novel, *Focus.* By the time he completed *All My Sons,* he had won many prizes: two Hopwood Awards for the college plays *No Villain* (1936) and *Honors at Dawn* (1937), a Theatre Guild Bureau of New Plays Prize for *They Too Arise* (1936), and a Theatre Guild National Award for *The Man Who Had All the Luck* (1944). But this recognition was as nothing compared to subsequent honors, which included New York Drama Critics Circle Awards for *All My Sons* (1947) and for *Death of a Salesman* (1949), a Pulitzer Prize for *Salesman,* and the Antoinette Perry Award for *The Crucible* (1953). Almost all the plays, the novel, and several short stories were adapted for radio, television, and motion pictures. *The Crucible* was turned into opera by Robert Ward in 1961, the same year that Roberto Rossellini presented an operatic version of *A View from the Bridge* (*Uno Sguardo dal Ponte*) in Italy.

The major plays were published and produced, usually in

translation, throughout the world—Sweden, The Netherlands, Belgium, Czechoslovakia, Russia, France, England, Ireland, Italy, Hungary, Spain, West Germany, Japan, Israel, Mexico, Argentina, and Brazil.[28] Success became manifest in other ways too. The playwright was named an "Outstanding Father of the Year" (1949); awarded an honorary degree at his alma mater (1956);[29] elected to the National Institute of Arts and Letters (1958), which voted him its Gold Medal for Drama the following year; and made president of P.E.N., an international literary organization (1965). Financial returns in these golden years were quite interesting—in an article entitled "Brooklyn Boy Makes Good," Robert Sylvester estimated that *Death of a Salesman* would earn for its author over two million dollars.[30] Finally, to crown his good fortune, Arthur Miller, the man who had all the luck, married Marilyn Monroe in 1956 after divorcing his first wife.[31]

II   *The Hearing*

As his characters discover, however, the wheel that raises also casts down; the decade of the 1950s brought censure as well as acclaim. During the Depression and World War II, Miller had been inspired by liberal reform programs designed to improve conditions in business, politics, and the arts. After the war he participated in those programs more actively. The situation in the theater particularly disturbed him: he saw a threat to free expression emerging that superseded "commercialization." "I may be wrong," he said, "but I sense that the playwrights have become more timid with experience and maturity, timid in ethical and social idea, theatrical method, and stylistic means. . . . We have an atmosphere of dread, an . . . accepted party line, a sanctified complex of moods and attitudes, proper and improper."[32]

This "atmosphere of dread" Miller ascribed in part to the inquiries concerning disloyalty then being conducted by certain federal agencies and Congressional committees. He believed that these investigations were planned to harass those with unpopular political views. He therefore wrote *The Crucible* to expose the process by which "terror . . . was being knowingly planned and consciously engineered. . . . Above all, above all horrors, I saw accepted the notion that conscience was no longer a private matter but one of state administration" (*C.P.*, 40, 47). He was not referring to any specific instance or individual—such as Senator Joseph

McCarthy, considered by many to be the most brutal of the official interrogators. Instead, he was "trying to tell people that the great 'issues' which the hysteria was allegedly about" in colonial as well as in contemporary America "were covers for petty ambitions, hardheaded political drives, and the fantasies of very small and vengeful minds."[33]

Then the playwright became a principal in the debate rather than merely a witness for the defense. Ironically, state authorities, by insisting that he inform on others and confess sins against the community, presented him with a challenge to "conscience" directly analogous to that which had confronted the protagonist of *The Crucible*.[34] In the play he had articulated his faith in the ability of the free individual to withstand irrational social pressures and to determine positive standards of citizenship. Now he demonstrated his faith through his conduct.

In March 1954, the State Department refused Miller a passport to visit Brussels for the Belgian première of *The Crucible*. His application was "rejected under regulations denying passports to persons believed to be supporting the Communist movement, whether or not they are members of the Communist party."[35] Miller indignantly denied "supporting any Communist movement." On July 3, he published a satire on the loyalty mania, patterned after Swift's "Modest Proposal," in which he sarcastically proposed formal specifications for judging treason that would be consistent with the policies he felt were actually operative. Among other things, it would be punishable to have "engaged in Conversations, talks, public or private meetings, lectures, visits, or communications, the nature of which is not illegal but on the other hand not Positively Conducive to the Defence of the Nation against the Enemy."[36]

But his difficulties had only begun. The next year, the Youth Board of New York City first suspended, then canceled, a contract with Miller to write a film script about juvenile delinquency in that city. A controversy on the matter raged for months and involved Mayor Robert Wagner, the Board of Estimate, the city's Investigations Commissioner, two citizens' organizations (the American Legion and Catholic War Veterans) that charged the author with leftist connections, and the New York Civil Liberties Union, which criticized the investigation on the grounds that "it is un-American to conduct investigations of political beliefs and associations unless they are necessary for security."[37] No evidence indicating disloyalty was found by the Investigations Commissioner but the script-writing plan was dropped, reportedly because of rumors that Miller was shortly to be called before a Congressional committee.

He appeared in June 1956 before the House Committee on Un-American Activities. He testified that, although he "had signed many appeals and protests issued by Red front groups in the last decade," he had never been "under Communist discipline."[38] As far as can be ascertained from public sources, Miller apparently had supported the following causes: Henry Wallace's visit to France to "set a pattern in this One World for the free interchange of opinions between the leaders and the people of all nations of good will" (1947),[39] a World Youth Festival in Prague (1947), a World Congress for Peace in Paris (1948), and a Peace Conference at the Waldorf-Astoria in New York (1949).[40] Moreover, he allegedly signed statements that defended Gerhart Eisler (later a high communist official in East Germany), criticized the House Committee on Un-American Activities, supported relief work in Communist China, and attacked the Smith Act (the act forbids teaching or advocating the overthrow of the United States Government by force). He also applied for enrollment in a study course on Marxism and, most important, attended four or five writers' meetings sponsored by the Communist party in 1947.[41]

Denying subversive intent, Miller freely admitted past associations (ending in 1950) with ultraliberal, leftist, or communist-front groups. But he risked a citation for contempt of Congress by refusing to identify persons he had seen at the communist-run meetings for writers. While he "would not support now a cause dominated by Communists," he said, "my conscience will not permit me to use the name of another person and bring trouble to him."[42] Indicted for contempt by a federal grand jury and brought to trial the following year, he claimed that being "forced to name other people whom I believe to be innocent of wrong-doing" was "not relevant to an investigation of passport abuses which was the subject matter of the investigation."[43] On May 31, 1957, he was found guilty, fined five hundred dollars, and given a suspended thirty-day jail sentence. A year later the conviction was reversed on appeal to the United States Court of Appeals for the District of Columbia.[44] The issue in contention has been described by Mary McCarthy: "the committee was not seeking information from Mr. Miller; it was applying a loyalty test. And for Mr. Miller it was not in reality a question of betraying specific people (who had already been denounced, so that his testimony could hardly have done them further harm), but of accepting the *principle* of betrayal as a norm of good citizenship."[45]

During this ordeal, Miller produced almost no important work. After *A View from the Bridge* and *A Memory of Two Mondays* in 1955, he published only a revision of *A View from the Bridge* (1956), a screenplay (*The Misfits*, 1961), and a number of essays and stories. He tried unsuccessfully to complete a play he had started in 1952, but not until the conclusion of his appeal, his divorce from Marilyn Monroe, and his marriage to Ingeborg Morath in 1962 was he able to finish *After the Fall* (*Incident at Vichy* followed in less than a year). The prolonged public debate may well have inhibited productivity; however, it confirmed Miller's theatrical and personal goals. While working on *After the Fall*, he said "I am trying to define what a human being should be, how he can survive in to-day's society without having to appear to be a different person from what he basically is."[46]

After the Fall was the inaugural presentation at the Lincoln Center Repertory Theater early in 1964. Miller's long-held hope for a publicly subsidized permanent company died quickly, however. By December he, along with producer Robert Whitehead and director Elia Kazan, ended their association with the New York group. He attributed the failure of this experiment to the intrusion of "marketplace laws" upon artistic needs.[47]

For the past fifteen years Miller has alternated between energetic public activity and long periods of work and hospitality at his country home near Roxbury, Connecticut.[48] He traveled extensively with his wife, a professional photographer who illustrated two journals reporting their experiences abroad, *In Russia* (1969) and *Chinese Encounters* (1979), and a journal recounting rural life in Connecticut, *In the Country* (1977). He has engaged in politics as a delegate to and critic of the Democratic presidential nominating conventions in 1968 and 1972.[49] From 1965 to 1969 he served as president of P.E.N., an international association of poets, playwrights, essayists, and novelists (8,500 members in fifty-one countries in 1969). As president he interceded on behalf of politically oppressed writers in many Western, Communist, and Asian countries. "P.E.N. is a weak reed," he wrote in 1971, "normally bankrupt, and in many ways a bumbling crew of idealistic people. The fact remains, awkward as it is, that but for its efforts more than one writer is alive today who wouldn't be, in the East and West."[50]

And Miller has worked hard in the theater. In addition to writing and participating in the production of three new works, *The Price* (1968), *The Creation of the World and Other Business* (1972), and *The Archbishop's Ceiling* (1977),[51] he assisted in revivals of earlier plays, adapted many for television (*Death of a Salesman, The Crucible, After the Fall, The Price, A Memory of Two Mondays*, his version of Ibsen's *An Enemy of the People*, and a short play entitled *Fame*), wrote and helped produce an antiwar film,[52] and collaborated with a composer on a musical version of *The Creation of the World*.[53] A desire to assert sanity and fair play continues to inform his work, his politics, and his private life. Early in 1979 Miller wrote that "the theater is practically a direct reflection of the preoccupations of society. . . . You change society because you sharpen its consciousness."[54] That conviction, which has both sustained and distracted him, remains constant.

CHAPTER 2

The Early Work

I Apprentice Pieces

ARTHUR Miller has always addressed his drama to "a whole people asking a basic question and demanding its answer."[1] From the beginning, however, he often presented his basic questions and answers in the form of generalized proposals. Ethical abstractions—usually of wide social relevance—dominate the early works, which include over thirty plays written for college, radio, and amateur performance (almost a dozen full-length plays were never produced). "Listen!" a character exclaims in *That They May Win* (1944),[2] a one-act work about war veterans: "We the people gotta go into politics. Politics is just another way of saying how much rent you'll pay. . . . You have to go to those Senators and Congressmen you elected and say, 'Listen here, Mister! We're your boss, and you have to work for us!'" Later, needless to say, Miller became more adept at shaping an outlook with the mannerisms as well as with the rational content of colloquial speech, but all his writing shows a tendency to make the themes explicit. The habit evidences high seriousness; unfortunately, it has also caused serious stylistic difficulties.

Another short play, a fantasy for radio called *The Pussycat and the Expert Plumber Who Was a Man* (1941),[3] carefully outlines one of the young playwright's favorite topics—the causal connection between occupational expertness and self-respect. A cynical talking cat with his eye on the presidency acts as the devil's advocate, scoffing at such a connection. "The one thing a man fears most next to death," he theorizes, "is the loss of his good name. Man is evil in his own eyes, my friends, worthless." To his dismay, a worthy human enters to teach him that "a man will actually prefer to stay poor because of an ideal. . . . Some useful men, like expert plumbers, are so proud of their usefulness that they don't need the

11

Salem Academy and College
Gramley Library
Winston-Salem, N.C. 27108

respect of their neighbors and so they aren't afraid to speak the truth." *They Too Arise* (1936), an unpublished version of the college play, *No Villain,* is also a typical apprentice piece: its abstractions mingle with homely, often comic dialect, and its male characters hope to find salvation in (or in spite of) their work. In this play a clothing manufacturer and his two sons struggle to stay solvent and honest at the same time. Arnold, the younger son, is the chief spokesman: "you can't start in small and get by [in business], and if you start in big you've got to be a louse to stay that way," he insists. "A strike is the way for the working people to gain power and bring Socialism to America."

They Too Arise, with its close-knit family that becomes disrupted by the father's business commitment, anticipates *All My Sons* and to a lesser degree *Death of a Salesman.* So too does *The Man Who Had All the Luck.* The relationship between Amos and Pat Beeves in *The Man Who Had All the Luck* is an embryonic form of the father-son antagonism that was to occupy the two later plays. In all three works, a well-meaning father forfeits the respect of his son by forcing him to accept his own standard of success (Pat Beeves tries to mold Amos into a baseball pitcher).[4] But this issue provides only a subplot for *The Man Who Had All the Luck;* the protagonist, David Frieber, has other troubles. Miller has summarized David's predicament. The play, he writes,

deals with a young man in a small town who, by the time he is in his mid-twenties, owns several growing businesses, has married the girl he loves, is the father of a child he has always wanted, and is daily becoming convinced that as his desires are gratified he is causing to accumulate around his own head an invisible but nearly palpable fund, so to speak, of retribution. The law of life, as he observes life around him, is that people are always frustrated in some important regard; and he conceives that he must be too, and the play is built around his conviction of impending disaster. (*C.P.,* 13–14)

Because of the verbiage that David and other characters employ to explicate this "conviction of impending disaster," the main story achieves less immediacy than the subplot. Unable to adjust to his ominous successes, the young man decides to end his uncertainty by launching a project—mink breeding—that will finally test his inherent capabilities and the world's rationality. If the mink die, he will know "that nothing came to me because of what I am, what I myself am worth. . . . I'm going to measure myself, once and for all. And mink can measure a man." In a resounding speech that sounds like a medieval condemnation of usury, David celebrates the beneficial effects of physical labor: "I stood in the world with money in my hands and everything was 'mine'! It was not *mine*, nothing is mine but what I'm good enough to make! . . . Money is a bitch, Hester, it's a whore bitch that'll bear for any man and what it bears can never be really yours."

David's friends speak as fatuously. Shory is the cynic of this play: "I'm not talkin' out of a book. A man is a jellyfish laying on the beach. A wave comes along and pulls him back into the sea, and he floats a while on a million currents he can't even feel, and he's back on the beach again never knowing why." Opposing his theory, with rhetoric almost as grandiose as the oratory in a play by Maxwell Anderson, Hester urges her husband to renounce his fearfulness: "you are the lightning, you are the banging hail! Do you see it, do you understand what happened? You are the god now; there was nothing in the sky that gave you things, nothing that could take them away! It was always you, Davey. Stand here! Smash it down!" Even though the mink die, Hester's influence proves to be more potent than Shory's. David explains his new self-confidence with a line that is limp as a jellyfish and vacuous as the sky: "I somehow don't feel ashamed . . . now."

All this self-conscious moralizing, dynamic neither in thought nor feeling, makes of Miller's "investigation to discover what exact part a man played in his own fate" (*C.P.*, 13) a contrived, hypothetical debate—despite the play's realistic "small-town" setting. In his first works Miller depended almost entirely upon explicit pronouncements to declare his point about a character's separation from the reality of achievement. As a result, his words failed to "measure a man."

II Focus

Miller understood that *The Man Who Had All the Luck*, which closed after four performances, was merely "a preparation, and possibly a necessary one, for those [plays] that followed" (*C.P.*, 14). It framed, however imperfectly, what he calls the most significant question serious drama can ask: "how may a man make of the outside world a home?"[5] In his novel, *Focus*,[6] he proposed the question far more coherently and forcefully, but he still relied on formal explanations of mental states and moral positions. This reliance will become apparent in a brief survey of the main character's progress.

As in several later works (particularly *All My Sons*), in *Focus* the writer first establishes a standard of "normal" behavior, then undermines that standard and initiates a journey from security to disillusionment. "Hours come when the familiar seems about to change its shape, verging on the strange and unexplored," he comments in the novel. Lawrence Newman, a personnel manager, is introduced as a stock type—an undistinguished, fastidious ("even in sleep he seemed to cling to his sense of propriety") middle-class drone whose house, occupation, and moral orientation have been prefabricated in accordance with certain conventional patterns. Conformity to those patterns aligns him with authoritative sources of strength and wisdom; the "Corporation" in Manhattan and his home neighborhood in Queens protect him in return for his loyalty to their standards. At work "he had toed the line, done his duty, carried off the ceaseless indignities that came from above. He was safe, would always be."

The principle that energizes this arrangement is racial exclusiveness. Since, naturally, one feels superior to persons whom one despises, it becomes possible to cultivate a "sense of power and self-purification" by finding decadent racial features in others. Thus Newman spends his daily subway ride cataloguing the attributes of minority groups. Assuming the validity of physical and behavioral stereotypes, he participates in a heartening, if passive, communion with those who share this outlook. In regard to Jews, "listening to reports of their avarice insensibly brought him closer to an appreciation of his own liberality, which seemed proven by the simple fact that he was not a Jew." Hating an abstraction called a "Jew" confirms his Gentile identity.

This hatred does no harm, he believes, because it merely acknowledges real facts. Sometimes, though, he indulges in a variation which, while slightly less innocent, gratifies the ego so much more. Reading a scurrilous insult scrawled on a subway pillar, he experiences a "titillation of danger," a premonition that "something was building up inside the city, something thunderous and exhilarating." A newspaper report of desecration in a Jewish cemetery arouses similar excitement: "there was a tang of violence to the story, the same threat of dark deeds and ruthless force that flowed out to him from the subway pillars. His eyes kept

massaging the two paragraphs as though to draw out the last wave of emotion from them."
The subway experience, his indifference to a Puerto Rican woman's cry for help, and interviews with Fred Carlson at home and Mr. Gargan at work indicate Newman's rigid mode of conduct. Then, in a moment, security and respectability vanish. The "familiar" order becomes transformed into a ghastly, surrealistic parody: "it was as though all the tokens of the known world had been switched, as though in a dream his own house numbers had been changed, . . . as though all the things that had been true were now all catastrophically untrue. . . . The horror of a nightmare, the ruthless but undefined force of an hallucination was upon him and he was striving to break out of it and understand what was happening to him."
He is led to this trial by circumstance, self-assertion, and sex. Gertrude's feminine ripeness quickens a dormant flair for manly daring; after their first encounter he feels sufficiently emboldened to protest his demotion in the company whose discriminatory policies he had diligently executed: "already, he thought, she was leading him into new paths." Besides stimulating his courage, Gertrude is inadvertently responsible for his first suspicion that his race-consciousness has been absurd. Sensuality, he finds, was not monopolized by Jews after all: "he was sitting there in the guilt of the fact that the vile nature of the Jews and their numberless deceits, especially their sensuous lust for women—of which he had daily proof in the dark folds of their eyes and their swarthy skin— all were the reflections of his own desires with which he had invested them."
Somewhat enlightened and greatly fortified, Newman begins to realize the consequences of anti-Semitism from the viewpoint of a Jew. The insults that he suffers after his new eyeglasses give his face a "Jewish" appearance extend his awareness. Finally, his vision focuses upon the individual rather than upon an illusory abstraction. He can sympathize with Finkelstein's furious refusal to be deprived of a personal identity: "looking at Finkelstein now, Newman saw that he had not really hated *him*, . . . he had passed this man each morning with the knowledge that he had in him the propensity for acting as Jews were supposed to; cheat, or be dirty, or loud." Newman wavers occasionally, intimidated by the old social pressures, but he acquits himself honorably during the last stage of his growth, the street fight—a trial by combat. His rage

impels him to an "honest five minutes" in which he achieves "independence and self-containment." His stand exemplifies the theory of heroic assertion Miller advanced in the essay, "Tragedy and the Common Man":

I think the tragic feeling is evoked in us when we are in the presence of a character who is ready to lay down his life, if need be, to secure one thing—his sense of personal dignity. From Orestes to Hamlet, Medea to Macbeth, the underlying struggle is that of the individual attempting to gain his "rightful" position in his society.... Its dominant force is indignation. Tragedy, then, is the consequence of a man's total compulsion to evaluate himself justly.[7]

Newman's history illustrates the conclusion that racial intolerance, when raised to a system of belief, frustrates this "compulsion" in the person who practices it as well as in the person victimized by it.

Miller develops his thesis, then, with a detailed third-person exposition of Newman's reactions. He also employs plainly labeled character types. Gertrude and Finkelstein not only catalyze but personify Newman's passions. Gertrude actualizes the long-held sex daydream of an ideally desirable woman ("she was like the woman of his vision"). Finkelstein, the persecuted Jew, configures the "defiance" engendered within the protagonist: "his clear anger, his relentless and controlled fury opened a wide channel into Newman's being, just as Gertrude's had."[8] In addition, Fred Carlson, Mr. Gargan, and the early Newman, intent upon classifying others according to racist formulas, are themselves human caricatures—stereotypes who rigidly follow predetermined behavior patterns.

A symbolic dream assists in the exposition. Several times Newman uncomprehendingly remembers the puzzling dream-vision that preludes his odyssey—a deserted carousel, senselessly rotating above an underground factory. The correct interpretation eventually occurs to him when he realizes that the innocent-seeming amusement in which he had indulged camouflaged an insidious purpose—the manufacture of irrational hatred and fear, "insanity in the darkness." Other significant images in the novel include the imposing "Corporation" and the hive-like neighborhood (monolithic institutions from which the wayward are cast), and the magical spectacles that focus Newman's eyes on reality. Symbolic images and characters, however, are of secondary importance in mediating between objective and psychological realms. The expository burden is borne largely by passages that baldly explicate mood or theme, but do not project internal states through gesture and dialogue. This commentary, furthermore, is too fluent to be acceptable as the thought of someone whose speech is as trite as Newman's. A character of small intelligence may experience moral regeneration; he does not as a result become splendidly articulate. Newman's concluding thought seems especially over-literate: "as he stood there about to reply, he longed deeply for a swift charge of lightning that would with a fiery stroke break away the categories of people and change them so that it would not be important to them what tribe they sprang from. It must not be important any more, he swore, even though in his life it had been of highest importance." Miller was not yet expert enough in *Focus* to create a subjective rather than a discursive analysis of "a man's total compulsion to evaluate himself justly."

III   All My Sons

All My Sons, Miller's first success on Broadway, represents a considerable advance in the author's ability to manipulate language. To a casual observer the dialogue may appear to be simply a phonographic imitation of a contemporary American idiom, replete with clichés and slang. In the opening scene, comfortable gossip circulated by the Kellers and their friends connotes the sense of security conventionally associated with everyday family and neighborhood life. The talk—ingenuous, friendly, relaxed—duplicates the good-natured banter one might expect to hear in any Midwestern suburban backyard on a pleasant Sunday morning.

This deliberate banality, however, encompasses more than mere linguistic verisimilitude: the common man's slangy syntax has been used for theatrical purposes. "The play begins in an atmosphere of undisturbed normality," Miller wrote. "Its first act was later called slow, but it was designed to be slow. It was made so that even boredom might threaten, so that when the first intimation of the crime is dropped a genuine horror might begin to move into the heart of the audience, a horror born of the contrast between the placidity of the civilization on view and the threat to it that a rage of conscience could create" (*C.P.*, 18).[9] Intruding upon the tensionless domestic world, with its chatter about want-ads, parsley, and Don Ameche, a terrible challenge to tranquillity becomes increasingly insistent, finally bursting apart the innocent verbal façade. The peaceful mood deceptively evoked by trite speech prepares the stage for desperate war.

A series of allusions that gradually reveal a hidden sin brings about the transition from tranquillity to fear—an Ibsenesque technique that Miller was to employ in later plays. The Kellers' elder son, Larry, was reported missing in action after a war-time flight; when a neighbor refers to Larry's memorial tree, which was "toppled" by a storm the night before, he sounds the first jarring note. As yet such references do not significantly affect the prevailing conversational tenor, pitched as it is to humorous trivia. Even Joe Keller's teasing a youngster about "jail" contributes to conviviality. But Joe and Chris, his other son, begin to worry about the impact that the tree's destruction will have on Mother, who still hopes for Larry's return. By the time she enters, then, the initial calm has already been somewhat disrupted. Her outburst of grief for the missing flier further disturbs that calm. "Because if he's not coming back," Kate cries, "then I'll kill myself! Laugh. . . . [She points to tree.] Laugh, but there are meanings in such things" (italics are omitted in quoting stage directions here and elsewhere).

Now another complication emerges: Kate refuses to allow Chris to marry his brother's fiancée because that would acknowledge Larry's death. The problem seems to involve mother and son, primarily, with Joe Keller standing by as a concerned spectator: "well, that's only your business, Chris," he comments. Yet the facts rapidly coming to light in the dozen or more oblique and direct allusions to an old scandal begin to place him in a more central position; they introduce a contradiction between his apparent neutrality and his actual involvement. His former partner in the machine shop, the spectator soon learns, has been serving a prison term for shipping defective cylinder heads that caused the death of twenty-one American pilots. "The story was," Keller recalls, "I pulled a fast one getting myself exonerated." And a friend comments, "everybody knows Joe pulled a fast one to get out of jail. . . . There's not a person on the block who doesn't know the truth."

A more dynamic style mirrors the rising apprehension felt by Keller and his wife as their secret rises from the past. Their questions, idly curious before, now become urgently incisive, demanding immediate solution: "now what's going to happen to Mother? Do you know?" "Why, Joe? What has Steve suddenly got to tell him that he takes an airplane to see him?" "She don't hold nothin' against me, does she? I mean if she was sent here to find out something?" (This last question is answered with another query: "Why? What is there to find out?") The need to "know"—the verb occurs almost two hundred times—assumes first importance. Within a family supposedly united by strong affection there is surprising uncertainty and, therefore, constant inquiry in respect to each other's motives: "I don't understand you, do I?" Keller asks Chris, a comment later echoed by Mother.[10]

The verbal contrast brings out a psychological contrast, as Keller's defensive questions reveal qualities not previously manifested by the industrialist: harshness starts to displace his simple folksiness, fearfulness displaces the comfortable self-assurance. The grave interrogation alternates with continued small talk. Keller dissembles his growing "nervousness" by performing as a homespun humorist: "I don't know, everybody's gettin' so Goddam educated in this country there'll be nobody to take away the garbage. . . . No kiddin'. It's a tragedy: you stand on the street today and spit, you're gonna hit a college man." But in the second act such pleasantries only bring his terror into sharper relief.

The Kellers attempt to seduce George, the jailed man's son, from his threatening demand for truth with the girl friends, grape juice, and homely clichés that remind him of his carefree existence as a boy in their town. Joe Keller almost succeeds in this verbal enterprise; he woos George with nostalgic reminiscences while discrediting his father with a show of gruff honesty. Then Kate ruins her husband's plan through an incriminating slip of the tongue—a venerable theatrical convention. As excitement builds to a climax, the hectic dialogue mixes the antithetical accents of normalcy and urgency. Keller stubbornly conceals the truth, Kate frantically evades it, and George persistently drives to uncover it ("what happened that day, Joe?"). At the same time, Chris and the neighbors, unaware of the impending crisis, cheerfully pursue avocations ranging from love to astrology.

When Chris discovers that his father had allowed the defective engine parts to be shipped, ordinary speech is unable to carry the intense stress and must be supplemented with exclamation and with violent action. Kate "smashes [Keller] across the face," and Chris in "overwhelming fury . . . pounds down upon his father's shoulder" (author's directions). In a confrontation that climaxes the

movement toward revelation at the end of the second act, the son
takes up the role of interrogator with a vengeance:

How could you do that? How? . . . What did you do? Explain it to me or
I'll tear you to pieces! . . . God in heaven, what kind of a man are you? . . .
Where do you live, where have you come from? . . . What the hell do you
think I was thinking of, the Goddam business? Is that as far as your mind
can see, the business? What is that, the world—the business? What the hell
do you mean, you did it for me? Don't you have a country? Don't you live
in the world? What the hell are you? You're not even an animal, no animal
kills his own, what are you? What must I do to you? I ought to tear the
tongue out of your mouth, what must I do? . . . What must I do, Jesus
God, what must I do?

An ethical disparity typical of Miller's "family" plays causes the
conflict between father and son. Joe Keller cares little for public
approval, everything for his son's admiration. To him, "the world
had a forty-foot front, it ended at the building line." "Nothin' is
bigger" than the family, in whose name even homicide can be
justified: "my only accomplishment is my son. . . . There's nothin'
he could do that I wouldn't forgive." "Joe Keller's trouble, in a
word," Miller has stated, "is not that he cannot tell right from
wrong but that his cast of mind cannot admit that he, personally,
has any viable connection with his world, his universe, or his
society" (*C.P.*, 19).
If the father is monomaniacal in his loyalty, the son qualifies *his*
familial devotion. Chris cares for his family—"you're the only one I
know who loves his parents," a friend remarks—but military
combat has taught him a higher principle. The men in his
command "killed themselves for each other. . . . Everything was
being destroyed, see, but it seemed to me that one new thing was
made. A kind of—responsibility. Man for man." His belief recalls
Lawrence Newman's final wish for a society founded upon
common welfare rather than upon self-interest and mutual ex-
clusion.[11]
After bringing the conflict to its brilliant culmination, Miller
mishandles the resolution. Joe Keller's sudden decision to commit
suicide is the most obvious sign of this mishandling. At first, Keller
holds firmly to his position; his obstinacy impels Chris to curse
himself and his father, then determine to give up his home, career,
and fiancée ("now I'm practical, and I spit on myself").[12] Instead of
sacrificing his own life, however, Chris brings about his father's

death by reading to Joe the letter in which Larry also had denounced his father and condemned himself. In this way, Chris damns Keller for Larry's suicide. More than that, the letter apparently demonstrates the validity of Chris's philosophy on universal brotherhood; for Keller hints at moral surrender in his cryptic statement before shooting himself: "sure, [Larry] was my son. But I think to him they were all my sons. And I guess they were, I guess they were."

If this vaguely worded last speech is supposed to indicate a sudden ethical conversion, it hardly suggests the process whereby Keller capitulates to an alien theory he had savagely resisted until that moment. More likely, and more appropriately after the gradual increase of tension during the first two acts, his suicide may be an emotional reaction to the rejection by both sons (he had warned that, should the bond with his surviving son be severed, "I'll put a bullet in my head"). But the speech does not express a feeling of deprivation strong enough to overcome Keller's staunch self-defense. The realization that he has driven one son to his death and alienated the other might well be unbearable to a character who has predicated his existence upon pride as a father. Yet the disintegration of such pride seems gratuitous when manifested so casually.[13]

The lameness of the ending is compounded by melodramatic plot devices: one familiar stage convention, an incriminating letter, leads to another, a suicide. Still others occur earlier in the play. There is coincidence: George's crucial interview with his long-imprisoned father takes place at the same time that Chris decides to marry Ann, George's sister. There is a prophetic symbol: the ruined tree portends the death of hope. And there is Kate's fatal slip of the tongue.[14] When such obvious conventions operate in concert with expository methods of some subtlety, as in the first two acts, they remain unobtrusive. When they become the chief narrative means, as in the finale, their awkwardness reaches distressing proportions.

The narrative crudeness and verbal obscurity at the conclusion of *All My Sons* may be symptomatic of a shift in interest from the indignant father to the outraged son. After the last question spoken by Chris in the second act—"what must I do?"—Keller's defense no longer commands central attention. Miller seems to have become captivated by a figure recurrent in his work—a maturing individual (a New-man) who proclaims, in abstract terms, the interdependence of all men. The third act betrays a drift toward the rhetorical style Miller has called upon so freely elsewhere: sententious declarations delivered by Chris and by three colleagues in disenchantment differ radically in style both from the simple-minded banter prominent in the first act and from the intense exclamation and interrogation prominent in the second.

Keller's attempt to justify his crime remains relatively concrete even when the appeal is made on hypothetical grounds: "did they ship a gun or a truck outa Detroit before they got their price? Is that clean? It's dollars and cents, nickels and dimes; war and peace, it's nickels and dimes, what's clean?" His questions, now self-answered, continue to expose his apprehension and his toughness; their specificity suits well the narrowness and the urgency of his commitment. On the other hand, Chris, though his diction is plain, argues his case for mutual responsibility with hazy generalities: "once and for all you can know there's a universe of people outside and you're responsible to it, and unless you know that, you threw away your son because that's why he died." Chris's wider concept is necessarily difficult to explain, but simplification of this kind does not clarify the idea.

No less than three other disillusioned, somewhat pretentious young men express disgust at the selfishness they encounter in the world. In so doing they reinforce the standpoint taken by Chris. Larry posthumously speaks his shame on learning of his father's indictment: "every day three or four men never come back and he sits back there doing business" (Act III). George has suffered from *his* father's disgrace: "when I was studying in the hospital it seemed sensible, but outside there doesn't seem to be much of a law" (Act II). And Jim gave up the dream of becoming a researcher: "these private little revolutions always die. The compromise is always made. . . . Every man does have a star. The star of one's honesty. And you spend your life groping for it, but once it's out it never lights again" (Act III).

These moralistic speeches place a disproportionate emphasis on the antagonist's position, a change in focus that may account for the inconclusiveness of Keller's pre-suicide statement, with its token acquiescence in Chris's theory. Besides interrupting the development of the main character, moreover, such judgments dissipate tension. They produce an effect opposite to that achieved early in the play by the judicious alternation of serious and comic moods. After the cleanly decisive second-act clash between father and son,

Chris's cynical wisdom comes as a wordy letdown: "we used to shoot a man who acted like a dog, but honor was real there, you were protecting something. But here? This is the land of the great big dogs, you don't love a man here, you eat him! That's the principle; the only one we live by—it just happened to kill a few people this time, that's all. The world's that way, how can I take it out on him? What sense does that make? This is a zoo, a zoo!" (Act III). (Similarly, Sue's long, misleading, and irrelevant criticism of Chris unduly slows the pace after the suspenseful conclusion of the first act.)

The playwright probably directed attention away from the father's loss to the son's in order to show the consequences of a thoroughgoing tribal outlook. "The fortress which *All My Sons* lays siege to," Miller stated, "is the fortress of unrelatedness" (*C.P.*, 19) But in taking that course he undercut the source of emotional power he had cultivated during most of the play. *All My Sons*, for two acts an extremely well constructed work, reveals clearly what is evident in almost every play Miller has written—the habit of following a carefully prepared movement to crisis with an anticlimactic denouement. His desire to formulate "social" truths has constricted his talent for capturing inward urgencies in colloquial language.

CHAPTER 3

Death of a Salesman

IN *All My Sons*, Miller's first important play, the protagonist's fall from dignity occurs within the narrative framework of an ancient family drama involving what Shakespeare in *King Lear* called "unnaturalness between the child and the parent"—"the bond crack'd 'twixt son and father." *Death of a Salesman*, Miller's most important play, repeats that archetypal plot in which a son (Biff) looks to his father (Willy Loman) for moral direction ("you know he admires you," Linda Loman tells her husband), instead finds corruption (Willy's adultery), and severs the bond of mutual respect ("you fake! You phony little fake!").[1]

After the breach of trust, shame and resentment prevent permanent reunion: "he thinks I've been spiting him all these years and it's eating him up," Biff remarks. The father, as outraged as the son, rigidly reasserts his ethical authority—"he'll see what I am", "I was right!"—thereby complicating the son's effort to derive a new basis for conduct (Biff: "will you let me go, for Christ's sake?"). Both undergo a crisis of self-knowledge. But Willy Loman, unlike Joe Keller, refuses to admit failure in his obsessive drive to attain personal fulfillment by molding a loyal, worthy son: "I won't take the rap for this, you hear?" Keller finally concedes his position to be untenable; the Salesman, on the other hand, commits suicide not simply as an escape from shame but as a last attempt to re-establish his own self-confidence and his family's integrity. "I always knew one way or another we were gonna make it, Biff and I!" he cries in his last speech. "That boy—that boy is going to be magnificent!" The two principal characters in *Death of a Salesman*, each desiring but thwarting the other's well-being, comprise the poles of an irreconcilable opposition.[2]

As a result of his discoveries about his father, Biff Loman (like Chris Keller) suffers an emotional and moral shock experienced by numerous other literary figures, including the biblical Adam and

24

many of Shakespeare's tragic heroes. He begins in security and innocence; proceeds through enlightenment, indignation, disillusion, and despair; and ends in cynical, sorrowful resignation. Miller diagnoses Biff's instability and kleptomania as a psychological illness that was initiated by the traumatic hotel-room encounter (young Biff finds his father with a woman), aggravated by Willy's insistence upon commercial achievement, and purged by belated insight. In a speech reminiscent of Chris's self-justification, Biff at last rejects the standards imposed upon him by his father, an imposition that had been more inimical than mere knowledge of the adultery. "I stole myself out of every good job since high school! And I never got anywhere because you blew me so full of hot air I could never stand taking orders from anybody! That's whose fault it is!" To his epitaph for his father—"he never knew who he was"—Biff could have added "or who I was."

While the playwright carefully surveys Biff's problem, however, he avoids the uncertain focus of *All My Sons* by concentrating attention (the attention that "must be finally paid") upon Willy's contribution to and apprehension of that problem.[3] To achieve this concentration, Miller fashions an impressive array of verbal, symbolic, and narrative techniques with a complexity and incisiveness he has equaled in no other work. These techniques exploit self-characterization. Willy Loman unwittingly reveals the moral limitations that prevent him from attaining the success he craves as a father and as a businessman.

I   *Verbal and Symbolic Technique*

Miller's characters delineate personal qualities through their particular usage of commonplace words and idioms: their language style reflects their style of conduct. Applications of this principle in *Death of a Salesman* range from the elementary to the sophisticated. At the elementary level there are a few explicit evaluations of the protagonist. Linda, for example, recites this estimate: "I don't say he's a great man. Willy Loman never made a lot of money. His name was never in the paper. He's not the finest character that ever lived. But he's a human being, and a terrible thing is happening to him. . . . A small man can be just as exhausted as a great man." ("He's only a little boat looking for a harbor," she adds later.) Charley also generalizes in plain terms: "Willy was a salesman. And for a salesman, there is no rock bottom to the life. He don't put a

bolt to a nut, he don't tell you the law or give you medicine. He's a
man way out there in the blue, riding on a smile and a shoeshine."
Whatever the accuracy of such evaluations, the trite metaphors
and informal syntax, at least, are appropriate to the subject.

The speech of almost everyone is the play mirrors a class, a
generation, and a way of life. "The boss is goin' crazy what kinda
leak he's got in the cash register," a waiter relates; "you put it in but
it don't come out." Clichés are abundant. Hap Loman is "gonna
beat this racket" and come out "number-one man" in order to
prove that his father "did not die in vain." His father excels in his
command of tasteless cant popular in the 1930s. "Well, bottoms
up! . . . And keep your pores open!" Willy calls, saluting his lady
friend. His most sorrowful laments are stock phrases: "where are
you guys, where are you?" he shouts to his sons; "the woods are
burning!" When he gropes for metaphoric originality, he cannot
escape staleness: "because you got a greatness in you, Biff,
remember that. . . . Like a young God. Hercules—something like
that. And the sun, the sun all around him." All the Lomans try to be
eloquent by leavening their lower-middle-class Brooklyn dialect
with high-class diction. They find words like "vengeful," "solidi-
fied," "consumes," "reconstruct," and "prohibit" (Willy), "feasible" and "characteristic" (Hap), "remiss" and "abrupt" (Biff),
"crestfallen" and "conquer" (Linda). In context, unhappily for the
speaker, such terms often sound incongruous.

Judged by these mannerisms, which Miller undoubtedly heard
in his own social milieu, Willy Loman can be seen simply as a
mediocrity native to American society. But Miller's objective, as in
All My Sons, goes beyond linguistic realism. The author customarily underscores his characters' banality with hackneyed phrases
and platitudes; here he practices that form of irony so deftly that
even the vaguest generalization becomes an instrument for self-
exposition.

Willy makes the superficiality of his belief in "personal attractiveness" clear through the way he advertises it. Childlike, he gains
assurance by repeating facile success formulas: "it's not what you
do, Ben. It's who you know and the smile on your face! It's
contacts, Ben, contacts! . . . A man can end with diamonds here on
the basis of being liked!" His trite slogans claim the rhythm as well
as the wisdom of aphorisms. "Because the man who makes an
appearance in the business world," he hopefully pontificates, "the
man who creates personal interest, is the man who gets ahead. Be

liked and you will never want." He invokes supposedly potent words as if repeating them would bring into existence the desired actualities: "I realized that selling was the greatest career a man could want. . . . There was personality in it, Howard. There was respect, and comradeship, and gratitude in it." Even his sons' names betoken his hearty, naïve optimism. His wife and younger son, indeed, echo the favorite magical cliché; Happy's compliment to Biff and Linda's to Willy is "you're well liked."

If the Lomans' favorite adjective is "well liked," one of their commonest—and most revealing—verbs is "make." This verb occurs forty-five times in thirty-three different usages ranging from standard English to slang—expressions such as "make mountains out of molehills," "makin' a hit," "makin' my future," "make me laugh," and "make a train." In the play this wide range of meanings tends to accent a materialistic business ethic. The various denotations are reducible to four general categories— fabrication, causation, execution, and acquisition. Since "a salesman," in Charley's words, "don't put a bolt to a nut, . . . tell you the law or give you medicine," Willy's attitude toward professional achievement stresses acquisition. "Make money" occurs no less than nine times, in addition to instances of seven related idioms like "make a living," "make good," "make the grade," "make a mark," and (simply) "make it." In context, furthermore, a majority of the usages denoting the other three primary senses *imply* attainment (or nonattainment) of success and money as, in the sense of execution, "the man who makes an appearance," "make a nice impression," and "you didn't make me, Willy. I picked you." Self-respect often depends, in Miller's works, upon constructive labor; here twenty-three idiomatic variants of a single verb (thirty-four examples in all) reiterate a contrary interpretation.

Thomas Mann has written, "no man was utterly wretched so long as he could still speak of his misery in high-sounding and noble words. One thing only was indispensable: the courage to call his life by large and fine names." Willy Loman possesses this courage in good measure, and probably his noblest word is the simple noun "man." His contradictory definitions of this word bring into view an unfortunate confusion. He conceives three distinct criteria: according to the interpretation of "make" that he habitually stresses, a man must acquire status and wealth; according to the interpretation of "make" that Willy honors but does not practice, a man must produce tangible goods; and to fulfill the goal he implies

in his catchword "well liked," a man must earn love through
"personal attractiveness." Willy perceives no inconsistency in his
statements on manliness. "A man who can't handle tools is not a
man." Yet "the man who makes an appearance . . . is the man who
gets ahead." Willy knows that "if a man is building something he
must be on the right track"—"a man has got to add up to
something." He learns little about masculine accomplishment,
however, from men who have elicited his respect: his late
employer, Mr. Wagner, "a masterful man"; his father, "an adven-
turous man," "a very great and a very wildhearted man"; his
brother Ben, "a man worth talking to," "the only man I ever met
who knew the answers"; and his neighbor Charley, "a man of few
words." Though Charley admonishes, "the only thing you got in
this world is what you can sell," Willy "always tried to think . . .
that if a man was impressive, and well liked," he could be (in Biff's
phrase) "a leader of men."

Because of his inconsistency, Willy fails to convince himself or
others of his right to the cherished title.[4] No label carries greater
censure for him than "boy" or "kid" ("you are not applying for a
boy's job," he instructs his ne'er-do-well son), but the appellations
others apply to him point to his own immaturity. Miller has
christened him "Lo-man"; his mistress calls him "drummer boy";
and nearly everyone else, including his sons, addresses him with
the diminutive "Willy" or "kid" (Ben, who had considered him fit
for heroic enterprises, employs the dignified form, "William").[5]
And Charley's taunt, "Willy, when are you going to grow up?"
infuriates him.

Willy's family participates in the attempt to define the goal of
manly endeavor. Linda supports her husband's rejection of "ad-
venturous" enterprise. She sees Willy as "a small man" whose best
hope lies with "the firm," not in Alaska. She advises Biff that "a man
is not a bird, to come and go with the springtime" ("you're such a
boy!"). Hap and Biff, however, have difficulty in adjusting to the
"measly manner of existence" demanded of those engaged in
"selling or buying." Hap asserts his virility by seducing the fiancées
of his company superiors ("maybe I just have an overdeveloped
sense of competition"). He would like to get into more manly work
in partnership with Biff—"raise cattle, use our muscles"—but will
not relinquish his "dream" of becoming "number-one man"—a
merchandise manager. His elder brother, more sensitive about his
shortcomings as a man, has been caught in the same deadly im-

passe. While "men built like we are should be working out in the open," "outdoor" work cannot really be considered a dignified vocation. So Biff broods, "I'm like a boy. I'm not married, I'm not in business, I just—I'm like a boy." Not until late in the play does he, unlike his brother and father, bring his occupational goal into line with his instinct for tangible production.

Willy Loman suggests his moral immaturity through logical as well as linguistic contradictions, especially when offering advice to Biff. Though he warns that "'Gee' is a boy's word," he uses the term frequently. He yells at his son, "not finding yourself at the age of thirty-four is a disgrace!" and soon adds, "greatest thing in the world for him was to bum around." "Biff is a lazy bum," he grumbles; then, "and such a hard worker. There's one thing about Biff—he's not lazy." He gives the following advice to Biff before the interview with Oliver: "walk in very serious. You are not applying for a boy's job. Money is to pass. Be quiet, fine, and serious. Everybody likes a kidder, but nobody lends him money." A few lines later Willy says, "walk in with a big laugh. Don't look worried. Start off with a couple of your good stories to lighten things up. It's not what you say, it's how you say it—because personality always wins the day." Memories of past conversations reproduce similar inconsistencies. Willy excused Biff's stealing a football: "sure, he's gotta practice with a regulation ball, doesn't he? Coach'll probably congratulate you on your initiative!" Yet he forgot this excuse: "he's giving it back, isn't he? Why is he stealing? What did I tell him? I never in my life told him anything but decent things." ("Why am I always being contradicted?" he wonders.)[6]

Willy Loman, then, exposes his peculiar "cast of mind" with his verbal idiosyncrasies. In addition, he projects his confusion symbolically; like Lawrence Newman, he admires two individuals who epitomize values that are equally important to him but incompatible. At one extreme stands Dave Singleman, recipient of a salesman's highest reward—he was *very* well liked. After being "remembered and loved and helped by so many different people" in "twenty or thirty different cities," he "died the death of a salesman" in a smoking car on the commuter train to Boston. Dave Singleman attained material gain through love; at the opposite pole, Willy's elder brother acquired goods through force. "Ben! . . . That man was success incarnate!" Willy exclaims, honoring the supreme exemplar of manliness. "The man knew what he wanted and went out and got it!"[7] Recalling the deeds of Ben and their

father, who made flutes and drove "a team right across the
country," Willy boasts "we've got quite a little streak of self-
reliance in our family." He displays this "streak" in his pursuit of
carpentry, gardening, and sports. For Willy, Biff's "greatest"
recognition was to be made captain of a high-school football team.
Biff comments after his father's death, "there's more of him in that
front stoop than in all the sales he ever made." Love of gardening,
another throwback to the pioneer's "self-reliance" personified by
his brother and remembered in his father, supplies the terminology
for an unconscious admission of moral impotence—"nothing's
planted. I don't have a thing in the ground."

Ben, though far more prominent than Dave Singleman in Willy's
memory, was less influential at a crucial point in Willy's career. The
energetic, self-made entrepreneur urged his brother to exploit the
Alaskan frontier ("screw on your fists and you can fight for a
fortune up there"), but Willy imagined that he and his sons could
make their fortune in the city and cultivate hardiness in their
Brooklyn backyard. He did not recognize the radical disparity
between slogans about "contacts" or "appearance" and Ben's
ritually repeated success story about walking into a jungle. Instead,
he invented a glib formula for child-rearing that amalgamated the
ideals of tough aggressiveness and genteel sociability: "that's just
the way I'm bringing them up, Ben—rugged, well liked, all-
around." It is not, therefore, simply the rejection of his brother's
mode of masculine action that leads Willy to catastrophe; he
founders on his unwillingness to come to terms with the consequences of that rejection. His desire to instill in Biff both a love of
"comradeship" and the spirit "to walk into a jungle" is frustrated by
"exhaustion," by financial insecurity, by disrespect from his sons,
customers, and employer, and above all by his inability to
distinguish between opposite values.[8] Biff's appraisal—"the man
didn't know who he was"—suits him perfectly.

II *Narrative Technique*

In telling his story Miller returned to a narrative technique he had
found useful before. The father's guilt in *All My Sons* becomes
apparent to the audience and to the antagonist after being hinted at
in a succession of fragmentary references to a hidden crime.
Though in *Death of a Salesman* the son already knows his father's
sin, the spectator learns the truth in a climactic revelation that

follows a series of covert allusions.[9] "There's one or two things depressing him," Biff says in the opening scene, inaugurating the series. Later he adds, "I know he's a fake and he doesn't like anybody around who knows!" Linda, blindly loyal, suspects nothing: "what has [Biff] got against you?" she asks her husband. Bernard, a neighbor, inquires into the secret shared by father and son: "what happened in Boston, Willy?" Willy's response, "I can't tell you," sums up his reticence on the topic.

Suggestive references of this kind, however, are relatively unimportant in this work. The chief narrative method for developing tension, temperament, and fact is dramatized memory, which allows the dramatist to represent time as "a mobile concurrency of past and present" rather than as a sequence of discrete, independent segments.[10] This subjective approach to delayed exposition brings to light not only crucial past events but also the emotional charges associated with them; Willy Loman oscillates between current and earlier guilt-feelings. The memories, generally concerned with the disintegration of his family and his professional aspirations, are released by analogous happenings in the present. Thus, after he is fired by Howard, Willy remembers his refusal of a vocational opportunity that might have led to magnificent accomplishment instead of the present ignominy. And Biff's unfavorable report on an attempt to acquire financial backing for a business turns Willy's mind back to the hotel room in which Biff discovered him with his mistress—a discovery that the father fears has initiated his son's failures.

Transitions in place and time are cleverly implemented by ingenious stage effects, a skeletonized house-set, multiple playing areas (apron, forestage, and two levels of the house), and the repetition of key words or topics before, during, and after each recollection. Miller's skill in executing imaginative, meaningful transitions is apparent in the opening scene, which introduces the subject of family disharmony. A conversation with Linda about his driving that day reminds Willy of the old "Chevvy" he owned when his boys still loved and obeyed him. As he "loses himself in reminiscences," sitting in his kitchen, interest moves to another playing level, the upstairs bedroom, where the brothers too have been discussing their father's careless driving. Then, when they recall their popularity with girls in their youth, they in turn are interrupted by Willy "mumbling" downstairs to an imaginary Biff on the same subject ("the girls pay for you? . . . Boy, you must really be makin' a hit"). Musical motifs, lighting arrangements, and scenic changes complete the preparation for the first vision, which opens, appropriately, with Willy admiring his popular teen-age sons as Biff polishes the "Chevvy."

During this transition, as in others, recurring themes are grouped in psychologically significant combinations. While Willy visualizes a joyful, affectionate family group, another intimate but less innocent scene from a still earlier time—again involving a "girl"— breaks in on the word "make":

> *Willy* [to Linda]: There's so much I want to make for—
> *The Woman*: Me? You didn't make me, Willy. I picked you.

Willy's family-dream returns, with Linda mending stockings (his mistress had asked for "a lot of stockings"), but since innocence has been corrupted now, shame colors the recollection. Now the mention of girls and cars, punctuated by "The Woman's laugh," denotes Biff's (and by implication, Willy's) irresponsibility, not worth. Changed to waking nightmare, the daydream disappears and leaves Willy alone in his kitchen, guiltily denying responsibility for his son's decline.

Two motives impel Willy to conjure the "reminiscences." He seeks *escape* from his problems by reliving a happier time ("how do we get back to all the great times? . . . Always some kind of good news coming up"). Disturbed by recurring troubles, however, he involuntarily recalls bad news that forces him to seek the *origin* of his and Biff's difficulties. "Why?" he continually asks, "what—what's the secret? . . . Why? Why! Bernard, that question has been trailing me like a ghost for the last fifteen years." Yet the same lack of self-awareness that caused his failure as a father keeps him from learning the "secret" contained in the visions. In contrast to Biff, who finally accepts his limitations, Willy remains unalterably determined that his son shall show the world "all kinds of greatness." His hallucinations thus measure the blind intensity of his ambition, which is strong enough to withstand not only galling indignities in the present but also agonizing internal re-creations of his inadequacy in the past.[11]

As circumstances become more threatening and as his remembrances become more explicit, leading Willy back to the central trauma of his life, his resistance to self-knowledge grows correspondingly more desperate. He stubbornly refuses to admit defeat. For example, when Charley offers him work as a way to salvage his pride, he "furiously" refuses. The effect of his growing anxiety is to steadily increase tension as the action progresses: Willy's agitated justifications gradually cumulate great excitement. When dealing with an intense character who concentrates his energies "upon the fixed point of his commitment," Miller writes, a playwright must design "scenes of high and open emotion, and plays constructed toward climax rather than the evocation of a mood alone or of bizarre spectacle" (*C.P.*, 7).[12]

Within the acts and scenes, he modifies this principle by interjecting moments of relative calm. The technique, practiced effectively in *All My Sons* and given additional flexibility by the temporal and spatial fluctuations in *Death of a Salesman*, can be easily observed in the first-act card game between Charley and Willy. The game begins quietly with good-natured small talk—a Miller specialty—that contrasts markedly with the strident finale ("the woods are burning!") of the hallucination just ended. "Can't we do something about the walls? You sneeze in here, and in my house hats blow off," Charley jokes. Seconds later, Willy loses his temper when his neighbor offers him a job, causing a moderately heated exchange. This anger quickly subsides, dispelled by Willy's sorrow over Biff ("I got nothin' to give him"); but in another minute Willy insults Charley again ("you're disgusting") and restores tension. At this point, Ben's image enters to complicate the succession of high and low emotional pitches. Suspense eases briefly during the dual conversation (Willy-Charley and Willy-Ben) as Ben proposes to send his brother to Alaska—the antecedent to Charley's more prosaic proposition—only to be renewed when Willy, remembering the pivotal choice of his career, irascibly terminates the game by accusing his friend of a misplay. This short episode—conducted almost entirely in stichomythic dialogue—contributes to a larger pattern of tensional variation: as an interlude between two stormy re-enactments of the past, it secures temporary relief from the ascending movement toward climax. At the same time, it sustains interest by mixing sorrow with anger. (Another discussion between Charley and Willy achieves similar effects in the second act.) Relatively subdued yet variegated in tone, the incident exemplifies the careful control of detail in Miller's finest writing.

The second act begins on an optimistic note: Biff has gone to request financial support for an undertaking—a sporting goods business—that he hopes will satisfy all the Loman criteria for masculine integrity. But tension increases sharply as Willy reaches the nadir of his profession—he is fired because no one likes him any longer. Finally, Willy's self-defense reaches its crisis. Insecurity, originally aroused by remembrance of The Woman, becomes unbearable with her re-entrance in the restaurant scene. This scene—a virtuoso orchestration of changing moods, times, themes, and stage effects—culminates the progression to climax. Simultaneously, it culminates the progression to truth; Willy unintentionally exhibits conclusive proof that his dishonesty, instability, and self-righteousness caused the father-son antagonism in the past and has perpetuated it in the present.

At first, Hap's amusing, worldly-wise manner with the comic waiter and with the "lavishly dressed" woman ("don't try, honey, try hard") provides respite from the relentlessly accumulating pressure. But Biff reinstitutes that pressure with his feverish recital of the debacle at his former employer's office. When Willy enters, shattered by an interview with *his* former employer, completely incommensurate attitudes are apparent—the elder brother's nervous determination to force his father to face "the truth," the father's frantic hopefulness regarding Biff's prospects, and the younger brother's blissful indifference to any problem weightier than seducing a pretty "girl." To further contort the grotesque interplay between optimism and dread, Biff's report triggers in Willy a recollection of the terrible hour in which his son saw him with The Woman in a Boston hotel room. The resulting dialogue is a polyphony of contrasting feelings: Hap tries to humor his father, brother, and girl friends; Biff revolves between rage and pity; Willy, recalling his mortification before his young son sixteen years earlier, and confusing present with past arguments, moves from wrath to anguish. Violent gestures, jarring trumpet notes, fading lights, and disembodied laughs jumble this well-ordered conversational chaos. Even the young ladies Hap has acquired add to the emotional diversity. From the depths of compassion Biff haltingly confesses, "Miss Forsythe, you've just seen a prince walk by. A fine, troubled prince. A hard-working, unappreciated prince. A pal, you understand? A good companion. Always for his boys." And Miss Forsythe insipidly replies, "That's so sweet"!

After Willy's impotent reassertion of authority in the restaurant's washroom ("I gave you an order!"), excitement modulates in descending stages to the closing quiet. By debating suicide with

"Ben," whose advice Willy now invents rather than recalls, the protagonist prepares himself (and the spectator) for release from anxiety. The urgency of his last argument with Biff is sharp but transient; when both verbalize their resentment—the restaurant turmoil hardly permitted anything so rational—at least token reconciliation is possible. Heartened by his son's love,[13] encouraged by his brother's imagined approval, driven by his consuming need to "make it, Biff and I," and accompanied by music that "crashes down in a frenzy of sound," Willy Loman insanely rushes off to gloss his tarnished image. This "frenzy" abruptly graduates to "the soft pulsation of a single cello string," and the play concludes with a sense of exhaustion suitable to the Salesman's end.

III   *The Ethical Implication*

The final assertion of personal worth ("a man has got to add up to something") turns out to be a final evasion of responsibility. With his suicide Willy intended to refute the indications that he had failed in his profession, in his family life, and, most important, in his self-estimation. But his insurance money could not possibly efface those indications because Biff has rejected a monetary standard of success—the "something" Willy decides to "add up to." Through a last profitless transaction the Salesman demonstrates again his obliviousness to the ethical implications of his acts. The other characters gain limited insights. In the short "requiem" they deliver conflicting evaluations: Charley will remember Willy's insecurity; Hap, his determination; Biff, his confusion. And each mourner reacts differently to the suicide: Charley—who had counseled that "nobody's worth nothin' dead"—must find an excuse for it; Hap misinterprets it; Biff condemns it; and Linda "can't understand it." (Willy's business associates pay no attention to it.)

What judgment should be rendered by the *spectator*, whose knowledge transcends these partial perceptions? Some spectators have declared Willy to be a passive victim of society—Miller's vehicle for an attack on American institutions or values. The following typical statement represents this opinion: "there is hardly an American of recent years who has stood wholly 'free and clear' of the sources of corruption which destroyed Willy Loman and baffled his sons: the insidious charm of advertised gadgets, the noisy glamor of school and college athletics, the dazzling authority of the Bitch Goddess, the concept of 'number one' and a certain readiness to cut corners in the sacred name of competition."[14] For another critic the play is "symbolic of the breakdown of the whole concept of salesmanship inherent in our society."[15] Eleanor Clark's comment on *Death of a Salesman* as "party line literature" has been quoted previously. Miller himself, despite his denial of "propagandist" intentions, has stated that he wished to counter "the law which says that a failure in society and in business has no right to live" with an "opposing system" based upon "love" (*C.P.*, 35–38).[16]

The play obviously alludes to attitudes and manners of the 1930s; the habits of a generation can, after all, be translated into dramatic dialogue. The slang, the references to knickers, old "Chevvies," and Hastings refrigerators, and the naïve definitions of success recall a specific period and a specific middle-class milieu. Willy's memories bring together some of the contradictions between ideals and actualities that characterized this era in the United States—contradictions between moral purity and self-indulgence, "rugged" independence and sentimental gregariousness, grand optimism and nagging insecurity, noble generosity and petty vulgarity. But Miller's technical apparatus—the colloquial language, the symbolic images, and the dramatized recollections—shapes the pride and the blindness of a mentality, not the evil influence of a social condition. If causal responsibility were to be assigned to any single source, that source would be the ego, presented throughout the work as the decisive arena of action. Indeed, in two later plays, *After the Fall* and *Incident at Vichy*, Miller quite explicitly proposed a practical lesson on the dangers of disregarding unpleasant psychological truths; one might with some justice draw an inference to that effect from *Death of a Salesman*. It seems futile, therefore, in view of the subjective perspective of the play, to exaggerate the importance of social causation by balancing admirable and unscrupulous characters[17] or by isolating pointed lines like Charley's observation that "for a salesman, there is no rock bottom to the life." The authority of *Death of a Salesman* can be located in its masterful visualization of Willy's longing and self-defeat.[18]

CHAPTER 4

Four "Social Plays"

I   The Crucible

AFTER *Focus, All My Sons,* and *Death of a Salesman,* many playgoers decided that Arthur Miller was a topical dramatist who dealt with injustices in American society such as anti-Semitism and capitalistic exploitation of the "common man." *The Crucible* confirmed their interpretation. This work, they assumed, addressed itself to that controversial subject of the early 1950s, Senator Joseph McCarthy's investigations of Communist subversion in the United States.[1] Miller had apparently camouflaged his condemnation of those proceedings with the tale of an equally notorious witch hunt conducted at Salem in 1692. The analogy seemed clear enough even though the setting of the play was a Massachusetts colony; the government, a Puritan "theocracy"; the prosecutor, Deputy Governor Danforth; and the subversives, Satan's agents disguised as ordinary townsfolk.

Miller did not deny the obvious contemporary relevance, but insisted that he was concerned with a problem larger than the current investigations. Senator McCarthy's activities, "a kind of personification of [moral] disintegration,"[2] symbolized a dehumanizing influence that might occur in any period. His subject was mass hysteria: he wished to show how it could be fomented by self-appointed (and self-seeking) saviors; what its social and psychological consequences might be; and how it must be averted. "It was not only the rise of 'McCarthyism' that moved me, but something which seemed much more weird and mysterious. It was the fact that a political, objective, knowledgeable campaign from the far Right was capable of creating not only a terror, but a new subjective reality, a veritable mystique which was gradually assuming even a holy resonance. . . . The terror in these people was being knowingly planned and consciously engineered, and yet

37

all they knew was terror" (*C.P.*, 39–40). *The Crucible* may well be called a "social play" since it analyzes a public phenomenon with historical precedent and current actuality. But it focuses on the "subjective reality" of that phenomenon; it cannot be judged merely on the literal accuracy or political aptness of its topical allusions.[3]

Miller explains the social and religious causes of the Puritan madness in a long commentary accompanying the play. Not everyone who contributed to that madness, he admits, was villainous. Some officials, like Danforth, Reverend Hale, and Judge Hathorne, committed the gravest wrongs in the name of the public welfare, as they conceived it. Salem was governed by "a combine of state and religious power whose function was to keep the community together, and to prevent any kind of disunity that might open it to destruction by material or ideological enemies." Any impatience with this power was curbed by harsh restrictive measures. The chief enemy to be exorcised was Satan; in formulating political policy, state authorities were able to enlist the Puritan's belief in the supernatural origin of good and evil. Miller's conclusion in this respect clearly refers to a contemporary situation: "the necessity of the Devil may become evident as a weapon, a weapon designed and used time and time again in every age to whip men into a surrender to a particular church or church-state. . . . A political policy is equated with moral right, and opposition to it with diabolical malevolence."

Greater harm, however, was done for personal than for political reasons. "Long-held hatreds of neighbors could now be openly expressed, and vengeance taken. . . . Land-lust . . . could now be elevated to the arena of morality." These egoistic motives are illustrated by minor details in the play: the quarrel between Putnam and Proctor over lumber, Reverend Parris's preoccupation with firewood and candleholders, and Giles's propensities for litigation. Selfish motives are also illustrated in the major incidents that magnify excitement prior to the explosion of hysteria. Miller sees bewitchment as a mental state that can be deliberately induced by unscrupulous individuals. The method used by malicious figures like Abigail and the Putnams to gain control over the frightened, the gullible, and the weak-willed is indeed diabolical. They first completely demoralize their victim, then subtly implant in him the terms of a confession that will release him from suspicion and at the same time achieve their own devious ends.

When *The Crucible* begins, the reported discovery of the girls' dancing has already instilled fear of demonic infiltration in the community. Reverend Parris, his daughter suspected of devil-worship, eagerly grasps at suggestions carefully insinuated by the Putnams, a couple bearing "many grievances." Mrs. Putnam thoroughly shakes the minister with her "vicious certainty" that his daughter Betty has commerced with the Devil, after which Putnam cunningly prescribes a plan to divert public notice: "you are not undone! Let you take hold here. Wait for no one to charge you—declare it yourself. You have discovered witchcraft." The terrified girl, as well as her intimidated father, seizes upon the words of this clever husband-wife team; overhearing Mrs. Putnam ask, "how high did she fly, how high?" Betty cries, "I'll fly to Mama. Let me fly!" In this way, knaves gain control of fools, brush aside the sane counsels of those who try to exert a calming influence, and initiate Salem's passion.

Reverend Hale, a scholarly expert on deviltry, signals the next stage in the growth of panic. Motivated by a "tasty love of intellectual pursuit" (author's note), he is more sincere than the Putnams, but he mercilessly continues the attack on poor whimpering Betty by driving at the theme introduced earlier by Mrs. Putnam (and taken up later by Abigail, the prime instigator of the witch hunt): "does someone afflict you, child? . . . Perhaps some bird invisible to others comes to you. . . . Is there some figure bids you fly?" When the chorus of interrogators—Hale, the Putnams, Abigail, and Parris—turns from Betty to Tituba, the impressionable Negro slave is so terrified that she eagerly reaches for the escape offered her by Hale and Putnam—a confession of complicity with the Devil ("we will protect you. . . . And we will bless you, Tituba"). The manner in which they elicit specific responses through suggestion may be observed in this exchange:

Hale: When the Devil comes to you does he ever come—with another person? . . .
Putnam: Sarah Good? Did you ever see Sarah Good with him? Or Osburn? . . .
Tituba: And then he come one stormy night to me, and he say, "Look! I have *white* people belong to me." And I look—and there was Goody Good. . . . Aye, sir, and Goody Osburn.

Abigail cleverly augments the uproar after Tituba's admission by adding her own. Her action induces frenzy in the other girls and accelerates the chain reaction of accusation and confession.

These incidents, Miller notes, may be considered a kind of introduction or "overture" to the trial.[4] Following a fairly long expository interval during which Abigail brings about the imprisonment of her rival, Elizabeth Proctor, the deliberate implantation of irrational notions in susceptible minds continues in the climactic episode. Several conventional narrative devices prepare the stage. At the beginning of Act Three, two unseen characters are heard in conversation—the offstage-actor technique invented by Aeschylus. Then there is the plot formula based on an unjust trial of a just man, with a heated debate on salvation and damnation. The trial at first involves traditional courtroom theatrics—fierce charges and countercharges by the participants, shouted objections and periodic clamor from the "townspeople"—[5] but Miller presently moves the hearing into a "vestry room" to create a more intimate stage setting. Another venerable plot convention, the fatal exposure of a lie, appears twice: once, when the court disproves Mary Warren's claim to be able to "pretend" fainting; again, when Governor Danforth discredits the veracity of John Proctor, the protagonist. In the second instance, as in *All My Sons*, a woman inadvertently betrays her husband, although here the basic device has been varied: Proctor is discredited, ironically, because the lie is *believed* (Elizabeth affirms his marital fidelity), while the truth (that Abigail, the adultress, wishes to supplant Elizabeth) is disbelieved.

With Proctor's case demolished, Abigail vigorously resumes her brilliant impersonation of a soul possessed. Pushed beyond the bounds of sanity by Abigail's performance, by the spectacular gyrations of her friends, and by that effective convincer, "confess yourself or you will hang," Mary Warren, who might have testified to Abigail's "private vengeance" against Elizabeth, breaks down—another victim of induced hysteria. Her ecstatic transports intensify the wildly melodramatic climax (the stage directions call for "gigantic screams" from the girls as they stare at an imaginary "bird"), and Proctor histrionically protests the triumph of unreason: "you are pulling Heaven down and raising up a whore!"

In constructing this "interior mechanism of confession and forgiveness" *(C.P., 40)*, Miller places special emphasis on the insidious role played by certain individuals. It would be an oversimplification, however, to say that he conceives the conflict as one between the innocent and wicked. The characters in *The Crucible* may better be described as either maturing or ethically fixed personalities—a distinction relevant to the contrast between Lawrence Newman and Carlson in *Focus,* Chris and Joe Keller in *All My Sons,* Biff and Willy Loman in *Death of a Salesman.* Whether self-righteous, vindictive, or merely escapist, those who share the responsibility for bringing on the disaster are mentally static or unstable, however dynamic they might be in action. They continue to enforce blindly, to manipulate ruthlessly, or to follow fearfully sanctified standards of conduct even when to do so becomes absurd and destructive.

Miller underlines their inflexibility by characterizing them in a mechanical fashion. Although Abigail has a few passionate lines as a jealous lover, she functions primarily as a catalyst in the intimidation-confession process. Others fall into more stereotyped patterns—Parris, the ranting paranoiac; Mary Warren and her friends, the malleable children; Tituba, the frightened, somewhat comic darky; Danforth, the uncompromising but misguided judge. Some of the wholly admirable figures are also stock types, like Giles Corey (the gruff, honest farmer) and Rebecca Nurse (the calm, comforting, wise old matriarch). For the reader, Miller's notes heighten the impression of static characterization when they anticipate a character's first lines, as in these instances:

Author's note: [Parris] believed he was being persecuted wherever he went, despite his best efforts to win people and God to his side.
Parris: I do not fathom it, why am I persecuted here? I cannot offer one proposition but there be a howling riot of argument. I have often wondered if the Devil be in it somewhere; I cannot understand you people otherwise.

Author's note: Danforth is a grave man in his sixties, of some humor and sophistication that does not, however, interfere with an exact loyalty to his position and his cause.
Danforth: While I speak God's law, I will not crack its voice with whimpering. If retaliation is your fear, know this—I should hang ten thousand that dared to rise against the law, and an ocean of salt tears could not melt the resolution of the statutes.

Resisting predetermined behavior patterns, three characters—at first deficient in "charity" and immersed in self-concern—eventually make humane, courageous, and rational adjustments to the

formidable challenges confronting them. The moral growth of
Reverend Hale and the Proctors contrasts on one hand with the
rigidity of Abigail, Hathorne, and Danforth, and on the other with
the instability of Tituba, Parris, and the girls. Reverend Hale seems
unpromising as a candidate for change. A note introduces him as a
stock figure—a smug intellectual with "the pride of the specialist
whose unique knowledge has at last been publicly called for." His
words bear out this description: "here is all the invisible world,
caught, defined, and calculated," he lectures; "in these books the
Devil stands stripped of all his brute disguises." But the "deeply
honest" minister, sickened at last by the gross injustice he has
abetted, denounces the judges. Elizabeth too arrives at greater
understanding. Initially adamant in her condemnation of her
husband's single adulterous act ("you forget nothin' and forgive
nothin'," Proctor complains; "learn charity, woman"), she acquires
a tolerance for human fallibility and an appreciation for human
goodness during her trial and imprisonment.

John Proctor does not advance, like Elizabeth and Hale, from
vanity to charity. He progresses in a different direction—from
shame to renewed assurance. For a time his humility as an
adulterer disposes him to accept the greater humiliation of
confessing to witchcraft; since he has already blackened his "good
name" by succumbing to and then publicly admitting lechery, he is
tempted to save at least his life. Indignation, however, compels
him to salvage self-respect. "How may I live without my name? . . .
Show honor now, show a stony heart and sink them with it." With
exalted victory-in-defeat rhetoric he proclaims his rediscovery of
what he thought had been lost—a "sense of personal invio-
lability. . . . That's what Proctor means near the end of the play
when he talks of his 'name.' He is really speaking about his identity,
which he cannot surrender."[6]

The Crucible, then, explores two contrary processes in the
context of a given social order—the generation of hysteria and the
achievement of moral honesty. How successfully are the two
processes integrated? The first three acts are very well structured.
Through an expository method Miller favored in earlier plays—
delayed revelation of past sins—he reveals, in retrospect, that the
central psycho-social issue of witchcraft arose from the private
issue involving Abigail, John and Elizabeth Proctor—a Puritanical
variant of the eternal triangle. Among the few covert early
allusions to the seduction are Parris's remark that Elizabeth "comes

so rarely to the church this year for she will not sit so close to something soiled [Abigail]," and Betty's comment to Abigail, "you drank a charm to kill Goody Proctor!" Abigail's passion for Proctor, which moves her to attack Elizabeth through the witch hunt, provides the chief causal link between the private and public issues even though it remains of secondary dramatic importance. The second act, a transitional interlude bridging the introductory and climactic episodes, builds suspense and develops the two subjects preparatory to their simultaneous resolution in the trial scene.[7] In the third act, Proctor and Hale cannot turn aside the forces maneuvered by Abigail, and the action ascends to its shrill emotional peak.

During this well-balanced ascent toward insanity, Proctor's personal difficulties are subordinate to Salem's ordeal. The conclusion abruptly reverses that relationship in a last-act shift of interest similar to, though not so disruptive as, the shift in *All My Sons*. Without warning, Miller's exhibition of devil-possession ceases.[8] Having sparked Salem's "fire," Abigail disappears; "the legend has it that Abigail turned up later as a prostitute in Boston," a footnote explains. Moreover, it seems that even as "terror" was spreading unchecked in Salem the condemnations were being called into question elsewhere in the area. The authority of the prosecutors has suddenly come to depend upon confession by those victims recently condemned, so that continued defiance by a highly regarded citizen like John Proctor will cure the town's fever. If Abigail's desire to supplant Elizabeth was the prime excitant of the madness, Proctor's desire to preserve his "name" becomes the prime depressant. When the protagonist realizes he cannot betray himself and his friends with a false confession, he at once completes his progression toward integrity and diverts Salem from its movement toward chaos.

The first consequence offers a consistent and positive, if unpleasant, denouement: facing execution in an irrational society, a man asserts his will to judge his own honesty and to oppose injustice. The second consequence, however, does not logically follow from the preceding action. Only some misgivings voiced by Parris and Hale support the premise that *Proctor's* salvation will ensure *Salem's* salvation. "Andover have thrown out the court, they say, and will have no part of witchcraft," Parris reports. "There be a faction here, feeding on that news, and I tell you true, sir, I fear there will be riot here." He protests to the judges that "it were

another sort that hanged till now. . . . These people have great
weight yet in the town." Hale alerts the governor to "orphans
wandering from house to house; abandoned cattle bellow on the
highroads, the stink of rotting crops hangs everywhere, and no
man knows when the harlots' cry will end his life—and you wonder
yet if rebellion's spoke?" This reportorial narration cannot carry
the heavy causal burden placed upon it. Nor can Proctor's last
brave speeches, inspiring as they sound, account for the fact that
after his hanging (Miller adds in a postscript) "the power of
theocracy in Massachusetts was broken." How does Proctor's
courage interrupt the "interior mechanism of confession and
forgiveness"? What psychological impact does self-sacrifice have
upon those who have triggered and those who have been crushed
by that mechanism? The notion implied in the conclusion, that
society may be redeemed by its maturest citizens, is an affirmative
one. But this optimistic expectation, while intellectually grati-
fying, does not jibe with the traumatic agitation of the climax or
with the quiet sorrow at the close.[9]

II   A View from the Bridge

Miller's characters function more intelligibly as fathers, sons,
husbands, or wives in a family setting than as citizens in society. Of
course, the protagonist of A View from the Bridge acts in a specific
social milieu that conditions his sense of guilt and his sense of
dignity. Yet for Eddie Carbone guilt and dignity derive from an
intimate attachment: his fatherly concern for his niece is as
obsessive as that shown by Joe Keller and Willy Loman for their
sons, his dramatic existence as dependent as theirs upon filial
allegiance, his grief after being deserted as sharp. His reactions
answer the question, to what lengths might a man go to protect his
prerogatives as a father? "I want my respect!" Eddie shouts,
repeating the demand made—often with the same words—by
Miller's chief characters.[10]

As in earlier plays, too, the "subjective reality" of the protagonist's trial assumes central artistic importance. For the first
time, however, in A View from the Bridge sexual desire and
jealousy become the dominant components of that reality.[11] Eddie
refuses to accept the implication that his fervent insistence on his
niece's loyalty carries with it the energy of physical attraction, but
like Willy Loman and Joe Keller he involuntarily bares his

emotional secret with his words and actions. From the beginning of the play his extreme possessiveness suggests the strength of a passion he will not acknowledge. The thought that Catherine could be contaminated by the world's wickedness or subjected to another man's authority is intolerable to him. Morbidly sensitive about her claim to adulthood, he dislikes her short skirts and clacking high heels, her "wavy" walk, her chats with Louis, and her plan to get a job. "You're a baby," he insists, though she is almost eighteen; "I guess I just never figured on one thing. . . . That you would ever grow up."

But Catherine *has* grown up, and her feminine maturity represents a potential threat to the innocent, affectionate rapport between uncle and niece. Beatrice, Eddie's wife, detects this threat. She feels obliged to warn the naïve girl not to throw "yourself at him like when you was twelve years old," not to appear "in front of him in your slip," not to sit "on the edge of the bathtub talkin' to him when he's shavin' in his underwear." "It's wonderful for a whole family to love each other," she argues, "but you're a grown woman and you're in the same house with a grown man." Alfieri, a lawyer, refers more directly to a sexual motive: "sometimes," he tells Eddie, "there is too much love for the daughter, there is too much love for the niece." Eddie's agitated responses to such statements attest to his unwillingness to admit the presence of this motive. "What're you talkin' about, marry me! I don't know what the hell you're talkin' about!" he "furiously" retorts, after Alfieri states, "she can't marry you, can she?" And Eddie is "shocked" and "horrified" (author's description) when Beatrice puts the problem quite bluntly: "you want somethin' else, Eddie, and you can never have her!" Eventually, in drunken, jealous rage, he expresses in gesture the secret he had denied in speech: "he reaches out suddenly, draws [Catherine] to him, and as she strives to free herself he kisses her on the mouth." (stage directions, italics omitted).[12]

Miller was particularly interested in the destructiveness of this inadmissible but irresistible passion—"a passion which, despite its contradicting the self-interest of the individual it inhabits, despite every kind of warning, despite even its destruction of the moral beliefs of the individual, proceeds to magnify its power over him until it destroys him" (*C.P.*, 48). The principal narrative convention Miller uses to "magnify its power" is a love-triangle. The rivalry arises immediately upon the entrance of Rodolpho and Marco,

brothers who have just illegally entered the United States from
Sicily, in a scene that splendidly illustrates Miller's ability to
encompass strong anxiety in commonplace talk. After the in-
troductions, Rodolpho gradually dominates the conversation,
impressing Catherine with his exuberant charm. Eddie had addressed his first remarks mainly to Marco, the elder brother; then,
eclipsed by the younger, he speaks progressively fewer lines. This
reticence, together with the defensive nature of his occasional
comments, subtly indicates his growing uneasiness and resentment. Finally, as Rodolpho crowns his dazzling self-exhibition by
singing a popular lyric, Eddie abruptly terminates the song and the
scene by reminding his guest of his uncertain legal status as an
immigrant. "Now," Alfieri declares, making the point explicit,
"there was a trouble that would not go away." Except for this
declaration, the inception of the sex-rivalry is conveyed entirely
through Eddie's ominous silences and through the connotations of
his sullen dialogue.[13]

Eddie's subsequent responses reveal the depth of his turmoil. He
insists that Rodolpho is an irresponsible "hit-and-run guy" who
wants to marry Catherine only to obtain American citizenship—he
is an "enemy" and a "thief" who breaks into a home, "makes a
stranger" of its head, and tries to carry off its treasure ("he's stealing
from me!"). This accusation, however inaccurate, is not nearly so
far-fetched as the next, that the blond Rodolpho must be a
homosexual as well as a thief. After all, he cooks, sews, and sings "in
a high tenor voice". "I mean he looked so sweet there, like an
angel—you could kiss him he was so sweet." Eddie enmeshes
himself so completely in his delusion that he impulsively tries to
prove it to his niece by kissing Rodolpho before her. The grossness
of this act and the irrationality of his accusations, which could have
no effect other than to further alienate Catherine, indicate the
intensity of the longshoreman's desperation.

Shame and hopelessness drive Eddie to a still more irrational
deed; seeking to protect his family's integrity, he destroys it. He
violates the Sicilian code of honor operative in his social world by
betraying the brothers—and, unintentionally, the relatives of a
friend—to the immigration authorities. Disgraced now both in his
neighborhood and in his home, he hazards a last defense of his
"name" in the manhood ritual of the duel with Marco, then is
delivered from humiliation by death. "Fear of being displaced, the
disaster inherent in being torn away from our chosen image of

what and who we are in this world,"[14] has driven him to a vindictive course of behavior that brings about a result opposite to what he had intended.

A View from the Bridge may thus be seen as an intriguing psychological study that shows the self-destructiveness of an inflexible, passionate individual; as such, the play resembles *All My Sons, Death of a Salesman,* and *The Crucible.* Again, however, Miller hoped to enlarge his scope beyond that of psychological analysis. He worked toward his end with Alfieri's commentary and with the vendetta between Eddie and Marco. As narrator, Alfieri— a contemporary substitute for the Greek chorus—establishes a rhetorical contrast with Eddie much greater than that between Chris and Joe Keller. His sonorous periodic sentences (he repeats the connective "and" in biblical fashion), his dignified diction, elegant imagery, and legendary allusions are obviously far removed from the protagonist's lower-class Brooklynese.[15] Alfieri succeeds in viewing Eddie's tortured protests from a rational perspective. But his formal explanations lessen the force of those protests by constantly interrupting the cumulation of tension. The most anticlimactic of his eight appearances, which divide the play into short, independent episodes, follows the emotional highpoint. After Eddie's startling performance in kissing Catherine and Rodolpho, the narrator intones, "and if I seem to tell this like a dream, it was that way. Several moments arrived in the course of the talks we had when it occurred to me how—almost transfixed I had come to feel." This deliberate slackening of pace must be compensated for later with some lively stage business—the police raid and the knife fight.

The philosophical content, as well as the style and timing of Alfieri's speeches, sustains a reflective, dispassionate "view." Eddie's fixation, the attorney announces, has an ancient lineage: "in some Caesar's year, in Calabria perhaps or on the cliff at Syracuse, another lawyer . . . heard the same complaint." It is caused by an objectively existing vital force: "soon I saw it was only a passion that had moved into his body, like a stranger." Its course is predetermined: "I knew where he was heading for, I knew where he was going to end." And it is elementally "pure." With this description, Alfieri elevates an abnormal emotional condition to a metaphysical plane where it is seen as legendary, objective, predictable, and sacred—even though Eddie's behavior reveals it to be idiosyncratic, subjective, erratic, and shameful. Eddie may be as fanatic and as uncompromising as a Greek tragic hero, but Alfieri's classical interpretation of his motives is foreign to Miller's twentieth-century "psycho-sexual" assumptions. Locating the origin of passion in a transcendent rather than in an inward source, the narrator proposes a psychological theory incompatible with that implied in the action. A chorus conferred many benefits upon Greek tragedy, but Alfieri's contribution to A View from the Bridge seems seriously limited.[16]

The contribution made by the vendetta situation—Marco takes on the obligation to avenge Eddie's disloyalty, Eddie in turn feels injured by Marco's insults—can also be questioned. Miller explains that he introduced the feud idea to broaden the ethical frame of reference and to cultivate a "myth-like feeling":

The mind of Eddie Carbone is not comprehensible apart from its relation to his neighborhood, his fellow workers, his social situation. His self-esteem depends upon their estimate of him, and his value is created largely by his fidelity to the code of his culture. . . . A certain size accrued to him as a result [of violating the code]. The importance of his interior psychological dilemma was magnified to the size it would have in life. What had seemed like a mere aberration had now risen to a fatal violation of an ancient law.[17]

That is, the urgency of his "interior dilemma" can be gauged by the fact that it drives him to break an "ancient law" of family loyalty.

This breach of "moral belief" does not come without preparation. Before deciding to inform, Eddie recounts the retaliation (ostracism) visited upon a neighbor who had broken the code. In addition, he tells Catherine that Rodolpho "could be picked up any day here and he's back pushin' taxis up the hill!" He warns the immigrant, "look, kid, you don't want to be picked up, do ya?" And he threatens, "watch your step, submarine. By rights they oughta throw you back in the water." These hints, however, do not simply prepare a violent ending to the struggle with Rodolpho; they introduce a conflict with a new antagonist—Marco. The younger brother, Eddie reasons, "didn't take my name; he's only a punk. Marco's got my name." Eddie's duel with Marco, who upholds a principle important in Sicilian society, transfers the defense of pride to a public arena, as Miller intended. But the contest for honor in society develops *after* the critical contest for love reaches its climax. When Eddie insists upon Marco's (and the community's) respect rather than Catherine's affection as his requisite for "self-esteem," the conclusion assumes a direction tangential to that established by the main action—a structural fault present also in *All My Sons* and in *The Crucible*. Reaching out for philosophical and social "laws," Miller again loosens his hold upon "interior" realities.[18]

III A Memory of Two Mondays

In 1955 Miller offered (together with the original production of *A View from the Bridge*) an admirable one-act play, *A Memory of Two Mondays*. The work was not, like those that had immediately preceded it, a psychological study with social connotations; it could be labeled a "social play" in the strictest sense of the term. "Nothing in this book was written with greater love," Miller wrote in the *Collected Plays*, "and for myself I love nothing printed here better than this play" (49). His satisfaction was understandable. He had found it possible, without resorting to turgid generalizations, farfetched "myths," or abrupt changes in narrative direction, to define the predicament of characters who are unable to understand or combat oppressive influences in their society. By tracing its imprint on their lives, he had implicated an "industrial apparatus which feeds [men] in body and leaves them to find sustenance for their souls as they may."[19]

In contrast to Miller's major figures in other works, the warehouse workers in *A Memory of Two Mondays* neither sustain with singleminded intensity their pursuit of personal goals nor despairingly seek release. For the grand outburst of a thwarted personality, the dramatist substituted unspectacular goings and comings of individuals divorced from all-consuming commitment; he "speaks not of obsession but of rent and hunger and the need for a little poetry in life" (C.P., 49). There is, therefore, no climax—a circumstance that may lead the reader to underestimate the emotional power of the play. Instead, there is a subdued movement from levity to sadness that recalls the alternation of moods practiced in *All My Sons*, although in *A Memory of Two Mondays* the humor has been exaggerated, the sorrow muted. Miller calls the play a "pathetic comedy."

The first Monday begins with the happy confusion of a farce. At one point, several employees try to revive sagging, stuporous Tom with face-washing and ear-blowing, with shouts, shakes, and whiskey. At the same time they argue with one another, serve customers, and placate the proprietor (the patient, on emerging from his drunken trance, announces, "no, no, Glen Wright was shortstop for Pittsburgh, not Honus Wagner"). "It's the same circus every Monday morning," the manager of the warehouse grumbles, giving the slapstick routine an apt name. The characters are comic types appropriate to this burlesque beginning: Raymond, the ringmaster; Tom, the perpetual alcoholic; Gus, a rowdy Falstaff; Jim, a faithful friend; Kenneth, poetic and aimless; Bert, innocent and wide-eyed; Agnes, the nervous spinster; Patricia, the uncertain ingénue; an unhappy husband; a hedonistic bachelor; an insensitive employer; two young smart-alecks; and a wonderfully ungrammatical mechanic.

The variety of accents emanating from this mélange suits the humorous re-creation of lower-class workaday life in a New York City automobile parts warehouse during the middle 1930s. As usual in Miller's writing, colloquial constructions make known a character's national origin, educational limitations, and personal idiosyncrasies. Gus, the stage instructions direct, "speaks with a gruff Slavic accent": "Aggie, come with me Atlantic City." Kenneth sports a rich Irish brogue: "it's a feast of crayons goin' on here every night," he says; "is that all yiz know of the world—filthy women and dirty jokes and the ignorance drippin' off your faces?" Kenneth's brogue invites the inevitable mimicry from a co-worker: "Jasus, me bye, y'r hair is fallin' like the dew of the evenin'." Then there is some choice American slang: "well, it ain't exactly off the manifold. It like sticks out, see, except, it don't stick out, it's like stuck in there. . . . I brung over a couple a friend of mines. . . . My boss says try all the other places first, because he says youse guys charge. But looks to me like we're stuck."

On the second Monday, six months later, the carnival hilarity gives way to resigned sadness and cynical resentment. From force of habit, Gus incites the regular week-opening bedlam. "Look at them goddam mice!" he calls:

He starts rocking the scale. . . . Patricia screams as mice come running out from under the scale. A mêlée of shouts begins, everyone dodging mice or swinging brooms and boxes at them. Raymond is pulling Gus away from the scale, yelling at him to stop it. Agnes rushes in and, seeing the mice, screams and rushes out. Jerry and Willy rush in and join in chasing the mice, laughing. Patricia, wearing leggins [sic], is helped onto the packing table by Larry, and Gus shouts up at her.

(stage directions)

But tired, good-natured old Gus, after his wife's death and twenty-two years at the warehouse, runs down at last; that night he ends his life "right." Larry, awakened from his dream of automotive glory, has sold his expensive car: "funny how you get an idea, and then suddenly you wake up and you look at it and it's like—dead or something. I can't afford a car." Agnes has become more tearfully sentimental; Patricia, coarse; Tom, sober, self-righteous, and boring.

As the city's grime dims his perception of natural and human beauty, Kenneth testifies to the fading of hope. The sadly funny result of his crusade to wash the windows—he succeeds only in bringing into sight an adjoining brothel—underscores for him the futility of resisting mental stagnation ("shouldn't have washed the windows, I guess," the boss observes). Deadened by monotony, Kenneth's mind loses its grasp upon his "chosen image" of what he is and wants to be. So he resigns himself to a dull future as a government clerk, concluding the play with his bittersweet song about a minstrel boy's romantic adventures. Only young Bert, more a spectator than a participant, escapes; the others attain at best a quiet maturity that enables them to endure.

The lack of a dramatic crisis is thus esthetically just. "*A Memory of Two Mondays* has a story but not a plot," Miller comments, "because the life it reflects appears to me to strip people of alternatives and will" (*C.P.*, 50). These characters do not suffer heroic disasters; they are simply worn down by drudgery and grime. Their visions of a freer, happier life slowly fade rather than suddenly turn into nightmare. They become minor mechanisms in company and society: the warehouse symbolizes their corporate existence, the source of both despair and stability. The author notes in his stage directions that "it is a little world, a home to which, unbelievably perhaps, these people like to come every Monday morning, despite what they say." To adapt a critic's remark in another context, Miller is concerned with two things: "the enmity of the machine age for the human spirit" and "the way humanity tries to persist through it."[20]

Fortunately, Miller manages to avoid, for the most part, abstractions such as these. He effects the transition from dream to necessity not only through simple changes in character, mood, and stage lighting ("the yellow light of summer . . . hardens to that of winter"), but also through changing modes of speech. Despite the daily futility and dinginess, strangely enough, several inhabitants of this cheerless universe—with its axles, weight scales, dust, litter, mice, dirty windows, and decrepit toilet—are part-time poets. "The place must seem dirty and unmanageably chaotic, but since it is seen in this play with two separate visions it is also romantic," Miller instructs.

Kenneth, the romanticist *manqué* of the warehouse, recites a sentimental little exhortation, quotes a few lines from Whitman's "The Ship of State," and sings Thomas Moore's fine ballad, "The Minstrel Boy." By the second Monday, however, he cannot "remember the bloody poems any more." Irony undercuts his yearning for lyric grace as he and Bert glimpse the mechanistic life with a clarity that dictates expression in simple free verse. Their reflections, if fairly pedestrian, are at least less pretentious than Alfieri's in *A View from the Bridge*. For example, Kenneth wonders,

> How's a man to live,
> Freezing all day in this palace of dust
> And night comes with one window and a bed
> And the streets full of strangers
> And not one of them's read a book through,
> Or seen a poem from beginning to end
> Or knows a song worth singing.

Gus, that coarse buffoon, summarizes his career in a moving prose elegy whose sole image is the automobile: "when there was Winton Six I was here. When was Minerva car I was here. When Stanley Steamer I was here, and Stearns Knight, and Marmon was good car; I was here all them times. . . ." With their everyday syntax and diction, their wasteland images, and their regular rhythms, Kenneth, Bert, and Gus apprehend—if only briefly and imperfectly— the pathos of their sad circus. Their lyrics and their lives poignantly tell of common men baffled by their "little world."

IV   The Misfits

"How may a man make of the outside world a home?" At those moments when his writing attains ethical clarity and technical proficiency, Arthur Miller answers this question by bringing forward the consequences—especially the psychological consequences—of a character's crucial decisions; and when (as in *A*

Memory of Two Mondays) there are no "alternatives and will," he brings forward the consequences that arise from an *absence* of moral choice. At other moments, he oversimplifies the problem of the individual's accommodation in society by ascribing a spurious public significance to private experiences. Then colloquial language loses its incisive force, structure loses balance, personality loses coherence. Except for the consistently excellent *Death of a Salesman*, Miller's plays contain both kinds of writing; in *The Misfits*, however, the second predominates. Undoubtedly the poorest product of the dramatist's mature years, this screenplay parodies—apparently without deliberate intent—the ordinary man's dream of living with extraordinary style.[21]

The work concerns four unemployed characters who, unwilling to accept conventional social roles or jobs, wander around Nevada seeking the liberated existence denied to the workers of *A Memory of Two Mondays*. Roslyn Taber "never had anybody much" as a girl; now she has just severed her only formal tie by divorcing her husband. Perce Howland rides the rodeo circuit gamely but unsuccessfully. Guido, owner of a derelict airplane and a half-built house, and Gay Langland, his closest friend, refuse to work regularly because, as they fondly repeat, "anything's better than wages"; they earn money sporadically by capturing wild horses. All take pride in performing expertly certain physical acts—flying a plane, building a house, roping a horse, riding a bull, making love, eating and drinking—but none can find a way to express that pride in a socially useful enterprise. Although they are outside the "industrial apparatus," they suffer the same plight bewailed by Kenneth and Bert in *A Memory of Two Mondays*: they cannot (to borrow a phrase from Miller's essay, "On Social Plays") "fulfill their subjective needs through social action." "I don't know what to *do*, but if I knew, I'd do it!" Roslyn declares.

Two symbols configure their isolation and their uselessness. Like the mustangs they chase during a last roundup, they are recalcitrant outcasts who serve no practical purpose in society. And the unfinished home—Guido ceased construction when his wife died—stands in the desert as an appropriate image of suspended creativity: "there is an abortive look to the place," Miller writes; "its very pointlessness is somehow poetic to Roslyn, like an unrealized longing nailed together." (Gay and Roslyn settle there temporarily, bringing joy to the bedroom and vegetable seeds to the garden.)

The question in *The Misfits*, then, is one that occurs in other works: how does one reconcile the desire for independence with the necessity for communal cooperation? Guido, Gay, and Roslyn recognize this problem; in fact, they spend much time analyzing it, when not driving, roping, or making love. Yet their words, as unpromising as their prospects, fail to describe either the self-sufficiency they zealously cultivate or the accommodation they spurn. Gay Langland, who pays particular attention to the first, advertises himself to Roslyn as a "damn good man—best man you'll ever see." In his Western drawl he modestly rationalizes the dangers of horse-roping, bull-riding, and woman-taming: "we all got to go sometime, reason or no reason. Dyin's as natural as livin'; man who's too afraid to die is too afraid to live, far as I've ever seen." This sophomoric claim to heroic status is far less meaningful than his simpler, heartfelt command, "how about some respect for me?" Miller's male characters—David Frieber; Ben, Willy and Biff Loman—often take pleasure in their skill at an occupation or avocation that involves manual ability. Gay turns this masculine satisfaction into a ludicrous cult of virility. Willy may have been a Lo-man and Lawrence a New-man, but Gay often sounds like No-man.

Informed by his love for Roslyn and disgusted by the slack market for mustangs, Gay eventually yields in his determination to achieve absolute self-reliance ("it's just ropin' a dream now") after a last exhibition of prowess with a lasso. His explanations remain amorphous: "Maybe the only thing is . . . the knowin'. 'Cause I know you now, Roslyn, I do know you. Maybe that's all the peace there is or can be. I never bothered to battle a woman before. And it was peaceful, but a lot like huggin' the air. This time, I thought I'd lay my hand on the air again—but it feels like I touched the whole world. I bless you, girl." Exactly what knowledge does he gain from Roslyn? What images encompass their rapport? The obscure references make Gay's rehabilitation hard to conceive. Guido also locates a whole world in Roslyn: "that big connection. You're really hooked in; whatever happens to anybody, it happens to you." The nature of this "big connection"—presumably Roslyn's unself-conscious feminine warmth and charity—can only be conjectured.

Since Roslyn also derives objective evaluations from sense impressions ("what is there that stays?"), she might be expected to clarify the meaning of the "gift of life" that makes her a "real woman." She does display a refreshing ingenuousness. "Birds must be brave to live out here," she exclaims gazing skyward. "Especially at night. . . . Whereas they're so small, you know?" And this on lettuce: "how tiny those seeds were—and still they know they're supposed to be lettuces!" On the subject of *human* life, however, her youthful wonderment changes to adolescent preciosity. "All the husbands and all the wives are dying every minute, and they are not teaching one another what they really know," she solemnly tells Guido. What they have to teach she never suggests. Even her hysterical denunciation of Gay's he-manship, perhaps her most credible act, abounds in vague generalizations: "big man! You're only living when you can watch something die! . . . You know everything except what it feels like to be alive." Again she leaves the point unclear.

In the published edition of the screenplay, Miller supplied introductory personality summaries similar in form to those in his notes to *The Crucible*. These summaries are even more abstruse than the dialogue. Guido looks like a "football-playing poet." Concerning Roslyn, the reader should try to imagine "a certain inwardness [that] lies coiled in her gaze." The male lead must convey the impression (somehow) "that he does not expect very much, but that he sets the rhythm for whoever he walks with because he cannot follow. And he has no desire to lead." Such descriptions, poor substitutes for self-exposition, tend to confuse rather than to stimulate the imagination.

Miller wished his work, he stated in a preface, to "have the peculiar immediacy of image and the reflective possibilities of the written word." Whatever "peculiar immediacy" *The Misfits* possesses appears mainly in the author's impressionistic locale sketches. Reno, for instance, amalgamates the contrasting vulgarities of city and country in its commercial rusticity. "No doubt about it, pardners," a radio announcer chuckles, "we are the Divorce Capital of the World. . . . For the third month a-runnin', we've beat out Las Vegas." In the desert immensities outside Reno, "night begins a few inches off the ground"; and in a "sterile white alkali waste" where the "desolation is almost supernatural," a town squats: "there is no tree, no bush, no pool of water. To right and left the blank white flatland stretches away, dampened here and there by acid stains of moisture left from the spring rains. Gradually a perverse beauty grows out of the place. It is so absolute, its ugliness is so direct and blatant as to take on honesty and the force of something perfectly defined, itself without remorse or excuse. . . ."

The attempt to distill ultimate values persists here too, but there is evident a colorful specificity that the dialogue, despite its homely Western syntax, lacks. When the dramatist, in his fanciful role as movie-maker, turns from designing scenery to directing actors, he surrenders the set to his lifelong enemy, "the reflective possibilities of the written word." His characters, striving to discover the secret of self-realization in an uncongenial environment, distort their banal diction into unrecognizable shapes. Their resolve to codify a vocabulary of integrity produces language that is neither natural nor rational. Lines spoken by individuals who lack verbal fluency are necessarily crude and tentative; they need not be outlandish and nonsensical.[22]

CHAPTER 5

After the Fall *and* Incident at Vichy

I   After the Fall

The Psychoanalytic Plan

AFTER an absence from the New York stage of eight years, Miller contributed *After the Fall* and a long one-act work, *Incident at Vichy*, to the Lincoln Center Repertory Theatre in its first two seasons. The plays, similar in theme, were radically different in technique. In *Incident at Vichy*, produced during the 1964–65 season, Miller's approach was that of conventional realism. *After the Fall*, produced about a year earlier, was the most introspective play he had written; it assumed the form of an interior dialogue, a progress in self-discovery accomplished without a psychiatrist. "This play," Miller wrote in the Foreword, "is a trial; the trial of a man by his own conscience, his own values, his own deeds. The 'Listener' [an unseen character addressed by Quentin, the protagonist], who to some will be a psychoanalyst, to others God, is Quentin himself turned at the edge of the abyss to look at his experience, his nature and his time."

The chief symptom of Quentin's malaise is loss of faith in self and in others. Having held the naïve belief that "underneath we're all profoundly friends," Quentin was severely shaken by disloyalty among husbands and wives, acquaintances, and business associates ("all this hatred isn't real to me!").[1] His own affairs proved exceptionally disappointing. He was "admired," "honored," "blessed," "loved," and "adored", yet he found that "these goddamned women have injured me." And he inflicted injury as well as received it; indeed, he wonders if he has "lived in good faith." The evidence of "good faith" that he reviews is not encouraging. He felt neither indignation nor compassion during a visit to the site of a Nazi extermination compound. His coldness rebuffed Holga, Louise, and Maggie: it drove his present fiancée to

57

tears, his first wife to psychotherapy, and his second wife to
suicide. Even his attitude toward his mother was ambiguous. He
honestly loved her—so much in fact that he was criticized for it.
Still, after she died he said, "I can't even mourn my own mother.
It's monstrous. . . . I don't seem to know how to grieve." The only
woman he remembers without unpleasant associations is Felice,
whose enthusiasm he did not reciprocate. "I have lived through all
the promises, you see?" he concludes; "I am bewildered by the
death of love. And my responsibility for it."

This bewilderment concerning sincerity was complicated by the
contradictory titles others gave him. On the positive side, his
mother saw him as "a light, a light in the world," and later admirers
compared him to a "pasha," "grand duke," "king," and "god."
Negatively, he was called a merciless "judge," a "little boy," an
"idiot," a "fraud," a "stranger," a "fag," an "ogre," a "liar," and a
"son of a bitch." "But where is *Quentin*?" he asks; "do you know
who I am? . . . I can't find myself." He ponders the angry remark
his father had directed to him as a youth: "Chrissake, *what are
you*?" His goal now is to "stop impersonating," to go "disguised no
more," and to "show what Quentin, Quentin, Quentin . . . is!"

The self-analysis follows a traditional pattern of psychoanalytic
treatment. Dispirited by maladjustment in his personal relations,
the subject seeks to understand the nature and origin of that
maladjustment; he reviews significant events in his childhood and
in his adult history for clues; finally, he perceives the cause of—
and, hopefully, the cure for—his inadequacies. Quentin's disorien-
tation had its roots in his youth: two memories, both of which show
his mother to be "treacherous," indicate that he was impressed
early with the instability of family relations. Once, his parents went
off on a vacation without telling him. "They sent me for a walk
with the maid. When I came back the house was empty for a week.
God, why is betrayal the only truth that sticks!" Another time, after
his father went bankrupt, his mother turned into a horribly
unforgiving "stranger" who cursed her husband's incompetence
and confessed to her impressionable young son the bitterness she
knew as a bride. She translated her "contempt" for her husband
into harsh advice: "I hope you learn how to disappoint people.
Especially women." In later years Quentin saw the drama of a
man's humiliation before and subservience to a woman re-enacted
by close friends. Elsie treated Lou, a law professor, with exaggerated condescension: she babied him with motherly attention

("your shirt's out, dear," "did you comb your hair today?");
warned him with "a sudden flash of contempt" not to publish a
controversial manuscript because he would be "incapable" of
defending himself; and comforted him in his despair—yet betrayed him by offering her body to another man.

Presumably—the point is not made entirely explicit—these
experiences taught Quentin that the secret enemy of a man's self-
respect was moral weakness or dependence (his brother commented of their parents, "without her he was never very much, you
know. He'll fall apart"). Assuming "guilt for what [he] did not do,"
Quentin shared the shame of his father and of his former professor,
figures who should have personified masculine dignity. He
presented a defensive if not antagonistic stance to women because
he felt that by engaging in wholehearted emotional communion he
might become vulnerable to some woman's patronizing "contempt" or infidelity. But his mistrust of intimacy led him to a
predicament in which the desire for independence ("be a man")
militated against the need for solace ("like a boy!"). Despite his
pessimism, Quentin requires love; gestures and words of affection
occupy a commanding place in his recollections.

Quentin recalls facts about his two marriages that illustrate this
predicament. While he urged his first wife to express herself freely,
he remained guardedly "distant" (Louise protested, "the moment I
begin to assert myself it seems to threaten you"). He agreed that he
had not been "very demonstrative," that "in seven years we had
never had a meeting." Still, he could not keep from "resenting" her
rigid self-righteousness or her "refusal to be brought down" and
assume a properly subordinate role. Because of his resentment,
Quentin ironically brought about the outcome he had feared.
Instead of comforting him, Louise ended by blaming him—as his
mother had blamed his father—and dismissed him with the same
contemptuous exclamation spoken by both Mother and Elsie,
"what an idiot!" By the time his marriage foundered, family life
had come to mean for Quentin the inevitable "death of love," for
estrangement always seemed to follow intimacy.

At that juncture he encountered Maggie—again, Quentin remembers those details that are psychologically relevant. A beauti-
ful creature unencumbered by moral or intellectual preconcep-
tions, she seemed to offer the perfect "cure" for his condition—
simple, unselfish, inexhaustible "idolatry." "You're all love, aren't
you?" he inquired; "that's all I am!" she responded. Unhappily, she

was extremely neurotic about love, partly the result (as with
Quentin) of childhood traumas. Her "moral" mother, who later
returned in dreams, tried to smother her.[2] Maggie never knew her
father. After a pathetic attempt to locate him, she adopted Quentin
as a father-surrogate of infinite wisdom and honesty ("you're like a
god!"). Her emotional dependence—she establishes her identity
by reminding herself, "I know who I am. I'm Quentin's friend"—
was irresistible.

But the wedding ceremony was hardly over before she exhibited
her "forbidden side," an insatiable appetite for total devotion—just
what Quentin could not give. "You need more love than I thought,"
he lamely admitted. Soon her "timid idolatry" changed to wrath,
exposing Quentin once again to a woman's scorn. Again he was
accused of not caring enough; again he saw this accusation
threatening his security (the stage directions refer to "the agony . . .
growing in his face, of total disintegration"); and again he ended by
sleeping alone on the living-room couch. In his wife's eyes he
metamorphosed from a father-figure into an "idiot," or an "ogre"
symbolizing "all the evil in the world." Maggie's "flash of
contemptuous anger" iterated Louise's earlier repudiation,
Mother's "growing contempt" for Father, and Elsie's "sudden flash
of contempt" for Lou. The hostility between Maggie and Quentin
marked another completion of the recurring cycle in which love, at
first freely proposed, was then selfishly withdrawn, a cycle in
which fidelity, hopefully sought, was soon bitterly lost.

When Quentin remembers these facts, he is willing to admit his
"complicity," but he does not attain this humility until relatively
late in his career. During most of his odyssey he thought himself
more sinned against than sinning. He considered both wives guilty
of "pride"—one vain about her virtue (in contrast to Louise, his
current girl friend does not seek a "moral victory"), the other vain
about her sexual attractiveness. He did glimpse his unconscious
"hypocrisy" and "fraud" in "playing God" ("can't even go to bed
without a principle!"). Not until his self-analysis, however, does he
fully comprehend the extent to which ego, the "power" of self-
assertion and of self-preservation, has directed his motives even
when they were ostensibly altruistic. "I loved them all, all!" he
realizes, "and gave them willingly to failure and to death that I
might live." He then understands the truth in Louise's notion that
"we are all separate people." This understanding serves as his
guide to sanity. He will "dare to love this world again," but now

love must be tempered by the humbling knowledge that any individual would "kill" those he holds dear to ensure his own survival (the play was originally subtitled *The Survivor*). Quentin's search for his real identity turns up a killer as well as a lover.

Technical Shortcomings

Because the action "takes place in the mind, thought, and memory of Quentin," Miller attempted to reproduce "the surging, flitting, instantaneousness of a mind questing over its own surfaces and into its depths" (stage directions). Technically, *After the Fall* bears a close resemblance to *Death of a Salesman*. In both, dramatized remembrance reveals the "inside of a man's head";[3] Quentin's transient recollections, like Willy Loman's, are a subjective version of the concept of delayed revelation Miller borrowed from Ibsen. Quentin's effort to recall the past is more self-conscious than Willy's, but the structural requirement remains the same: although the disoriented protagonist may not always appreciate the significance of past events, the spectator should perceive an underlying psychological unity.

The playwright works to achieve that unity in *After the Fall* through factual details contained within the memories (whether deliberately or involuntarily recalled), through interpretive comments Quentin addresses to an invisible auditor, and through the juxtaposition of incidents or words. The last device, important also in *Death of a Salesman*, calls attention to key motifs with abrupt transitions in the train of thought. For example, when reminded of the title—"idiot"—that he had received from both wives, Quentin conveys his anxiety and his need for reassurance by recalling his question to Holga, "you love me, don't you?" On another occasion, his mind quickly replaces two disturbing memories (Elsie treating Lou like a child and Mother shouting "idiot" at his father) with two comforting memories—Holga's affirmative answer to his repeated question to her and Felice's benediction, "I'll always bless you!" Sudden transitions of this kind also bring out the idea of his "complicity." After he poses his leading problem ("why can't I be innocent?"), two images briefly interrupt his thinking. Each image draws from him a variant of the original query: the memory of a ruined watchtower elicits the question, "why does something in me bow its head like an accomplice in this place!" and a memory of his indignant mother triggers the question, "why is the world so treacherous? Shall we lay it all to mothers?"[4] Such associations implement Miller's method of joining narrative fragments in a mosaic that configures a personality.

The fragments, however, are not so well put together as in *Death of a Salesman*; the explanation of Quentin's motivation presented in this discussion may have misleadingly suggested a more logical organization of data than the play exhibits. Quentin certainly is more sincere, intelligent, and articulate than Willy Loman. Where Willy, overwhelmed by failure, rejects the message his story outlines, Quentin tries to arrive at a constructive solution to his troubles. Yet, though Quentin knows more, he shows less. He never manages to conceive his aversions and sympathies clearly or to integrate them meaningfully; his memories and his evaluations remain obscure. This obscurity may be what has prevented many playgoers from seeing any issue of greater seriousness than whether Maggie really *is* Marilyn Monroe, or any "code" more mature than the one discovered by a reviewer for *Time*: "when life seems unbearable, find a new woman and start a new life."[5]

One weakness of *After the Fall* lies in its abbreviated characterization. Since time and personal histories have been condensed, reactions often seem disproportionate to causes: Elsie and Louise justly describe the behavior of two other characters as "incredible." Felice showers blessings on Quentin "because you really listened to me and didn't just try to roll me over" (first edition). Holga, contrarily, was deeply hurt when he merely "fended off her hand." Maggie, careening from ecstasy to violent hatred, attributes her success as a singer to "just the way you looked at me" and her decline to reading his note about an inability to love anyone except his daughter. These explanations do little to measure Quentin's "power," Felice's gratitude, Holga's pique, or Maggie's volatility— even when they are supplemented by the information that Felice's husband cared too much for his Volkswagen, Holga's relatives were high-ranking Nazis, and Maggie's mother smoked cigarettes inside a closet. Miller may have exaggerated certain responses to stress the distortion of memory or the irrationality of lovers, but grotesqueness does not emerge as his stylistic goal, apart from Felice's obviously comic gestures.

Similarly, many recollections—necessarily random and abrupt in order to preserve an illusion of the mind's "instantaneousness"— are unintelligible because they are not sufficiently prepared for by preliminary exposition. The early scenes are especially puzzling. Before the first act is half over Quentin has referred to a bewildering assortment of things—the deserted tower, Mother's contempt, Father's grief, Holga's dream, Louise's revolt, and Lou's fear. Some events, such as Mother's attack upon her husband, appear to be unrelated to Quentin's problem until they are reviewed in the light of subsequent information. The short hospital scene cannot succeed as a simple exercise in pathos since at that premature stage Father's utter dependence has been manifested only in a few bald declarations like "she was my right hand"; nor does the incident enunciate Quentin's "hardness," except in equally direct assertions ("is it simply that I am crueler than he?"). The complex episode involving Lou, Elsie, and Mickey ends in a deadly argument over loyalty among former Communist party members, but only in retrospect does one see that this enmity was less frightening to Quentin than Elsie's insult, which duplicated his mother's. Finally, the momentary interruptions by Mother, Holga, Felice, and Louise, if ultimately relevant, are too incomplete to make readily comprehensible the part each character played in the failure of love. Quentin's confusion becomes the spectator's.

References to irrationality in society at large are even more nebulous than those to family disharmony. Quentin, a lawyer, fails to promote a convincing case for his own incrimination in the slaughter of Jews during the war. He does try to throttle Maggie, of course, and he could be termed "murderous" in a figurative sense when he selfishly disregards the feelings of others in order to preserve his well-being. But can common self-interest be equated with genocide? If everyone possesses the urge to kill, is everyone equally guilty for actual murders? Are no distinctions to be made between insults to the body and to pride, between killing in self-defense and in malice? To what degree does a sense of "complicity" justify emotional passivity? Quentin does not accumulate enough data to answer these questions. His "fleeting," disconnected memories of towers, congressional hearings, and suicidal ex-socialists hardly demonstrate how the will to survive operates in public life.[6]

The playgoer who finds this procession of images confusing gets little guidance from Quentin's commentary. Quentin tries to extract objective truths from his self-analysis; unfortunately, as in most of Miller's works, objectivity is often identified with formality and affected elegance. In his last speech he takes up a theme sounded by Gay Langland in *The Misfits*, then proceeds to develop it with rhetoric far more flowery—though no more comprehensible—than the cowboy's plain diction. "Is the knowing all? To know, and even happily, that we meet unblessed; not in some garden of wax fruit and painted trees, that lie of Eden, but after, after the Fall, after many, many deaths. Is the knowing all?" Here and elsewhere Quentin enunciates some rather vague concepts in the florid style of Alfieri:

And that vision sometimes hangs behind my head, blind now, bleached out like the moon in the morning; and if I could only let in some necessary darkness it would shine again.

.   .   .   .

We conspired to violate the past, and the past is holy and its horrors are holiest of all!

.   .   .   .

"To live" we cried, and "Now" we cried. And loved each other's innocence, as though to love enough what was not there would cover up what was. But there is an angel, and night and day he brings back to us exactly what we want to lose. So you must love him because he keeps truth in the world.

After speculating on the meaning of two divorces, two suicides, and the annihilation of six million Jews, he finds this kind of bombast necessary—the artificial metaphors and analogies, the ornate vocabulary, the portentous tone—to get at the elementary idea that, in spite of man's wish to believe otherwise, ego directs all motives. (He puts the matter quite simply in a less poetic moment: "we are very dangerous.")[7]

To transform his private observations into universal principles, Quentin typically employs impersonal nouns like "one," "whoever," "man," "the world," and the collective "we" or "you." "Why is the world so treacherous?" he asks, elevating himself and his mother to "sons" and "mothers." To lend further authority to the behavioral laws he fabricates, he invokes contemporary and biblical symbols. The "blasted stone tower" of the concentration camp reminds him of humanity's destructive impulses. His "crucifixion" gesture, which calls forth the image of suffering Jesus, signifies Everyman's unfulfilled desire to "love everybody."

It is fitting for Quentin to balance a symbol of evil with one of good since he conceives his principles as polar extremes. Man falls from blissful "innocence" to a soul-harrowing consciousness of "guilt," "complicity," and "blame." In the before-and-after terminology, "love" contrasts with "hatred," "life" with "death," and "lie" with "truth." Once there was "solidarity," an "unseen web of connection," and "constancy"; there was "good faith," "final hope," "absolute necessity," "deep belief," and "blessing." And there were "promises," "proofs," "believers," "brothers," and "profound friends." Then "the world ended, it all fell down, and nobody was innocent again." All that remained was "despair" and the "pointless litigation of existence before an empty bench." A few recurring words span the two poles. As a "little boy," Quentin was literally without knowledge of evil; and later he sees himself as a "boy" in a figurative sense, retaining hope in human decency. When Maggie calls him a "little boy" or a "kid," on the other hand, she considers him naïve and irresponsible. "Idiot" also connotes opposite meanings: Mother, Louise, and Maggie use the term pejoratively, whereas Quentin and Holga represent life as an "idiot child" that must be embraced despite its deformity. Most key words, however, lack even this relatively limited versatility. Endlessly repeated, they merely reinforce a simplistic dualism that has slight bearing on the complex emotional problem troubling Quentin.[8]

The wisdom that Quentin promulgates does not, in short, fulfill the high expectations he raises during the intricate process of gaining it. As objective "truth" it is superficial; as subjective insight, obscure. Quentin occasionally recognizes the absurdity of his pronouncements on love and salvation. He impatiently asks, "why do I make such stupid statements?" He acutely remarks, "it's all true, but it isn't the truth." And he belatedly realizes that Maggie "had the truth that day, I brought the lie that she had to be 'saved'!" He goes so far as to vow "to live in good faith if only with my guts!" Yet good intentions scarcely deter him from an infatuation with his own sapience. He continues to formulate "abstractions" at the same time that he acknowledges their incompatibility with emotional commitment. He practices his last and greatest deceit upon himself.[9]

The play thus becomes an excursion in psychological deception, not revelation—the opposite of what its subjective design and its protagonist's announcements lead the spectator to await. It reflects too well Quentin's chaotic oscillation between withdrawal and engagement, between the mature awareness proposed by Louise and the adamant innocence demanded by Maggie. *After the Fall* recapitulates the dilemma Miller has never satisfactorily solved:

how are the languages of mind and heart to be reconciled? As T. S. Eliot asks, "after such knowledge, what forgiveness?"

Autobiographical and Literary Allusion

Though Miller customarily alludes to actual persons or incidents, he does so to an unusual extent in *After the Fall*. In addition, he invokes literary as well as autobiographical sources to give substance to and extend the relevance of his fictional account. His protagonist's ordeal—the ordeal occurring when a character who has enjoyed comfortable security reacts violently to irrationality in society or to treachery in a loved one—imitates a crisis that exists as an "objective fact" in his own history, in his earlier plays, and in two major works by other authors.

Miller's purpose in referring to his personal experience has been widely misunderstood. When *After the Fall* was produced in 1964, many spectators questioned the propriety of bringing to public notice matters they considered offensive, embarrassing, or distracting. Among the lay critics, one woman called Miller "nauseating as a lover." Others derided his ungallant attitude toward the female sex generally; scorned his "cheap, sensational revelation" of intimacies with Marilyn Monroe ("I hope Mr. Miller doesn't meet Joe DiMaggio on a dark street"); and denounced his advice to "a pretty girl . . . to have an operation on her nose." Their consensus was that the work "is not art but a self-indulgent foray into personal catharsis."[10] The professional critics were equally scandalized. Leslie Hanscom in *Newsweek* remarked that although the playwright was normally a "fugitive from familiarity," he had "written what is undoubtedly the most nakedly autobiographical drama ever put on public view."[11] Robert Brustein in the *New Republic* indignantly commented that "he has created a shameless piece of tabloid gossip, an act of exhibitionism which makes us all voyeurs."[12] An anonymous reviewer in *Time* summed up all the biographical interpretations: "his new play is a memory book of betrayals, a soliloquy with his conscience, an exorcism of guilt, an intimate manual of bad marriages, a chronicle of the birth of a writer, a dirge for the death of love, and underlying all, a tormented but intellectualized quest for self-justification."[13]

Annoyed, Miller defended himself by denying any autobiographical intention whatsoever. "That man up there isn't me," he retorted in reference to Quentin; "a playwright doesn't put himself on the stage, he only dramatizes certain forces within himself."[14]

Furthermore, he insisted, "the character of Maggie, which in great part seems to underlie the fuss, is not in fact Marilyn Monroe."[15] In a literal sense this point is well taken; the "game of identification," as Miller terms it, has no doubt been overplayed. But while one can only guess at the degree of psychological correspondence between his characters and their prototypes, certain important factual parallels are undeniable.

The chief character and the author have much in common. They were born about the same time (the text places Quentin "in his forties" in 1964). During the Depression Quentin's genial, foreign-born father, like Miller's , lost a sizable business.[16] Some years after this first crisis in their lives, both young men left home to make their own way; in both family histories, an elder brother stayed to help his father re-establish himself in business. Like Miller, Quentin sought in socialism a "brotherhood opposed to all the world's injustice," became disillusioned with leftist causes, appeared before "the Committee"—presumably the House Committee on Un-American Activities—and wondered why (to paraphrase John Proctor in *The Crucible*) the accuser had now become holy. And he too decided as a matter of conscience to remain loyal to associates who had been "subpoenaed," parting company with a close friend who "named names."[17]

Quentin relates his spiritual anguish to the torment suffered by European Jews during World War II. Is he a Jew? Miller, of course, was reared in a Jewish family and neighborhood. His novel, two short stories,[18] and a later play, *Incident at Vichy*, deal with problems of Jewish identity; and several characters in other works speak at times with a Yiddish accent. *They Too Arise*, for instance, contains flavorful idioms such as "he needs them like a hole in the head, he needs them," "all the worries I got on my head," and "what do you want I should kill myself?"[19] Quentin's mother, in the original version of *After the Fall*, employs similar expressions: "what are you talking about, I didn't end up calling all the Turkish baths the night my bother Herbert got married?" she says, indulging in an unmistakably Yiddish construction, and again when she mimics, "'Mama, I'm in love!' And with what? With who?" In his revision, however, Miller deleted these locutions. Quentin, who decides he has as much affinity with the wartime persecutors as with the persecuted, does not identify himself as a Jew.

Whatever his religion, the protagonist's marital career certainly parallels Miller's. Quentin met his first wife when both were college students; like Mary Grace Slattery, she was a quiet, introspective type. That marriage ended in divorce after lasting more than a decade. His present fiancée, a foreign professional woman, suggests Miller's present wife, Ingeborg Morath, a Swiss photographer. And his second wife, despite Miller's protest, greatly resembles Marilyn Monroe. The two women experienced the same unpleasant childhood: each was an illegitimate girl who tried unsuccessfully to locate her father, a fact that contributed, as did the mother's instability, to loneliness and insecurity in adult life. Though neither was graduated from high school, both nevertheless rose to the highest rank in popular entertainment with an arresting combination of sexual attractiveness and girlish charm.[20] Some of Maggie's pronouncements capture the delightful simplicity of the typical Marilynism:

I was christening a submarine in the Groton shipyard; 'cause I was voted the favorite of all the workers! And I made them bring about ten workers up on the platform, whereas they're the ones built it, right? And you know what the admiral said? I better watch out or I'll be a Communist. And suddenly I thought of you and I said, "I don't know what's so terrible; they're for the poor people."

.   .   .   .

I was with a lot of men but I never got anything for it. It was like charity, see. My analyst said I gave to those in need. Whereas, I'm not an institution!

Upon meeting Quentin-Arthur, Maggie-Marilyn was so favorably impressed that she kept his photograph in her bedroom, but the relationship went awry after several years of marriage. Each woman became extremely difficult to live or work with, brooded about people taking her as a "joke," broke contracts, and finally ended her life with an overdose of sleeping pills.

In establishing these parallels Miller probably hoped to authenticate with the testimony of an eyewitness his theme on the disintegration and subsequent reintegration of self-confidence. Autoplagiarism, a form of allusion less obvious than autobiography in *After the Fall*, serves a similar purpose. If Miller affirms the reality of Quentin's "fall" by pointing to analogous characters and episodes in his personal experience, he does so also by duplicating lines and situations in his previous writing. His many repetitions of earlier dialogue review in coda-fashion his principal motif.

A few general similarities exist between *After the Fall* and minor works such as *Focus, The Man Who Had All the Luck,* and the short story, "I Don't Need You Any More." But Miller borrows most extensively from his major plays. Before his troubles Quentin naïvely embraced the same "blind," "limitless" power of love that, according to Alfieri, took possession of Eddie Carbone in *A View from the Bridge* (one of Quentin's comments even recalls Eddie's niece-fixation: "the only one I will ever love is my daughter"). Maggie was the chief object of his passion, and he encouraged her just as Willy Loman encouraged his son: "see everybody smiling, adoring you? . . . Everybody loves you, darling!" (Willy: "thousands of people will be rooting for you and loving you"). In return, simple, good-hearted Maggie (and Felice) conferred a "blessing" upon him, as Roslyn blessed Gay Langland in *The Misfits.* Elsie adored him also; her affection ("you know how she admires you") was brought to Quentin's notice in words nearly identical with those Linda used to describe Biff's feeling for his father in *Death of a Salesman* ("you know how he admires you").

In addition to love, Quentin enjoyed that elusive recognition ("they respect you") pursued by Willy ("one thing about Charley. . . . They respect him"), Eddie ("I want my respect"), and Gay ("how about some respect for me?"). Quentin worshiped at the altar of integrity, which he called his "name"; so did Eddie ("I want my name!") and John Proctor ("how may I live without my name?"). He would not tolerate any suspicion of unworthiness in himself or in those he loved, worrying in regard to Maggie ("'cause I think . . . you were ashamed once") what Joe Keller (*All My Sons*) had worried about in regard to Chris ("because sometimes I think you're . . . ashamed of the money") and what David Frieber (*The Man Who Had All the Luck*) had ceased worrying about in respect to himself ("I somehow don't feel ashamed . . . now") [Miller's ellipses]. Even so, Quentin occasionally marveled at his own motives, his exclamation, "my God, I—How could I do that?" sounding like Willy's "my God, I was yelling at him! How could I!" He was no less amazed at the actions of others: "all this hatred isn't real to me"; and Chris Keller is told "you don't realize how people can hate." In brief, Quentin was "like a boy" in optimism and impracticality: criticisms proffered by Maggie ("you're like a little boy") and Felice (*her* husband also "was always so childish")[21] echo his own statement as well as evaluations made by figures in other plays—Biff Loman's self-criticism, "I'm like a boy"; Charley's rejoinder to Willy, "when the hell are you going to grow up?"; Shory's comment to David Frieber, "when are you going to stop being a little boy?"; and Sue's assertion in *All My Sons* that "men are like little boys."

Miller's characters do not remain peacefully childlike for long. The bond joining friends falls apart: "I turned out to be the only friend he had," Quentin says of Lou; and Willy remarks, "Charley, you're the only friend I got." Employers are ungrateful. Quentin's short, sharp "I've been fired" duplicates Willy's startling announcement, "I was just fired" (Mickey delivers a similar line—"I've been subpoenaed"). Family members inflict the cruelest wounds. Along with Chris Keller and Biff Loman, young Quentin is shamed by his father's humiliation, but in *After the Fall* the father rather than the son asks Chris's accusing question, "what are you?" Later, as a husband, Quentin receives further evidence that familiarity breeds contempt. His complaint to his wife, "what I resent is being forever on trial, Louise," condenses Proctor's to his: "I cannot speak but I am doubted, every moment judged for lies, as though I come into a court when I come into this house!" "Say hello to me," Guido pleads in *The Misfits*, anticipating the exchange of hellos that concludes *After the Fall*. When communication fails, Louise reiterates Willy's insult to Charley, "you are disgusting!"

After estrangement, the despondency is profound. Quentin ("what's the cure!") and Willy ("what's the secret?") grope for a solution, but as Quentin finds (first edition), "it's very hard to see the death of love, and simply walk away," or to quote Willy, "but if you can't walk away?" Though Lou in *After the Fall* and Willy Loman sometimes remember the "great times" of the past with fondness, Quentin considers them with dismay. He sees the inadequacy of former beliefs ("it's a dream, now"), an insight similar to Gay's ("it's just ropin' a dream now"). At his journey's end Quentin turns from faith in loving to faith in knowing, a change consistent with Miller's usual denouement. "He had never known such calm ... for what he understood he no longer feared," Lawrence Newman reflects in *Focus*; "you've got to know ... once and for all," Hester commands David Frieber; "I know all about the world," Chris Keller mourns; "you know something, Charley, ... he never knew who he was. ... I know who I am," Biff Loman concludes at his father's funeral (Maggie repeats the second claim during her euphoric stage). "God knows how black my sins are!" Proctor declares; "I don't know anything," Bert frets as he leaves the warehouse in *A Memory of Two Mondays*; Eddie Carbone "allowed himself to be wholly known," Alfieri eulogizes; "maybe the only thing is . . . the knowin'," Gay drawls; and Quentin soberly admits, "I know how to kill . . . I know, I know." Both Quentin and Gay ask rhetorically, "is the knowing all?" The implied answer is "yes."

In addition to his works, Miller alludes to two other literary sources. He owes an obvious debt to the Old Testament, and in his Foreword he acknowledges his interest in the Adam and Cain narratives. He takes the biblical account of the Fall to allegorize man's loss of innocence through self-knowledge: "presumably we are being told that the human being becomes 'himself' in the act of becoming aware of his sinfulness." Yet awareness of potential depravity may have disastrous consequences if it undermines faith in one's self. Paradoxically, the grand corrupter is not pride, which preserves the illusion of innocence ("that lie of Eden," Quentin calls it), but self-knowledge, the enervating sense of guilt and limitation. In Genesis, God predicts death as the penalty for learning to distinguish good from evil; analogously, Quentin's understanding of "hatred" causes spiritual torpor: "strength comes from a clear conscience or a dead one. Not to see one's own evil—there's power!"

To forestall the dissipation of his animal energies by shame, Quentin is tempted (as is every man) to spurn insight and to choose instead "Cain's alternative"—"to express without limit one's un-bridled inner compulsion, in this case to murder, and to plead unawareness as a virtue and a defense. . . . Through Quentin's agony in this play there runs the everlasting temptation of Innocence, that deep desire to return to when, it seems, he was in fact without blame" (author's Foreword). "Not to see, not see! To be innocent!" Quentin muses; indeed, in his "own blood-covered name" he "turns his back" upon those he loves. Perhaps his "brothers" did die in a Nazi concentration camp, "but my brothers built this place." Cain's way, however, forfeits the only chance man has to locate a peaceful home in the world. While "the wish to kill is never killed," Quentin finds it is possible to pacify the destructive impulse. It is possible, in sorrow and in exile, to nurture "hope," "love," "courage," and "forgiveness." One may achieve redemption in the service of an enlightened ego.[22]

Notwithstanding the biblical allusions and the numerous references to "God," the play, like everything else Miller has written (including *The Crucible*), does not require the existence of supernatural power to explain damnation and salvation. In his Foreword the author specifically advises against taking Quentin's unseen auditor (the "Listener") to be God. When Quentin retells the story of Jesus and Lazarus, he does so only to give figurative emphasis to his idea that the human capacity for love is extremely limited; to mock his own amorous pretentions, he twice "spreads his arms in crucifixion" (stage directions). The Christ-image is metaphorical here, the term "God" a verbal habit—though uttered perhaps with an overtone of deprivation. Quentin neither seeks nor experiences rapport with divinity: "it's so damned clear I've chosen what I do," he laments, "it cuts the strings between my hands and heaven" ("it's a mistake to ever look for hope outside one's self," his fiancée says). Miller interprets Old and New Testament ethical concepts in a wholly secular manner.

To further support his thesis on human inconstancy, Miller may have turned to Albert Camus, the late French novelist, playwright, and essayist. Although Miller does not verify this in his Foreword, correspondences are too marked to be coincidental. His title immediately suggests an engagement with Camus's version of the Adam story, *The Fall* (*La Chute*), a novel published in France in 1956 and translated the following year.[23] The two plots are similar in most important respects. In *The Fall* Jean-Baptiste Clamence, a middle-aged lawyer like Quentin, delivers an account of his disenchantment with humanity to an unspecified listener whose rejoinders are indicated solely through the narrator's comments (the novel, written in the first person, is a monologue). "Showered with blessings" and enjoying a brilliant career, Clamence (like Quentin) had won the greatest success with his clients, friends, and lovers. He took pride in his "innocence" and his faultless virtue. "You would really have thought that justice slept with me every night. . . . I freely held sway bathed in a light as of Eden" (Quentin: "the world so wonderfully threatened by injustices I was born to correct! . . . Like some kind of paradise. . . . It's Eden!"). And moral wholeness implied moral authority or "power."

Exile—the decay of self-esteem—began when Clamence disregarded the cries of a drowning woman, just as Quentin figuratively "turned his back" on various women needing help (Holga tells of a stranger who *did* care enough to prevent her from leaping off a bridge). Each lawyer heard a mocking laugh; each found that he shared the base instincts of other men, his "accomplices"; each became, to quote Miller's description of Quentin, "weighed down with a sense of his own pointlessness and the world's." Eventually, both adjust to their shocking insight in similar ways. Clamence vows to confess his lies and to become a "judge-penitent" dedicated to showing others their "guilt." Likewise, Quentin receives the title of "judgey" when he orders Maggie to "do the hardest thing of all—see your own hatred, and live!" Neither lawyer appeals for divine intercession, though Clamence recalls "the references, purely verbal, that I often made to God." For him "there is no giving of absolution or blessing," while Quentin hopes to "meet unblessed" with others in mutual forgiveness.

Additional verbal and thematic correspondences indicate that Miller may have studied other works of Camus. Quentin ("we are killing one another with abstractions") sounds like a character in *The Plague* (1947) who warns against "abstraction . . . killing you."[24] *The Rebel* (1951), a long philosophical treatise, addresses the same question implied in *After the Fall*: "whether innocence, the moment it becomes involved in action, can avoid committing murder."[25] (Interestingly, Camus advances an affirmative answer, in contrast to that arrived at by Quentin, who hopes for pardon only after inevitable acts of inhumanity.) Finally, like Meursault in *The Stranger* (1942; first English translation, 1946), Quentin has no strong desire for professional success, restricts his involvement with women, feels little grief after his mother's death, and reveals an unsuspected murder-instinct. "I'm a stranger to my life," he asserts; his father calls him "a stranger"; Louise is "like a stranger I had never gotten to know"; Maggie says "I'm like a stranger here" on her wedding day; Holga "senses an estrangement"; and even his parents are "strangers" to each other.[26]

It would be a mistake to conclude that these similarities in idea, narrative structure, and phrasing represent a decisive debt either to the French Nobel Prize winner or to the Bible. Miller has shown a strong interest in the fall theme—the crisis of disillusionment— from the start of his career during the early 1940s. In almost every work, and apparently in his life as well, self-knowledge offers the only tenable alternative to self-defeat. The allusions in *After the Fall* attest to the constancy of his concern and support the validity of his solution. They strengthen the credibility of a thesis that is

imperfectly realized in the portentous dialogue and tortuous
structure of this ambitious play.

II Incident at Vichy

Playwrights deal with recurring human phenomena or merely
with biographical and historical details; they interject implicit
biases or explicit messages; they view their material in a subjective
perspective or avoid psychological penetration. At his best, Miller
performs the first activity in each of these categories. For his
subject he invariably turns to a recurrent phenomenon even
when, as in *Incident at Vichy,* he refers extensively to an actual
happening. Historical reference in that play—like the historical,
biographical, and literary references in preceding works—augments the authenticity and objectivity of his treatment without
restricting him to a political or topical scope. Miller is not primarily
interested in the reactions of specific Jews to anti-Semitism in
France during World War II, just as in *Focus* and in *The Crucible*
he does more than retell stories about the persecution of Jews in
New York City and witches in Salem. Historical facts establish a
suitable context for the demonstration of a point that could have
been made as well, the author believes, with evidence drawn from
Harlem or Vietnam.[27]

In an essay entitled "Our Guilt for the World's Evil," Miller
attributes the factual basis of *Incident at Vichy* to a story he heard
from a friend. In 1942 a certain Jew (Leduc in the play) was
arrested in Vichy, France, which though still unoccupied was
subject to Nazi racial policies. As he waited to be interrogated,
together with others suspected of being Jewish, he realized that a
death sentence was inevitable. Before his turn arrived to enter the
police office, however, a Gentile suspect (Prince Von Berg in the
play) who had just been freed enabled the Jewish prisoner to
escape at the cost of his own life. The story came to signify to Miller
not the heroism of the Gentile nor the suffering of the Jew but the
inhumanity and "common want of solidarity" of *both*: "what is
dark if not unknown is the relationship between those who side
with justice and their implication in the evils they oppose." Von
Berg, "the hero of the play," sides with justice; he "comes into the
detention room with his pride of being on the humane side, the
right side." Yet he (like Leduc) shortly discovers "his own
complicity with the force he despises." Miller's "lesson" is that "it is

immensely difficult to be human precisely because we cannot
detect our own hostility in our own actions. It is tragic, fatal
blindness. . . ."[28]

The play teaches this lesson just about as explicitly as the essay
does. Miller's analysis of the human hate-mechanism follows
closely that in *Focus,* in *The Crucible,* and in *After the Fall,* but in
Incident at Vichy it proceeds almost entirely along discursive lines.
Leduc (a psychiatrist) explains, "Jew is only the name we give to
that stranger" within everyone.[29] Recognition of this "stranger"
would threaten one's sense of purity and power, so each individual
finds it necessary to blame someone else for his own inadequacies:
"each man has his Jew, it is the other."[30] The "other"—a visible
embodiment of death and degradation—can be purged from the
social body; indeed, it is a positive if not holy deed to do so.
Lebeau, a Jewish artist, shows the effect of this attitude upon the
scapegoat: "they keep saying such terrible things about us, and you
can't answer. And after years and years of it, you . . . I wouldn't say
you believe it, but . . . you do, a little . . . You get tired of believing
in the truth" (Leduc adds, more pointedly, "we have been trained
to die"). As long as man chooses not to tolerate his fallibility,
sacrificial murder "will be repeated again and again forever."[31] But
murder is negation, "and that is why there is nothing and will be
nothing," Leduc states. To quote words spoken by a German
major, "there will never be persons again. What do I care if you
love me?" By refusing to countenance his destructiveness, man
becomes infinitely destructive. "I am only angry," Leduc laments,
sounding the key idea postulated also by Quentin in *After the Fall,*
"that I should have been born before the day when man has
accepted his own nature; that he is *not* reasonable, that he is full of
murder, that his ideals are only the little tax he pays for the right to
hate and kill with a clear conscience."

"What can ever save us?" Von Berg despairs, as the discussion
moves from diagnosis to prognosis. Leduc tells the nobleman that
there "will be nothing—until you face your own complicity." To
affirm their "humanity," men must charitably accept their common failings and selfishness. The humiliation resulting from this
acceptance can be meliorated by exchanging "guilt" for "responsibility." Salvation for Miller's characters lies in self-knowledge.

The playwright does not penetrate below this argumentative
surface. None of the speakers supports his position with the
psychological data that give substance to other works by Miller or

to a play like Jean-Paul Sartre's *The Victors* (*Mort sans sépulture*, 1946). *The Victors* involves a similar situation—civilians await interrogation and probably execution in Nazi-dominated France— but intimacies brought up during a frantic self-evaluation supply an experiential basis for Sartre's philosophical stand. In *Incident at Vichy*, Miller does not specify, except for a few incidental details, the personal impetus behind the claims and counterclaims. His characters, whether blind or visionary, are merely vehicles for theoretical assertion.

The blind, frozen in their respective postures, refuse to admit their "implication in the evils they oppose." Each jealously defends his accustomed identity (which is mainly a function of his profession), denies the worth of his brother, and proves that "the Jews have their Jews" ("what a crew! I mean the animosity!" one character exclaims). The businessman guarding his propriety sits as far removed from communication with his fellow prisoners as the gypsy guarding his broken pot, and the Old Jew's unbroken silence, culminating in an explosion of feathers, adequately symbolizes the absence of "solidarity." The others make the point clear in a long debate. Lebeau cannot find "meaning" in the attitudes of friend or enemy. Bayard, an electrician, defends the socialist cause ("class interest makes history, not individuals"); he is refuted by Lebeau, Leduc, and Von Berg. Monceau, an actor, offers a façade of outward confidence ("the important thing is not to look like a victim"); his collegues judge that inadequate also.

Before their epiphanies, the prince and the psychiatrist take leading roles in the futile debate. Von Berg, an esthete, interprets Nazi terror not as a meaningless accident, a capitalist conspiracy, or a personality test, but as an "outburst of vulgarity." Leduc sees *his* position delimited in argument with the Austrian aristocrat, the Jewish actor, and the German officer. Then Leduc and Von Berg attain insight—as in all Miller's plays, moral growth offsets moral rigidity—and Von Berg carries out the play's only significant action in giving up his life for his friend. Yet the process by which the two attain insight receives little attention. Leduc suddenly perceives his own enmity after a momentary urge to take "vengeance" on his wife ("what scum we are!"). The prince understands his "complicity" as abruptly when his tolerance for a Nazi cousin is pointed out to him.

Miller has certainly verified his ability to portray mental complexities attendant upon "the fear of being torn away from our chosen image." In this instance he chose to illustrate the universality of his theory on evil and responsibility with a symposium conducted by simple personality types.[32] And he succeeds in stating his argument cogently—although his article "Our Guilt for the World's Evil," does so equally well. What he does not do in *Incident at Vichy* is lend an emotional shape to the "hatred" he finds resident in all men.

CHAPTER 6

The Price *and*
The Creation of the World

I   The Price

They Too Arise, The Man Who Had All the Luck, All My Sons, Death of a Salesman, After the Fall—all these plays involve a problematic relationship troubling two brothers and their father. Typically, one brother is faithful to the father during some financial or moral crisis, while the other becomes ambivalent toward him and turns to goals outside the family. The son who leaves home, usually to follow a career, strives for independence and self-realization but experiences severe distress; he may feel insecure, immature, or guilty of betrayal, and he may also feel the persistent influence of his father's values after discrediting them. His success in the "outside world," in short, continues to be jeopardized by an unresolved psychological problem that originated in the "home" before his eighteenth year. Until he reevaluates his attachment to his father he remains disoriented and perhaps self-destructive.

The Price and *The Creation of the World and Other Business* repeat this theme of filial disloyalty.[1] There are, of course, major differences among the seven plays. In *After the Fall*, for example, Miller reduced the recurring situation to a subplot. *The Price* features a confrontation not between father and son, as in *All My Sons* and *Death of a Salesman*, but between the brothers, focusing on the one who stays behind. Victor Franz took on a policeman's job at the age of twenty-two in order to support his spiritually and financially bankrupt father, a businessman victimized a decade earlier by the economic crash of 1929. About the same time, his older brother Walter (now a prominent and wealthy surgeon) left home to further his education. Their father lacked sufficient

78

emotional resilience to return to business, or even to social activity: "the man," Victor remembers, "was a beaten dog, ashamed to walk in the street. . . . There was no mercy. . . . One day you're head of a house, . . . and suddenly you're shit."[2] Victor nevertheless retained his "faith" and "confidence" in him, and carried out his "responsibility." He did not need to make a conscious decision: he merely responded to his father's need.

At present, unsettled by the prospect of retirement and by the task of selling his parents' stored furniture (the father has been dead some sixteen years), Victor reflects on the consequences of his loyalty. He wonders whether he may have made a fatal mistake when he became a policeman—for Miller, one's life in good part amounts to one's work. He wonders too whether he exaggerated his father's predicament or importance ("I acted like some kind of mountain crashed"). The elapsed years—and his sense of their worth—seem like a "dream" that has come to "nothing." "You've got to make decisions before you know what's involved, but you're stuck with the results anyway. . . . I'm not even sure any more what I was trying to accomplish." He suspects that he "lay down his life. . . . I look back now, and all I can see is a long, brainless walk in the street." "It's all pointless," he muses, "the whole thing doesn't matter to me!" Victor, who associates his father with a "massive" and outdated armchair, finds "it difficult to decide if the stuff [furniture] is impressive or merely over-heavy and ugly" (stage directions); nor can he decide if his allegiance was "impressive" or merely sentimental and "pointless." Yet when Walter offers him money ($12,000) and a good job on condition that he acknowledge his futility, he stubbornly refuses, clarifies his ethical position, and reaffirms the value of his conduct in the past.

Walter views that conduct as a refutation of his own position. "You must certainly see now how extreme a thing it was," he asserts "to stick with him [their father] like that?" If Victor was right to stay, then Walter must have been wrong to leave. One brother laments that he may have betrayed himself by keeping faith; the other, beset by guilt rather than regret, fears that he may have betrayed himself by *not* keeping faith. Before his nervous breakdown, Walter worked for professional success as insurance against repeating his father's fall:

Suddenly I saw . . . terror. In dead center, directing my brains, my hands, my ambition—for thirty years. . . . Overnight, for no reason, to find

yourself degraded and thrown-down. . . . I thought I wanted to be tops,
but what it was was untouchable.

But by avoiding close ties to others he paid a "price" for security
("the respect, the career, the money"), just as Victor paid to honor
his "responsibility." As Victor remarks, "you've got no wife, you've
lost your family, you're rattling around," and Walter concurs:
"there's too much to learn and far too little time to learn it. And
there's a price you have to pay for that."

Walter renounced this "fanaticism," but the fact that it once
compelled him to desert his father still undermines his peace of
mind. So, supported by Victor's wife, Esther he tries to justify
himself by attacking his brother. He has, he insists, reached truer
insights and more honest convictions than Victor, whose fidelity
was not even founded on mutual affection. Their father believed in
success, not love; he had greater respect for Walter's achievements
than for Victor's sacrifice. "There was no love in this house. There
was no loyalty." Victor should realize that for twenty-three years
his concern for his parent was motivated by an "illusion," and that
he "invented a life of self-sacrifice, a life of duty." Esther agrees:
his life has been a "farce," a "dream, . . . a nightmare."

Despite his earlier misgivings, Victor contradicts his wife and
brother. To accept Walter's reasoning—along with the money and
job—would be to repudiate the commitment he made forty years
ago and the life-style that resulted from it. Loyalty to his father
dignified his existence then and justifies it now; like Willy Loman,
Joe Keller, and Eddie Carbone, he seeks self-respect in a vexing
but emotionally potent parent-child bond. "I can't behave as
though nothing ever happened," he exclaims in his understated
manner; "you're not turning me into a walking fifty-year-old
mistake. . . . Can you go home and start all over again from
scratch?" For Victor, derogatory information about the old man—
who may have selfishly manipulated his sons—is irrelevant. He
judges not his father but what he did for his father.

Neither Victor nor Walter, therefore, will invalidate or "walk
away" (Willy Loman's term) from a long-held basis for self-
esteem. In Miller's later works individuals always reaffirm their
choices, whether those choices are instinctive and altruistic (Victor, Von Berg, Gay, and Roslyn) or reflective and self-centered
(Walter, Leduc, Quentin). Victor finds it important "to believe in
one another" as a felt response, while Walter opts to "risk

believing" as a willed decision. The brothers represent two incompatible personality types Miller has contrasted since his apprentice years—the Innocent and the Cynic. Victor, the phlegmatic, humble sentimentalist resists Walter the nervous, aggressive pragmatist. In a "production note," Miller observes that "as the world now operates, the qualities of both brothers are necessary to it; surely their respective psychologies and moral values conflict at the heart of the social dilemma." Reconciliation seems both desirable and attainable, for (as Walter comments) the two simply took "different roads out of the same trap. It's almost as though we're like two halves of the same guy. As though we can't quite move ahead—alone." But they come together only in "conflict," as competitors. Walter is not rational or practical enough to see Victor's need as ultimately the same as his own: "your failure does not give you moral authority!" he protests—"you will never, never again make me ashamed!" And Victor is not compassionate or idealistic enough to remove the "hook" of remorse from his distressed brother: "you won't get it [reassurance], not till I get mine! . . . there's nothing to give." Neither can follow the course suggested by Quentin and Leduc—to confront our complicity in "evil," to understand how we try to serve ourselves by dishonoring our brothers.[3]

In *The Price*, then, Miller continues to study father-son love and loyalty as the battleground for self-justification. The play shares with *All My Sons*, *Death of a Salesman*, and *After the Fall* many details in respect not only to moral issue, plot, and characterization but also to tensional progression and even phrasing. To different degrees these works are all retrospective, since the protagonist's discovery (or more accurately, rediscovery) of certain information concerning past events precipitates a crisis in the present; the drive to secure justice turns into a journey toward self-knowledge. Repeating the technique he first employed effectively in *All My Sons*, Miller builds tension in *The Price* by gradually introducing uncomfortable subjects into commonplace family discussion: both plays begin with homey middle-class jokes and complaints. Surrounded by his parents' old-fashioned furniture in the attic of his boyhood home, a Manhattan brownstone scheduled for demolition, Victor recalls pleasant times ("people were friendlier") but Esther disturbs his peace by raising worrisome issues (as Kate does in *All My Sons*). She frets about aging (Victor will soon be fifty), about the necessity to bargain with the dealer, about

Walter's "moral debt" to her husband and failure to return their phone calls (the brothers have not met since their father's death), about the uncertainties connected with Victor's retirement and financial insecurity, and (the most aggravating subject) about the emptiness of their lives. Before the elderly Jewish dealer arrives and dissipates the tension momentarily with his comic mannerisms, Esther's impatience erupts in a demand for money. The scene neatly illustrates Miller's favorite method of exposing facts and the stress associated with those facts.

Although this tactic was modified in *After the Fall* to suit the subjective nature of the review conducted by Quentin, Miller's two plays of the 1960s bear a close resemblance. Young Quentin's mother castigates her husband for losing the family fortune during the Depression; in the same situation, Victor's mother vomits on her husband. Like Walter, Quentin leaves his indigent father to be cared for by his brother while he goes off to college to launch his career. Quentin expresses perfectly both the tough self-interest and guilt of the successful brother in *The Price*: "I felt a power in the going . . . and treason in it. . . . Because there's failure, and you turn your back on failure."

For its prototype, however, *The Price* takes *Death of a Salesman*.[4] Walter accuses his brother of "sacrificing his life to vengeance"; Willy Loman accuses his elder son of the same thing: "you cut down your life for spite! . . . you vengeful, spiteful mut!" "You lay down and quit," Walter shouts at Victor, just as Willy says of Biff, "he . . . laid down and died." Biff Loman feels "like a boy," and his father claims he "never grew up." Similarly, Esther calls Victor ineffectual with his brother: "you're still eighteen years old with that man!" Biff thinks that he failed as a dutiful son ("I've been remiss. . . . But now I'll stay"), which is what Victor thinks of Walter ("you had a responsibility here and you walked on it"). Though he stood by his father, Victor doubts whether he achieved anything by it: "I look at my life and the whole thing is incomprehensible to me. . . . It ends up—nothing." Willy (as well as Biff) reveals this sort of insecurity when he protests against "ringing up a zero. . . . A man has got to add up to something. . . . What's the answer?"

Though he has doubts, Victor justifies himself to his wife. "You don't understand *anything* any more!" he tells her—a line that repeats Linda's perplexity concerning Willy ("I don't understand it"). Female characters—Esther, Linda Loman, Kate Keller, Eliza-

beth Proctor, and Quentin's two wives—always pay "attention" to
Miller's protagonists (all of whom are male except Roslyn in *The
Misfits*), but they rarely "understand" them. At a trying time Victor
lacks Esther's support ("Where have you been?") just as Willy
lacked the support of his sons ("Where are you guys, where are
you?"). "What are you trying to do," he asks her, "turn it all into a
dream?"

Unfortunately, life does pass like a "dream." Gregory Solomon,
the furniture dealer, uses the term to describe his own past; Hap, to
describe his ambition ("that's what I dream about"); Biff, to describe his father's obsession ("take that phony dream and burn
it"). The dream favored by Willy and Hap is "to come out
number-one man"—a motive once celebrated by Walter and now
lamented by Solomon ("everybody wants to be number one").
Willy's realities, in short, are located for the most part "inside his
head" (the original title of *Death of a Salesman*); and when Victor
shows concern for his father's shame he asks, "what about the
inside of his head?" Subjective realities may be important, Esther
concedes, but not when they distort facts: "what's so dreadful
about telling the truth?" In similar fashion Biff claims that his father
"never told the truth." Biff requests "the facts"; Solomon offers
"facts" to Victor. As a salesman Solomon is realistic ("that I can
sell"), in contrast to the wishful thinking of Hap ("we could sell
sporting goods!") and Willy ("I could sell them!").

To summarize, Miller's "family" plays (excluding *A View from
the Bridge*) exhibit, as a result of their similar story elements, four
recurring characters: two brothers separated by the different
degrees of affection they give to and receive from their father, a
father who demands fidelity from his sons after his fall in status or
financial position, and a mother who, whether or not she respects
her husband, does not understand him.[5] In addition, a fifth character type occurs in most of these and Miller's other plays—a choric
commentator, a friend and adviser to the protagonist whose
observations are sensible, well-meant, but usually futile. He can do
little to moderate the pain or passion he sees. He acknowledges the
flux of human fortunes, tolerates the idiosyncracies of those he
cares for, and holds to principles of common sense, sanity, and
survival. He is a sympathetic yet realistic kibitzer. Shory in *The
Man Who Had All the Luck*, Jim Bayliss in *All My Sons*, Charley
and Ben in *Death of a Salesman*, Alfieri in *A View from the Bridge*,
and Kenneth in *A Memory of Two Mondays* play this role (it is

taken over by the protagonist in *Incident at Vichy* and *After the Fall*; it is omitted in *The Crucible*).

The Price offers a comic version. "Water I don't need," Gregory Solomon gasps in his Russian-Yiddish accent after climbing up to the attic; "a little blood I could use." (He concludes the play with a fit of "howling laughter.") More seriously, Solomon tries—like similar characters in the other plays—to ease the despair of the chief actor. He understands Victor because he too has discovered that "it's impossible to know what is important." In retrospect his life appears as unreal as a "dream"; for instance, he could not keep his daughter from suicide, and even if she were still alive, he speculates, "what would I say to her?" Puzzled by the problem of reaching beyond the self toward profitable connection with others, Solomon and Victor finally support each other in that enterprise. Solomon resumes his own constructive endeavors by taking on the "responsibility" of the furniture (literally, the title of the play refers to the amount he offers). And at the same time he acts as a model of good faith for Victor. Just as he works equitably to "pick up the pieces" after deaths and divorces, so does Victor equitably appraise his own estate under the paternal influence of the aged Jew.

Solomon speaks with conviction, *as if* his commerce possessed dignity and purpose. Living is "the same like [selling] secondhand furniture," he argues: "the whole thing is a viewpoint. It's a mental world." Work, cooperation, mutual respect combat the fear of "nothing" that (as Quentin discovered) deadens the will. With the practical wisdom of his namesake he tells Victor that "if you want to do business a little bit you gotta believe [trust one another] or you can't do it. . . . Nothing in the world you believe, nothing you respect—how can you live?" He models as well as enunciates this doctrine by patiently, charitably, vivaciously establishing rapport with his suspicious client ("I'm not sociable," Victor insists). At first Victor has trouble evaluating the man: he cannot tell whether Solomon—like the obsolete furniture and his kindness to his father—is "pointless" or "impressive." Eventually his skepticism and reserve give way before Solomon's charm and good will. His positive accommodation to the dealer, which Solomon maintains is essential for a valid financial transaction, prepares him to make a positive accommodation to his father; in each relationship he bases decisions about monetary dealings upon judgments about moral dealings. Walter has paid for freedom from guilt with emotional detachment. Victor, who bought freedom from guilt with good faith, reaffirms the kind of "belief" that allies him to Solomon.[6]

Solomon thus contributes more to the protagonist's rehabilitation than do any of Miller's other choric types. His contribution should not be exaggerated: stressing the idiosyncracies of his speech and the infirmities of his age, Miller centers serious interest on Victor's crisis. A kibitzer, after all, should not displace the principal player. The relative importance of Solomon, however, points to a change of emphasis in Miller's plays after *A View from the Bridge*. Victor (with Solomon's help), Quentin, and Leduc formulate a policy for survival whose origins can be seen in the "realism" expounded by commentators from Jim Bayliss and Charley to Alfieri. Moving away from the disillusion, paralysis, and isolation experienced by Chris Keller, Biff Loman, and Walter Franz, they propose a compromise that avoids two radical attitudes toward intimacy—at one extreme, total withdrawal, and at the other, violent possessiveness. They explore the feasibility of temperate, unselfish, rational commitments (a positive lesson for the playgoer) rather than demonstrate the consequences of frantic, egocentric, deeply distressed commitments (a negative lesson). They try to escape the traditional masculine dominant-subordinate relation, whereby one man's quest for self-realization requires his brother's (or son's) self-effacement. They redefine the procedure whereby an individual seeking justice interprets what "happened" in the past.

They have partly succeeded. There is certainly a great difference in outlook between Chris Keller's conclusion, "now I'm practical, and I spit on myself," and the conclusion reached by Quentin: "even now . . . I could dare love the world again!" Miller's recent optimists speak with a sober maturity that contrasts with the superficiality of Chris, Lawrence Newman, and Gay Langland. Furthermore, by placing their priority on survival they circumvent John Proctor's noble sacrifice: they wish to *live* with honor.[7] Yet their efforts to articulate a rational mode of interaction—the lifetime goal of a persistent, humane playwright—still seem to be incomplete. Victor validates himself but cannot extend his "belief" to Walter; desiring neither to dominate nor to be dominated, he fails to find a way to love his brother. And Walter's hope for salvation ("Now I'm a realist, yet love is still possible!") expresses a wishful thought unsupported by past experience. In his honesty Miller cannot visualize a productive exchange between

individuals as an immediate reality. It occurs only in the future
(Quentin and Holga), the past (Victor and his father), or an instant
of the present (Leduc and Von Berg).

These characters have attempted to fathom the "world's evil."
Earlier figures like Willy Loman and Eddie Carbone were not
able to contemplate their frailty or failure; their stubbornness
ensured their defeat as well as their vitality. From the time of
Aeschylus, in fact, theater audiences have gained profit from the
spectacle of a prideful, obsessive male passionately asserting and
destroying himself as a father or citizen.[8] Can an equally effective
dramatic language be devised to show the spectacle of a compassionate, creative male intelligently offering and fulfilling himself in
his family or society? Can masculine egos ever be reconciled?
Arthur Miller, after investigating the traditional tragic formula as
skillfully as any other modern playwright, has devoted the second
half of his career to these questions. They are unanswered but
invaluable extensions of his original question, "how may a man
make of the outside world a home?"

II The Creation of the World and Other Business

The "respective psychologies and moral values" of Walter and
Victor Franz "conflict at the heart of the social dilemma" in a
recurring father-son situation. The same can be said of the
irreconcilable argument between God and Lucifer in *The Creation
of the World and Other Business*.[9] This time, Genesis supplies the
family configuration composed of a father (Adam), his wife (Eve),
two dissimilar sons (Cain and Abel), and the grandest kibitzer of all
(Lucifer). The conflicting values are debated not by the brothers,
as in *The Price*, or by father and son (*All My Sons, Death of a
Salesman*), but by the commentator and the father's father (God)
in a legalistic, argumentative format similar to the prosecution-
defense interplay between Walter and Victor, Keller and Chris, the
witchhunters and John Proctor, Alfieri and Eddie, or Leduc and
Von Berg. Each debater pushes his position to an extreme: realism
versus idealism, survival or success versus respect or love, disillusioned detachment versus innocent faith. In other plays, a few
characters refuse to "settle for half" (Alfieri's phrase) and manage
to bridge, at least tentatively, these dualisms—Quentin in theory,
Von Berg and Leduc in a cooperative action, and Solomon in the
force of his personality. More often, caring individuals try but fail,

like Chris and Joe Keller, Gay and Roslyn, Gus and Kenneth, or Biff
and Miller's most complex failure, Willy Loman—who both
idealizes the practical life (as symbolized by Ben) and pragmatizes
the caring life (as symbolized by Dave Singleman). In *The
Creation of the World*, however, there is neither pathetic failure
nor limited success, merely an illustrated discussion between
Miller's principal adversaries.

The story of Adam and Eve had been in Miller's mind when he
wrote *The Price* and (obviously) *After the Fall*. It suggested to him
another way of contrasting the standpoints in his ongoing argument. On one hand, man seems dedicated to self-aggrandize-
ment. As the knowing Solomon says, "it's already in the Bible, the
rat race. . . . The minute she [Eve] laid her hand on the apple,
that's it. . . . There's always a rat race, you can't stay out of it." On
the other hand, as the hopeful Quentin speculates, knowing this to
be true may not preclude "forgiveness." "Courage" and "love"
may still be "feasible":

Is the knowing all? To know, and even happily that we meet unblessed;
not in some garden of wax fruit and painted trees, that lie of Eden, but
after, after the Fall, after many, many deaths.

In *The Creation of the World* these standpoints are discussed at
length by God and Lucifer. God builds his relationship with the
first humans on mutual trust, then tests that bond by ordering them
to stay away from the Tree of Knowledge, and later by (according
to Lucifer) "setting them up for a murder." Even after Adam and
Cain fail these tests, love continues to be God's chief gift and man's
central choice. Humanity will be properly guided

only if the eye of God opens in the heart of everyman; only if each himself
will choose the way of life, not death. . . . I made them [humans] not of
dust alone, but dust and love; and by dust alone they will not, cannot long
be governed.

Appropriately, Adam ends the play with a plea to Eve and "to the
world" for "mercy."

Lucifer, who presents his case even more loquaciously than God,
advocates freedom from such responsibility. He proposes that
God do away with priority between good and evil in order to
prevent strife between the two allegiances. Dissent among rival

factions in society or within the individual would cease: "so people
would never come to hate themselves, and there's the end of guilt.
Another Eden, and everybody innocent again." God calls this "a
cosmic comedy where good and evil are the same." But Lucifer
intends to free men from the obligation to make moral distinctions
because he disbelieves in their capacity to live honorably ("what is
Man beyond his appetite?"). Indeed, after the murder of Abel an
"outraged" God concurs: "you are all worthless! This is a chaos you
want, and him [Lucifer] you shall have—the God who judges
nothing, the God of infinite permission. . . . I see now that your
hearts' desire is anarchy."

Lucifer particularly abhors guilty consciences. He tries to avert
the first murder to forestall the consequent "remorse" and "fear of
God" that will keep men dependent on divine forgiveness,
perpetually suspended between "high promise and deadly terror."
So he demands that Cain "face him [Abel] with indifference":

> Kill love, Cain, kill whatever in you cares;
> Murder now is but another sort of praise to God!
> Don't praise Him with a death! . . .
> If man will not kill man, God is unnecessary!

Without love there would be no jealousy, hatred, and murder when
love is rejected, no "fear of being unacceptable," no guilty
subservience, no cyclic alternation between the violation and the
renewal of trust. "There is no consolation, woman!" Lucifer
declares to Eve after Abel's death; "unless you want the lie of God,
the false tears of a killer repenting!" And to Cain: "you're the one
free, guiltless man. Tell God you have no need for Him! Speak out
your freedom and save the world!" Miller's nontraditional, amoral
Devil wants to prevent crime, not cause it ("I've got to keep them
out of trouble, not get them into it").

His concern for mankind is motivated by concern for his own
welfare, both being rooted in his cardinal principle, self-interest.
"And will I ever be more than a ridiculous angel until I murder His
[hopes]?" On Cain's "shoulders may I climb the throne." God
understands this motive. Regarding Lucifer's campaign to ac-
quaint Adam and Eve with forbidden knowledge, He comments
"that's all you're after, to grind away their respect for Me. . . .
Nothing is real to you. Except your appetite for distinction and
power. . . . It's only his power this Angel loves!" For Lucifer,

however, self-interest is universal: he thinks God has tempted Adam with the apple so that enlightened humans will "magnify Your glory to the last degree." He also accuses God of "setting up" Abel's death to perpetuate His authority. "God wants a murder from you," he informs Cain,

> So he[*sic*] may stand above your crime, the blameless God,
> The only assurance of Mankind, and his [*sic*] power is safe.
> God wants power, not morals!

Each antagonist sees the will to power animating the other, and they agree that it animates man too. God makes sexual innocence the sign of obedience, self-control, respect, and love, but the emergence of lust signals the birth of self-will. "You had to have power, and power is in you now," He rebukes Adam, "but not Eden any more." Cain, who "killed for pride and power and in the name of love," also sacrifices rapport with God. God conceives self-will as man's fall, Lucifer conceives it as man's hope.[10]

One may object on two counts to Miller's reinterpretation of the biblical stories. As a dramatic piece it lacks dynamic speech and characterization, except for a few poignant lines spoken by Eve and Cain. This point needs no elaboration; the sex-humor at the beginning is particularly inane. Second, as a philosophical exposition of Miller's hard-won conclusions about human potentials the work lacks logical clarity, especially in regard to Lucifer's stand on love and guilt. According to Lucifer, people would not "come to hate themselves" if guilt were nonexistent: they would be as unoppressed by conscience as animals. Each individual would live in Satanic ignorance, worshiping only himself, with no capacity to value virtue (the worship of all creation). Since guilt comes from *knowing* one has chosen evil even though good is preferable, Lucifer wishes to do away with distinctions between the two ("there is no sin or innocence"). When he seduces Eve by introducing her to the principle of egoism, he hopes to weaken her dependence on God and to enlist her in his own service. But in encouraging her disobedience he ironically enables her and Adam to learn how *to distinguish between good and evil*, and so attain a new kind of understanding that makes moral choice possible. The specific consequence of the first prideful act defeats his purpose, for having once acquired such understanding how can humans follow Lucifer's request to behave as if they had none? Under what conditions can a self-conscious person unlearn moral awareness, refuse to evaluate, and achieve "indifference"? For that matter, with what weapons can Cain "kill love," that is, deaden his God-given ability to perceive and respond to virtue?

Miller, of course, may have intended to show Lucifer's position to be false or self-contradictory. If, for further illustration of this point, Lucifer desires a world in which "there is no sin or innocence," how could he remain "perfectly evil"? If self-love were elevated to an absolute status, how could it and its contrary be "equally real"? If, like Walter and Victor, Lucifer and God represent incompatible values (one a "God of what-they-are," the other "in charge of improvement"), then God (like Victor) correctly rejects the attempt at reconciliation. But where does this leave Cain? Neither God nor Lucifer wants him to commit murder; the archetypal outcast, he identifies with neither party. Yet he kills in the name of *both*—to satisfy his ego, and out of love for God! Cain's involvement with these opposing principles requires an explanation more precise than that offered by God in the remark, "Cain killed for pride and power and in the name of love." Because God and Lucifer polarize their attitudes, their commentary works against clarifying the complexities suggested by Cain's "dilemma." Lucifer's notion that "if man will not kill man, God is unnecessary" might be true. One cannot judge its truth, however, without further information about the distress mechanisms that interrupt love and motivate murder.

The Creation of the World simplifies the continuing dialogue in Miller's writing, but it is a difficult dialogue to conduct. As Miller sees them, one value or motive inevitably negates the other: self-interest ends in guilt when a need to care for others speaks out, and dedication to others ends in betrayal when a need to gratify the self speaks out. As polarized constructs, neither possesses absolute validity. If egoism appears mean and directionless, the alternative to Lucifer's specious cynicism appears to be equally unworkable, since man will not love his God or his brother for long. Translated into particular commitments (as opposed to philosophical debates), love turns out to be dangerous and unstable. Neither tendency can triumph, nor can the two coexist, a paradox that has challenged and frustrated Arthur Miller throughout his career.

CHAPTER 7

The Perspective of a Playwright

I *Thesis*

ARTHUR MILLER has focused upon a single subject—"the struggle . . . of the individual attempting to gain his 'rightful' position in his society" and in his family. Miller's chief characters, whether they eventually revise their objectives or remain rigidly defensive, are motivated by an obsession to justify themselves; they fix their identities through radical acts of ego-assertion.[1] "However one might dislike this man, who does all sorts of frightful things," the dramatist comments of Eddie Carbone, "he possesses or exemplifies the wondrous and humane fact that he too can be driven to what in the last analysis is a sacrifice of himself for his conception, however misguided, of right, dignity, and justice" (*C.P.*, 51). High rank or noble status does not distinguish such figures. "The commonest of men," Miller states in "Tragedy and the Common Man" (1949), "may take on [tragic] stature to the extent of his willingness to throw all he has into the contest." "The closer a man approaches tragedy the more intense is his concentration of emotion upon the fixed point of his commitment, which is to say the closer he approaches what in life we call fanaticism" (*C.P.*, 7).

Fanatical self-assertion may bring an individual into violent opposition with his society. Tragic antagonism arises because the "unchangeable [social] environment" often "suppresses man, perverts the flowing out of his love and creative instinct" ("Tragedy and the Common Man"). According to Miller, in "The Shadows of the Gods" (1958), conflict between father and son prefigures tragedy's "revolutionary questioning" when the child affirms his independence after confronting an intolerant parental authority. Later the mature hero, in life and in art, directs his protest against restrictive forces more potent than the father's, for "in truth the parent, powerful as he appears, is not the source of injustice but its deputy" (43).

Society, however, is not the sole tragic villain. Miller admires his hero's obsessive claim to a given "right," and he sorrows at its frustration. At the same time, he realizes that total self-concern can lead to total self-defeat; "conscience," if not tempered by humility and informed by reason, may degenerate into a savagely destructive faculty. When opposed by "forces of disintegration," Miller's major figures react in either of two ways, depending upon the flexibility of their ethical posture. They may reexamine their criteria, as in the case of David Frieber, Lawrence Newman, Chris Keller, Biff Loman, John Proctor, Gay Langland, Quentin, Prince Von Berg, and Victor Franz. Or they may persist in their assertion even though persistence brings catastrophe to themselves and to those for whom they care. That is the course chosen by Joe Keller, Willy Loman, Eddie Carbone, Maggie, and Cain, each of whom arrives at "the end of his justifications."[2] In the first instance, accommodation is directed by realistic self-knowledge; in the second, "constancy" to an ideal of self-love remains the paramount value. The fanatic rejects "truth," which he fears will undermine his "power," alienate him from others, and negate his longing for "respect" and "peace." Despite the nagging pressure of guilt-feelings, he commits the grossest acts, even suicide, in order to maintain the sanctity of his "name"—pride in his adequacy as a father or lover, citizen or businessman—and to prevent the exposure of his secret weakness, dependence, malice, or shame. "To perceive somehow our own complicity with evil is a horror not to be borne."[3]

The author's moral bias is clearly evident in these divergent reactions. Individuals can buttress their own and society's stability by resisting "hatred" and "exclusiveness." Or individuals can upset social equilibrium by enforcing the exaggerated demands of a narrow egoism. Lawrence Newman and John Proctor (among others) strengthen their communities even though they defy popular standards; Willy Loman and Joe Keller adopt popular standards but become estranged from both family and society because of their uncompromising self-will. Extreme egocentrism inevitably thwarts a man's constructive energies: the only way to acquire dignity is to respect the dignity of others.

Miller has proposed his version of the Golden Rule in many essays. He has denounced writers who conform to commercial specifications, businessmen and politicians who exploit other men's insecurities, informers who betray friends in order to preserve their own reputations, civilians who passively tolerate wartime atrocities, and veterans who quickly forget the comradeship they knew during combat. He encountered the last while gathering material in American army camps for a movie. In his journal of the tour, *Situation Normal* (1944), he reports that soldiers, after sharing a common purpose in battle, lose their "unity of feeling" on returning to the United States: "civilian life in America is private, it is always striving for exclusiveness" (158).

Whatever the specific situation, his point on the necessity for communication between individuals and their institutional sources of value remains the same. He repeatedly stresses the idea that the proper business of serious drama is to demonstrate the feasibility of such communication and the disastrous results of its absence. The protagonist of this drama must enter into meaningful social relationships, if only to challenge conventional norms. He should possess "the worth, the innate dignity, of a whole people asking a basic question and demanding its answer" ("On Social Plays," 1955, 8). The "identity" he molds within the intimate bonds of his family must be tried in an inhospitable world. Society as a whole, Miller explains in "The Family in Modern Drama" (1956), is "mutable, accidental, and consequently of a profoundly arbitrary nature to us." A limited theater will therefore restrict its scope to the family, which symbolizes what is "real" and abiding in human affairs. But a writer "cannot hope to achieve truly high excellence short of an investigation into the whole gamut of causation of which society is a manifest and crucial part." He must answer the essential question, "how may man make for himself a home in that vastness of strangers and how may he transform that vastness into a home?" (37, 40–41).

Ibsen, Miller believes, conducted this evaluation, but dramatists after Ibsen have been unable to "bridge the widening gap between the private life and the social life." They usually precipitate one or the other component from the tragic equation: "our lack of tragedy may be partially accounted for by the turn which modern literature has taken toward the purely psychiatric view of life, or the purely sociological" ("Tragedy and the Common Man"). This fragmented literature reflects contemporary experience: the complexity of society militates against a tragic configuration of its irrationality. "We are so atomized socially that

no character in a play can conceivably stand as our vanguard, as
our heroic questioner. . . . To think of an individual fulfilling his
subjective needs through social action . . . is difficult for us to
imagine" ("On Social Plays," 6). Great drama will not be produced
until "a play mixes 'I' with 'we' in a significantly original way. . . .
The only materials for a possible new trend in the U.S. are new
insights into social and psychological mechanisms; the next
original interpretation of these elements, one with the other, will
establish a new form."[4]

The task of creating this "new form" has presented Miller—and
most notable dramatists of this century—with the severest challenge. How does a writer introduce a social milieu so that its
"codes" assume a recognizable and influential presence? How
does he show "indignation" as a function of personality—whether
the indignation of a rebellious son, a betrayed father, a down-
trodden worker, a persecuted citizen, or some combination of
these and other identities—rather than as an intellectual abstraction? In short, how does a playwright translate his "way of looking"
into a character's way of acting? A character may discuss public
issues fluently, but the job of depicting those issues in concrete
terms is a formidable one; he may easily exclaim "I know who I
am," but the difficulties involved in giving that self-awareness an
emotional content are immense. The solutions Miller proposes in
his essays and in his plays supply the index to his achievement as a
dramatist. His lifelong effort to integrate the radical "I" with the
reactionary "we" has been an impressive one. His shortcomings
may well verify his opinion that, given the facts of contemporary
life, total success in such an enterprise is inconceivable.

II *The Search for "a New Form"*

Miller has never seemed to be particularly intimidated by the
problem of finding a dramatic means to interrelate "social and
psychological mechanisms." In 1947 he said, "my development is
toward an ever-greater examination of human nature. So many
people are talking about new form. This to me is an evasion of the
problem of playwriting, which is a revelation of human motives
regardless of form."[5] A decade later he added, "however important considerations of style and form have been to me, they are
only means, tools to pry up the well-worn, 'inevitable' surfaces of
experience behind which swarm the living thoughts and feelings

whose expression is the essential purpose of art" (*C.P.*, 52). The words "regardless" and "only" belie the tremendous concern Miller has shown for his "tools" throughout his career. If his "examination of human nature" has centered on a single subject, his methods have certainly undergone much modification. In several analyses of his own plays he illuminates those changing artistic strategies and his continuous struggle with the technical questions entailed by his thematic interests.

The most penetrating and comprehensive analysis is his long Introduction to the *Collected Plays*. In it he indicates his involvement with three stylistic modes prevalent in modern drama, which may be labeled the realistic, the expressionistic, and the rhetorical.[6] "I have stood squarely in conventional realism" (52), he declares, and an acknowledgment of a major debt to Ibsen supports the statement. Although he had gained an appreciation for the power of "hard facts" from Dostoyevsky's *The Brothers Karamazov*, he learned how "to make the moral world . . . real and evident" by observing Ibsen's "ability to forge a play upon a factual bedrock. A situation in his plays is never stated but revealed in terms of hard actions, irrevocable deeds" (19). More specifically, Ibsen helped Miller answer the "biggest single [expository] problem, namely, how to dramatize what has gone before":

If his plays, and his method, do nothing else they reveal the evolutionary quality of life. One is constantly aware, in watching his plays, of process, change, development. . . . It is therefore wrong to imagine that because his first and sometimes his second acts devote so much time to a studied revelation of antecedent material, his view is static compared to our own. In truth, it is profoundly dynamic, for that enormous past was always heavily documented to the end that the present be comprehended with wholeness, as a moment in a flow of time, and not—as with so many modern plays—as a situation without roots. (21)

"What I was after," Miller recalls, "was the wonder in the fact that consequences of actions are as real as the actions themselves" (18).

While he embraced words, gestures, and shapes of the familiar world, however, he "tried to expand [realism] with an imposition of various forms in order to speak more directly . . . of what has moved me behind the visible façades of life" (52). He expanded in two directions. From the start of his career he wished to enrich the realistic style with an "evaluation of life"—a conscious articulation of ethical judgment. Quite early that wish led to a vexing predicament: in *The Man Who Had All the Luck,* he realized soon after completing the work, he had not been able to avoid a rhetorical, or discursive, presentation of his theme. With the next play he determined to "forego" any sentiments that did not arise naturally from the action. The plan in *All My Sons* was "to seek cause and effect, hard actions, facts, the geometry of relationships, and to hold back any tendency to express an idea in itself unless it was literally forced out of a character's mouth" (15–16). In this way Miller thought he would find it possible to elicit a "relatively sharp definition of the social aspects" (22) without resorting to the discursiveness of the earlier play.

Then he saw that the most significant consequences composing a character's inheritance from past decisions might be emotional, not physical. In *Death of a Salesman,* therefore, he introduced an "expressionistic element" to get at the "passion" residing "behind the visible façades." "From the theatrical viewpoint that play . . . broke the bounds, I believe, of a long convention of realism. . . . I had willingly employed expressionism but always to create a subjective truth. . . . I had always been attracted and repelled by the brilliance of German expressionism after World War I, and one aim in *Salesman* was to employ its quite marvelous shorthand for humane, 'felt' characterizations rather than for purposes of demonstration for which the Germans had used it" (39).[7] This "shorthand" reproduced the psychological immediacy of past events: "the *Salesman* image was from the beginning absorbed with the concept that nothing in life comes 'next' but that everything exists together and at the same time within us" (23).

All My Sons represented a compromise between an explicit moralism and a realistic "geometry" of causation; *Death of a Salesman* represented a compromise between rhetorical, realistic, and expressionistic modes. After *Death of a Salesman,* a "preference for plays which seek causation not only in psychology but in society" (36) compelled Miller to curtail his exploration of subjective processes and to return to a more objective frame of reference. In writing *The Crucible* he was still bemused by "a kind of interior mechanism," but he hoped to "lift" his study "out of the morass of subjectivism" (40–41) with historical data and with evaluative declamation. "It seemed to me then," he writes in a 1960 Introduction to *A View from the Bridge,* "that the theater was retreating into an area of psycho-sexual romanticism, and this at the very moment when great events both at home and abroad cried out for recognition and analytic inspection" (vi).

Having "taken a step toward a more self-aware drama" with *The Crucible*, Miller continues in this preface, he decided to advance further into the realm ruled by "codes and ideas of social and ethical importance": the fanaticism of Eddie Carbone can be measured by his willingness to violate "the code of his culture" (vi, viii). In another essay, "On Social Plays," Miller states that by the time he wrote *A View from the Bridge* he had abandoned his theory of "interior" causation in favor of "bare" facts and rational commentary. At an earlier stage he probably would have told the story in temporal depth; now he did not want to write "a slowly evolving drama through which the hero's antecedent life forces might, one by one, be brought to light" (16). Without subjective clinical detail interrupting "that clear, clean line of [Eddie's] catastrophe," the "events themselves" could be related swiftly, and the breach of social law would reverberate with "mystery" and "wonderment" (17-18).[8] In *After the Fall*, again, Miller intended to objectify the "psychological question"—to "present the psychology of men not for its own sake, . . . but primarily as it issues forth in its public importance."[9]

Miller's experimentation with expressionistic, realistic, and rhetorical styles, then, has been conditioned by his overriding desire to declare objective truths about man in society: "our standards of right and wrong, good taste and bad, must in some way come into either conflict or agreement with social standards" (*C.P.*, 10-11). A playwright's goal should be to merge "surfaces of experience" (the objective) with "cogent emotional life" (the subjective) and "philosophically or socially meaningful themes" (the analytic) so as to make known the public significance of private engagements. "Drama is akin to the other inventions of man in that it ought to help us to know more, and not merely to spend our feelings. The ultimate justification for a genuine new form is the new and heightened consciousness it creates and makes possible—a consciousness of causation in the light of known but hitherto inexplicable effects" (*C.P.*, 8, 13, 52-53). Miller's aim as a craftsman has been to "make real on stage as in life that part of man which, through passion, seeks awareness. There is no contradiction between the two."[10]

III   *The Problem of Perspective*

Arthur Miller and Eugene O'Neill have done more than other
American dramatists to "relate the subjective to the objective
truth":[11] *Death of a Salesman* and O'Neill's *Long Day's Journey
into Night* are two of the finest works in the American theater.[12]
Contrary to Miller's assertion, however, there *is* in his plays a
contradiction between passion and awareness, between irrational
impulse and rational concept. His best dialogue mirrors psychological conditions, yet he constantly returns to the formal generalization; he can skillfully manipulate emotional tension, yet he seeks
esthetic detachment; his figures act most intelligibly in a family
context, yet he feels obliged to make explicit their connection with
a social "environment." Miller sees his principal subject—the drive
for self-justification—primarily as an *internal* process activated by
"mechanisms" that repress or involuntarily recall shameful memories and motives, that effect rapid transitions between taut and
relaxed moods. When his characters fervently defend egocentric
attitudes, their futility evokes a genuine sense of terror and pathos
that indirectly but powerfully reinforces his thesis on the necessity
for "meaningful" accommodation in society. When, on the other
hand, his characters intelligently reform, their self-knowledge
remains only a rhetorical promise. After their fall and recovery the
mature new-men—Lawrence Newman, David Frieber, Chris
Keller, Biff Loman, John Proctor, Gay Langland, Quentin, Leduc,
Von Berg, and the Franz brothers—predicate rather than model
their liberating insights. A tendency to impose judgment upon
action—the tendency Miller worried about after writing his first
Broadway play, *The Man Who Had All the Luck*—has prevented
him from achieving the harmony of styles he has long sought. His
attempt to enlarge the "interior psychological question" with
"codes and ideas of social and ethical importance" has distorted his
subjective perspective and so compromised his exceptional talent.

A review of his symbolic, structural, and verbal techniques
substantiates this conclusion. Miller has been relatively fortunate in
finding apt metaphors to signify the implications of a "gap
between the private life and the social life." Most of his symbolic
images, it is true, are drawn along simple lines—a carousel that
conceals hatred (*Focus*); a fruitful tree destroyed in its prime (*All
My Sons*); "green leaves" blotted out by the hard outlines of
apartment buildings, a flute song displaced by childish nonsense

from a wire recorder, a wife's praise erased by a whore's laugh (*Death of a Salesman*); a dingy warehouse harboring hopeless inmates (*A Memory of Two Mondays*); a herd of mustangs moving toward extinction (*The Misfits*); a ruined tower that memorializes horrors committed by "ordinary" men (*After the Fall*); feathers and a broken pot guarded as if they were life itself (*Incident at Vichy*); a "massive," discarded armchair (*The Price*).

Just as obviously, many of Miller's workers—a fearful personnel manager in an anti-Semitic corporation (*Focus*) and an unscrupulous industrialist (*All My Sons*), a frustrated salesman (*Death of a Salesman*) and a dispirited policeman (*The Price*), dehumanized laborers (*A Memory of Two Mondays*) and displaced cowboys (*The Misfits*)—find little spiritual "sustenance" in their trades.[13] Men who look for a satisfying social role in a productive occupation—Chris Keller, Biff Loman, Kenneth and Bert, Gay Langland, Quentin, and Walter Franz—are disappointed; even the reborn Lawrence Newman faces a future as a "glorified usher to salesmen." In *Incident at Vichy*, one of only two plays set in a foreign locale, the situation is worse: none of the prisoners—from Leduc, a psychiatrist, to Von Berg, an aristocratic non-worker, to the Gypsy, who does odd (or illegal) jobs—can possibly make positive use of his abilities in his country. Despite his acquaintance with a wide variety of trades as a youth, Miller never envisioned a profession—except, perhaps, his own—that could unite its practitioner with his society in mutually beneficial labor.

Taken symbolically, these vocations and images could be said to indicate the misuse of natural talent brought about by an incongruity between personal and social objectives in contemporary urban culture. As such, they are rather facile indications. A subtler, more extended occupational metaphor that objectively represents the individual's malaise in society is the pursuit of justice through law. In Miller's plays, with their rhythm of accusation and defense, the defendant invariably fails to obtain equity and must resort to extralegal means to protect his rights.

Lawrence Newman forges a new code of conduct after he perceives the inadequacy of the mores to which he had subscribed and the inability of the law to relieve racial discrimination. In *All My Sons*, a courtroom drama in essence if not in setting, the trial metaphor assumes greater importance. Joe Keller commits fraud and involuntary homicide, conspires to incriminate his partner, and evades detection until his son (with the help of George, a lawyer) prosecutes, finds him guilty, rejects his appeal, and delivers what amounts to a death sentence. Both Chris and his father call upon principles beyond the jurisdiction of formal law; each defends his principle with a fierceness that makes the legal question seem petty in comparison. In *Death of a Salesman*, again a minor character, Bernard, chooses law as his profession, and again a father stands accused, then condemned by his son for a breach of trust far more serious than, though associated with, his technical transgression (adultery).

Eddie Carbone brings on disaster by upholding a statute (against illegal immigration), not by violating one, but—as with Joe Keller, Willy Loman, and Eddie's accuser, Marco—his justification transcends the realm of jurisprudence. Institutional procedures are powerless to secure for him his paternal "rights" or to prevent Rodolpho from "stealing" his niece. "The law is not interested in this," his impassive attorney tells him; "you have no recourse in the law." Victor Franz, retiring from police work, sees his career as "a little unreal," and in *The Creation of the World* man comes out guilty even when God argues for him. Miller's central metaphorical statement of the law's insufficiency occurs in *After the Fall*, whose protagonist rejects the legal profession after having adopted its mode of operation in his personal life.[14] Quentin learns (as does Eddie Carbone) that the great limitation of the legal mode is an incapacity to account for, much less to deal with, emotional needs. Although his original outlook persists—he continues to discuss human behavior in terms of moralistic formulas ("this pointless litigation of existence before an empty bench")—he gives up his practice in the hope of arriving at more humane knowledge.

In these works the legal system for redress of grievance is seen to be almost irrelevant to the protagonist's defense of a "conception, however misguided, of right, dignity, and justice." In *Incident at Vichy*, in *The Crucible*, and in Miller's adaptation of Ibsen's *An Enemy of the People*, the system of public morality becomes, through agents acting in its name, the active perpetrator of injustice. The trial of integrity is consequently tied more closely to a courtroom or jail terminology. *Incident at Vichy* deals with the supreme perverters of law in recent times. As in Kafka's *The Trial*, the rationale that justifies political murder ("there are no persons anymore") appears bizarre and irrational to those victimized by it. Only Von Berg penetrates the ethical obscurity by reasserting, in an act of self-sacrifice, the responsibility of individual conscience.

Similarly, John Proctor gives up his life to confirm a principle of enlightened self-determination intolerable to the Salem judges. (Before the hearing and the ordeal in jail, Proctor suffered a private trial at home: "I come into a court when I come into this house!" he complained to his wife, who would not forgive his liaison with Abigail.)[15]

In his adaptation of Ibsen's *An Enemy of the People* (1950), Miller reiterated with an abundance of legalistic set-speeches his belief that public antipathy can provide a grueling test for a nonconformist who dares question social standards. As in *Focus*, *The Crucible*, and *Incident at Vichy*, a community's insanity arouses indignation in a "lonely" battler. The issue is almost allegorical in its polarization of good and evil: Honesty, personified by brave Dr. Stockmann, debates (again in a trial setting) with Evil, personified by smug middle-class materialists—the "people." During the debate Stockmann exposes the bourgeois immorality, self-interest, and blindness that had masqueraded as communal justice, enterprise, and wisdom. "The majority," he declares, "is never right until it *does* right."[16] The fact that Stockmann, in common with most of Miller's chief figures, is forced to look beyond juridical criteria for a tenable standard of justice calls into question the social order founded upon those criteria. "There doesn't seem to be much of a law," a character laments in *All My Sons*; "all the law is not in a book," Marco states in *A View from the Bridge*. Where law is superfluous or malign, the trial process becomes an ironic metaphor for the pursuit of self-respect.[17]

Miller incorporated the accusation-defense rhythm of a trial into almost all his major plays. Despite his wide-ranging experiments with form, the narrative schemes of *All My Sons, Death of a Salesman, The Crucible, A View from the Bridge*, and *After the Fall* are remarkably alike.[18] In each work hidden guilt is first referred to covertly, then bared in a climactic revelation—a scheme based upon Ibsen's exhibitions of the inescapable causal movement from past action to present reaction. The secrets and the methods with which they are brought to light vary. Eddie Carbone obstinately suppresses *two* secrets—betrayal of the immigrants (an objective fact) and ardor for his niece (a "cast of mind"). Joe Keller and Willy Loman also conceal both their crimes and their moral frailty; John Proctor *confesses* his sins; Quentin concludes that *all* men are guilty. In *All My Sons*, in *The Crucible*, and in *A View from the Bridge*, the sin is suggested by verbal

allusions and by the protagonist's behavior; *Death of a Salesman*
and *After the Fall* modify that procedure with memory-surveys.
Since the protagonist fears discovery—he usually hesitates to
admit his offenses even to himself—gradual exposition generates
suspense by exploiting the discrepancy between inward reality
and outward appearance. "Who can ever know what will be
discovered?" Alfieri muses.

Revelation ensures a surprising transition from one issue to
another. As the secret comes into view, an antagonism developed
at the beginning of each play gives way to a more urgent
opposition. Thus attention is transferred from an argument
between Chris and Kate to an argument between Chris and Joe
(*All My Sons*); from a present to a past father-son dilemma (*Death
of a Salesman*); from a struggle between the Proctors and Abigail
to one between John Proctor and the judges who have condemned
him (*The Crucible*); from the Eddie-Rodolpho to the Eddie-
Marco duel (*A View from the Bridge*); and from Quentin's
dialogue with Louise to that with Maggie (*After the Fall*). Both
before and after the transfer, dramatic interest centers on only one
of the combatants: Keller's fear replaces his wife's as the crucial
subject; Willy's failures in the past, his failures in the present;
Proctor's final decision, Abigail's machinations; Eddie's response
to Marco, the response to Rodolpho; Quentin's self-justification in
the second marriage, that in the first.

This complex format has an outstanding weakness: the resolution of the second issue tends to occur after the emotional climax,
an outcome that is likely to reduce the impact and coherence of the
primary progression of character in the preceding action. Chris
Keller's first engagement with his father was emotionally climactic
but ethically inconclusive. The subsequent rematch forfeits excitement generated by the gradual development of Joe Keller's
anxiety; during the last act Chris diverts attention from the
protagonist's standpoint with speeches on social responsibility.
Although the focus of interest belatedly shifts from the harried
father to the outraged son, however, the decisive conflict is at least
confined to a single set of opponents. In *The Crucible*, contrarily,
the public problem of witchcraft (which supersedes the private
problem of love-jealousy) splits into two relatively separate power
struggles: one involves Abigail, Proctor, and the girls during the
hearing; the other, Proctor and his jailors after it. These struggles,
loosely joined by Miller's implied theory that society can be saved

by its morally mature citizens, come to *independent crises* ending respectively in mass hysteria (the melodramatic highpoint) and personal honesty (Proctor's refusal to confess to witchcraft). Until the fourth act, the social implications of the play arise directly from psychological origins; then the causal connection is abruptly severed. *A View from the Bridge* displays another anticlimactic resolution. The emergence of a second antagonist moves the battle for respect from a family to a community arena, but it blurs "that clear, clean line" of the original (and critical) confrontation, a result compounded by the narrator's propensity for myth-making.

Eager to advance his concept of social "relatedness," Miller fails to honor in these plays the structural rule he observed in Ibsen, Beethoven, and Dostoyevsky: "above all, the precise collision of inner themes during, not before or after, the high dramatic scenes. . . . The holding back of climax until it was ready, the grasp of the rising line and the unwillingness to divert to an easy climax until the true one was ready" (*C.P.*, 16)[19] He avoids anticlimax in *After the Fall* by unfolding Quentin's problem and solution concurrently, allowing only a summary statement of the solution at the ending. Unfortunately, the skeletal, poorly integrated memory sequences inhibit the movement toward significant climax. The double-issue design is wholly successful only in *Death of a Salesman* because there the articulation of value does not become narratively (or verbally) intrusive. Like Chris Keller, Biff Loman goes home again to clarify his "revolutionary questioning," and others also offer interpretive comments. But this activity, far from redirecting attention from one character or issue to another after the play's tensional peak, merely expedites the outcome already predicted by the Salesman's spiritual collapse and makes possible a measured transition from the chaos of the climax to the numbed calm of the denouement. Willy Loman consistently channels the flow of tension; his "fanaticism" unifies psychological and sociological sources of tragedy.

Miller's construction, if rarely flawless, is never formless. His metaphors, if sometimes obvious, are sometimes subtle. It is the dialogue that swings between extremes of brilliance and insipidity. Colloquial speech may be heard in an amazing variety of accents— Irish, Swedish, German, Sicilian, Slavic, Barbados, Yiddish, Puritan, Brooklyn, Southwestern, and Midwestern. *After the Fall* and *Incident at Vichy*, in fact, were the first works that did not make extensive use of subliterate English (except for Maggie's New York locutions and childish inanities, which convey a certain charm and a certain mental barrenness). Whether in historical, regional, or foreign dialect, Miller's dialogue is most telling when it works by implication, not by explication.

Explicit analyses of motivation may, of course, serve a legitimate and even commendable purpose by establishing a rational perspective. Thus Biff Loman and Charley reflect on the meaning of Willy's existence; the misfits as philosophers explain the misfits as doers; Quentin during his psychoanalysis contemplates Quentin before; Leduc and Von Berg answer the question puzzling the other prisoners; the debates in *The Price* and *The Creation of the World* propose policies to secure deliverance from guilt. Rhetorical differences corresponding to differences in perceptiveness are often pronounced: the abstruseness of Shory, Hester, and David Frieber contrasts with the folksiness of their friends in *The Man Who Had All the Luck*; the incisiveness of Newman's thoughts contrasts with the triteness of his conversation; Chris Keller's abstractness, with his father's solidity; Proctor's eloquence, with the girls' incoherence; Alfieri's fluency, with Eddie's awkwardness; the lyricism of *A Memory of Two Mondays* with the slanginess; Gay's pretentiousness, with Roslyn's naiveté; Walter's formality, with Solomon's simplicity. Too often in these instances, however, "analytic inspection" receives disproportionate emphasis, produces artificial wisdom, and unbalances the interplay between idiomatically authentic, emotionally intense, and ethically rational language styles.

At other times, trivial homespun talk, unable to bridge the "gap" separating passion from formal communication, dumbly masks unspeakable humiliation, wrath, or sorrow. Then Miller's writing attains its greatest power. Joe Keller's bluff words resound with increasing apprehension: "because it's good money, there's nothing wrong with that money. . . . What have I got to hide? What the hell is the matter with you?" Interrogating his son with driving insistence, Keller harshly answers each question he raises:

Jail? You want me to go to jail? If you want me to go, say so! . . . I'll tell you why you can't say it. Because you know I don't belong there. Because you know! . . . Who worked for nothin' in that war? When they work for nothin', I'll work for nothin'. Did they ship a gun or a truck outa Detroit before they got their price? Is that clean? It's dollars and cents, nickels and dimes; war and peace, it's nickels and dimes, what's clean? Half the Goddam country is gotta go if I go! That's why you can't tell me.

The conviction ringing in these rhetorical questions derives less from a businessman's self-righteousness than from a father's desperation.[20]

In a similar way Willy Loman's commonplace locutions define uncommon motives. "He won't starve. None a them starve," Charley advises concerning Biff, "forget about him." Willy answers with the poignantly simple sentence, "then what have I got to remember?"[21] Longer passages touch upon, rather than belabor, specific ideas exposed by the action. In her concluding remark Linda alludes quite laconically to her financial insecurity, to her efforts to keep the "home" intact, and above all to her inability to comprehend her husband's strange compulsion: "why did you do it? I search and search and I search, and I can't understand it, Willy. I made the last payment on the house today. Today, dear. And there'll be nobody home. . . . We're free and clear. We're free."

The Crucible, like *Death of a Salesman* (and all of Miller's plays), contains some self-conscious oratory. In neither work does this detract from the dynamics of character, theme, and tension (perhaps the long historical footnotes in *The Crucible* helped assuage Miller's speculative bent). The Puritan dialect may sound archaic and formal to a present-day audience, but it can be as impressive in its monosyllabic directness as contemporary English.[22] "It were a fearsome man," Rebecca eulogizes over one of the witch-hunt victims. "Spite only keeps me silent," Proctor says; "it is hard to give the lie to dogs." A few fanciful metaphors relieve the verbal plainness ("I see now your spirit twists around the single error of my life, and I will never tear it free!"), and Tituba's exotic, faintly humorous Barbados inflection contributes additional color.

Like Tituba, Joe Keller, and Willy Loman, Eddie Carbone in *A View from the Bridge* expresses fearfulness through a comfortably ungrammatical, sometimes comic idiom. "Listen," he warns Catherine, "I could tell you things about Louis which you wouldn't wave to him no more." His contorted syntax registers sharper pain as, ashamed and embarrassed, he tries to dissuade his niece from marriage. In one passage his words wander about in a sobbing rhythm before stumbling to their apologetic petition:

I was just tellin' Beatrice . . . if you wanna go out, like . . . I mean I realize maybe I kept you home too much. Because he's the first guy you ever knew, y'know? I mean now that you got a job, you might meet some fellas, and you get a different idea, y'know? I mean you could always come back to him, you're still only kids, the both of yiz. What's the hurry? Maybe you'll get around a little bit, you grow up a little more, maybe you'll see different in a couple of months. I mean you be surprised, it don't have to be him. [Miller's ellipses]

When suppressed feeling threatens to burst the everyday verbal "façade" in lines such as these, the common man's language becomes emotionally resonant. That resonance marks the distinctive quality of Arthur Miller's achievement.

APPENDIX

"The Absence of the Tension": A Conversation with Arthur Miller

I wanted to see what Arthur Miller was thinking before I finished the second edition of my book on his life and work. On a hot summer afternoon, July 27, 1979, he greeted my sister Toby Gutwill and me at his home in the country near Roxbury, Connecticut. Tall with a bit of a paunch, dressed in shorts and sounding almost as gravel-voiced as George Burns, he showed us a simple graceful chair he had designed and put together from pre-Revolutionary wood salvaged from his barn.

His manner was as simple and graceful as his chair. He was comfortable, enthusiastic, sensible, anecdotal—a wholly satisfying conversationalist. At sixty-four, Arthur Miller is in a good place, and I do not refer only to the pleasant hills around Roxbury.

We left him, after three hours, heading for a chore with a shovel.

I *The Absence of the Tension*

Arthur Miller: What do you want to talk about?

Leonard Moss: I want to say hello. I'm not going to conduct an interview. I don't have a list of questions to ask.

AM: Well, that's a relief! Have you been to New York to see *The Price*?

LM: I saw the original production but not this revival.

AM: It's properly done this time. It wasn't the other time because we had a lot of bad luck. One man got taken to the hospital a few days before we opened, and the other conked out after a week. We had to recast. But it wasn't that so much as my redirecting it in an atmosphere of emergency after the director and actors fell out.

LM: Do you remember my letter asking about the relationship between the two brothers and their father?

AM: Yes. But it's fundamentally a social or moral problem, it isn't simply a psychological problem. The play is examining what you might call the architecture of sacrifice. And of course society depends on sacrifice; everybody has got to do a social duty. We expect the police or the authorities to do that, certainly. There has to be the sort of a person who gets gratification from doing it or you're not going to have a society. And Victor, of course, is a policeman.

LM: Isn't it possible to get some kind of amalgamation of the two points of view, so that you don't have to get the super-egoistic type, and neither do you have to rely on the sacrificial type?

AM: Yeah, hopefully you could, but you ain't gonna get anything if the ironies don't get lifted into view. See, a guy like the older brother frequently is the one who invents new procedures because he is not bound by any reverence for what exists; he's perfectly selfish and temperamental and idiosyncratic. Whether it be in physics or automobile engineering or business, those types add something new to the way the world goes. But they're hell on their relatives—their wives and their children! And the other brother is a terrific husband and father.

LM: You were talking about one of the actors in the original cast who almost died before opening night. Does the idea of dying worry you?

AM: I've been dealing with that for years and years and years. I used to say that plays such as I write are written from the lip of the grave, as though the ultimate judgment was lying upon us all and the object was to find out what it was, if possible. It wasn't that I was attempting to deal with my own death. I thought about the world that way, perhaps simplistically, as though there was a judgment that could be made. I can't imagine trying to write tragedies or anything approaching them without that in mind. You can write comedies with everything left in abeyance, but if you think of any of the Greeks shrugging their shoulders and saying "I don't know what anything means," it's not possible with their structure; it is too pointed, it's too definite, it's too much like an arrow trying to reach a target, as compared with let's say a Chekhovian play, which can end with one foot in the air.

LM: Sometimes I think it's a *negative* judgment—getting back to *The Price* as well as Greek tragedy—on the failure of some of our institutions or values.

AM: It's getting clearer now why we're in such trouble—clearer than maybe ten years ago. And it's that, first of all, history is taking place at a velocity that is unbearable. Tremendous movements begin and end in a year or two. Take something with tremendous meaning for us, like Vietnam, which was maybe the most important event in the history of this country in the twentieth century (apart from the Depression), something that turned us around more violently than anything else. In a space of a few years, Vietnam has become another failed ideal. We had to create a kind of ideal out of it—those of us who hated the war—at least a negative ideal.

A lot of people—this is almost impossible to digest—have a feeling that there is no hope about anything. It's not that they particularly hoped about Vietnam—it's an exemplary situation. I have gone through this now maybe ten times, from the Spanish Civil War. It's been one after another, where of necessity a younger generation believes in an ideal which promptly collapsed or became something else or degenerated.

Now it gets repeated at a quicker velocity—the Soviet Union went from 1919 or '20 for about twenty-five years before a final judgment could be laid upon it, though some people out there still refuse to make any judgment. The Chinese went from '49 to at least '66 before any kind of real doubt could be leveled, and that's a long time. Now it takes about a year or two—take the so-called revolutions in the Third World, like Africa. The revolution takes place on Tuesday, by the next Thursday they're lining people up and shooting them down, and we're back where we started from as far as creating a just society is concerned.

LM: But isn't there some handwriting on the wall? It could be just a long transition to working out a new temperamental type— say, between the two brothers in *The Price*.

AM: Well, my only question is this. When one side wins too thoroughly there is a real question in my mind whether, given the contemporary means for indoctrination and social control that exist—secret police and radio and television and the rest—I wonder what chance remains. We take for granted that both sides are going to persist.

To a degree that's true—they will. Take Czechoslovakia. The Czechs are in an exemplary condition. There's a country that was democratic in our sense of the term—people got elected and they got thrown out. And in a real sense the power resided in the people. It was set up by Wilsonian democrats, and that's the way it was. It wasn't a case of people inured to thousands of years of tyranny and not knowing any different. And they knew they were advanced technologically—they made the best cars in Europe.

OK—they get invaded by the Russians, who very intelligently decided that what they had to do was destroy the cultural inventors, especially those who really were wedded to some other kind of vision, whatever it might be. It might be a Catholic vision—it needn't be West European capitalism—or it might be a Communist vision that was anti-Soviet. They have driven out an army of intellectuals, who now live in Western Europe and some in America.

I had one of them here who still lives in Czechoslovakia. In a moment of candor he wondered whether the spirit, which is skeptical and courageous—the counterforce—could really go on or be quite completely wiped off the face of the earth. This has happened. Many people there really don't understand what this kind of guy's doing by resisting the regime, and the reason is that physical conditions of life there are not all that horrible. They still have an underlying technology that they use—it's crippled, it could be far better utilized if it were not sat on by these oafs—but people still get their beer and live a lot better than people live in Moscow because they naturally do things more efficiently.

So you have to raise a question about time. You are saying "a long-term transition." OK, but I can see a transition too, to something else, to where that imagining of what you could call a voluntary kind of life is crushed.

And a lot of Americans don't have it anymore. When you talk to them about it, in between not wanting to hear about it, they're scared. See, it's a very fragile kind of plant that exists in history only a few years. In the United States, only since the Civil War up until maybe 1930 is when its heyday was; then it got knocked out of existence, apart from the Communists. There is an internal mechanism working in both systems—no question about it—to integrate everybody into the system.

I think that's why people instinctively make so much of writers, who really don't deserve all that much attention most of the time: they're not that smart and they're not that good. Most writing is not worth the paper it's written on, except it gives us amusement of some sort. But there's a sense that these anarchistic people are trying at least to create something new; there is an instinct that something in the procedure of art is our last gasp. We are the reminders of independent craftsmanship.

LM: Analogous to the procedure that has to be incorporated in our lives.

AM: Right. See, everybody wants to be an artist now. I get invitations, probably ten a week—a writer's workshop, a playwright's workshop, a lecture here, a talk there. "Tell us something."

It wasn't that way when I was growing up. Take my old neighborhood. All types—football players, saxophone players, dentists; I was the only one who ever came to be a writer. You read *Studs Lonigan* or any book about a neighborhood. You didn't find people walking around saying, "I'm going to be a writer or an artist." I'm sure that if you wrote the same sort of book about a later generation, I'm sure more people dream at least of escaping the system by being an artist. Don't you think there's more of that now?

LM: I can't see it. There's a lot of people who go for the money in writing, but I don't see the idea there that it's a creative thing to do.

AM: But all these courses! When I went to the University of Michigan it was the only school in the United States that gave a playwriting course. It was the only school that I was aware of where a student could enter a writing contest and win money. It was so rare—that they actually thought that much about writing. And of course Harvard would never have a course in creative writing because they felt that it wasn't serious.

LM: It's become more respectable—

AM: and more widespread.

LM: But as you once said, "many writers, few plays."

AM: Oh, I don't mean that they actually create anything—that's got nothing to do with it. It's this image of the Bohemian, of the free man who doesn't go to work every morning, and out of himself creates his *living*—that's what I'm talking about. It's really the reincarnation of the old shopkeeper who lived upstairs and went down, opened his store, and sent nine children through college and raised eleven dentists.

LM: Somehow I can't see a generation of writers or artists at the present time leading the way. It seems to me it's going to come from somewhere else, maybe even the politicians, unlikely as that seems. There aren't many on the horizon right now who—

AM: who will do what?

LM: Who will give us models for living differently, more creatively, more openly.

AM: My prejudice is that for a great many people the enviable model is the writer.

LM: Where are we going to get models for the kind of life that you keep talking about in your plays and getting your characters to approach—some kind of amalgamation of the two Franz brothers in *The Price*?

AM: That would be great! The only thing I worry about is not so much the amalgamation but the tension, the unhappiness of not having that model. The tension, for example, is terrific between the two brothers, that they give way completely.

LM: But that tension has gone on for thousands of years.

AM: We have lost a lot of it. I used to know a guy who lived around the corner; he's dead now. His name was Theodore K. Quinn. Nobody ever heard of him. He used to be the Vice President of General Electric Corporation, but he was an old Populist underneath all that. He helped buy out one business after another for General Electric, and he was the witness to what he thought was a disaster.

The guys who ran the little businesses were terrific spiritually. They were independent, they were tough, they were witty, ironical, and they talked back. The Company would buy out their businesses, pay them very well, and make them the managers. So they were doing absolutely everything they had done before, except one thing: they no longer worked independently, they were parts of this gigantic octopus.

And he told me that he realized he was witnessing the end of an era, and the end of a kind of person. 'Cause what happened was they grew more and more irresponsible. The idea was "don't make waves." They would see something's not going to work and say nothing: "Be quiet—it'll collapse, and when it collapses it'll change by itself." So what becomes of the virtues of science? He wrote several books. He tried to stop this monopolization, with very little success.

The point is the integration of everybody into one unit; we've simply lost the sense of real independence.

LM: It *could* happen that integration could work in a creative way.

AM: Yes, very often. But at a tremendous cost.

LM: We are still talking in traditional terms—the either/or. Either we'll become mindless robots or—

AM: Well, you have to be ready to concede something to make this compromise. It depends on what. I'll tell you one thing: in the East (for example, China), that particular tension is gone—or never really existed. You educate yourself with only one thought in mind: to find your niche in the hive. Which is of course largely true here. The artist is the only one who has any independence at all, such as he has. Since that philosophy and that system occupy most of the world, the question is how we proceed from here.

LM: What I heard you saying before was that we keep the tension between the two poles intact.

AM: If possible.

LM: That doesn't give you the final answer.

AM: Without the tension you'd have no question. My problem is that I can't see people asking these questions. Here's the irony: the Socialist idea is an integrationist one; they claim a rational society where your talents are used instead of wasted. The irony is that up to this point—the Soviet Union has been around for sixty-five years or so—the fundamental equipment has been taken from *us*, brought into being by these "half-mad liberals" whose existence the other system would suppress. And it's a real question in my mind whether the time will come when they will slowly bind themselves into a well-integrated *stop*. It's not just a question of Capitalism-Communism. It's hard to find a difference. The tension has gone.

LM: So what's going to happen?

AM: Now they have to turn themselves around. Chrysler Motor Company is practically out of business. They sold a big plant to Volkswagen. Symptomatic—they build a brand-new plant in Pennsylvania, never occupied. They never manufactured a *bolt* in there. Volkswagen moved in with a small car and they can't build enough of them. Wait six months here for a Volkswagen. You ain't gonna wait two minutes for a Chrysler; they're paying you two dollars for gas money to come to a Chrysler showroom.

This is all that brick that forms in the head; the concrete slowly settles down. They seem to have lost the strength to bear the tension of conflict and growth. Their ingenuity left them. They got so well integrated that they weren't even capable of competing with another capitalist industry. It's a good example of the absence of the tension.

LM: How does the tension get renewed?
AM: This is a hard question.

II *Can't See the End*

LM: Do you have a personal model in the moral world—
anybody or any work?
AM: There used to be. There isn't any longer because I've used
up all my capacities to emulate. I used to think very often of
Chekhov as a person, but I know that I'm not like him. In terms of
works, I would have liked to live in Greece with the tragedies.

I attach myself to Ibsen because I saw him as a contemporary
Greek, and I suppose it's because there was a terrific reliance in
him as there was in the Greeks on the idea of the continuity
between the distant past and the present. "The birds came home to
roost"—they always did; your character was your fate. I like that
immensely. Beyond that, there was something about Ibsen's
character I didn't like; personally he would have been insufferable.
Lots of writers are totally unreliable, selfish, consumed with their
own psyches, vain.

LM: Sounds like Walter again, in *The Price*. Anyone else?
AM: Only bits and pieces. When I grew up I couldn't stand
Eugene O'Neill's plays. It seemed to me the dialogue was so
phony: you laughed at that kind of dialogue. It was fit for old
melodramas, it wasn't serious, you couldn't read that stuff.
Nobody I knew spoke that way; nobody I knew spoke good
English—what kind of Americans spoke like *that*? Nobody. So I
couldn't stand that.

And then it seemed to me the plays were so weighed down with
the psychological task he had set himself, like being a modern
Aeschylus, that I couldn't see the life in it. He wrote a couple of
marvelous things; the best thing he wrote was *Long Day's Journey
into Night*, his last play. But a lot of the rest is just plain academic
stuff, and I have a feeling one reason his reputation grew was that it
became available to academics.

But as time went on I felt more and more the weight of his
seriousness, finally; despite all, he was pitting his life on his next
discovery, which no other writer I knew was doing. Fitzgerald did
it; Hemingway didn't do it (Hemingway goofed off); Dreiser did
it. So I was moved by that.

But I could never identify myself with him as a person. He

seemed to have to consume his own children. I can't identify myself with that.

I've never become involved in writing as an avocation. I don't enjoy, after ten minutes, too many theoretical discussions, or literary discussions. I will admit that when I was starting out I used to read a lot of criticism about anybody, especially Marxist criticism. It was a new idea at the time to locate the society in the novel; this I had never thought of. Especially during the Spanish Civil War.

I don't know, I've got tremendous notebooks full of stuff I can't finish. There must be 100,000 words.

LM: What's in your way?

AM: Can't see the end of it. A thing to be something has to not be something else. I sometimes read three novels in a week and then I make a note of what I felt about them. I do that because I will not remember a month hence anything about them. Anything. It'll get all fused with all the other things. In other words, it failed not to be everything else! It succeeded in being *everything*! It's terrible. You take the characters and you find you can put them in a different book. It's a rare work that is stamped with real creation, very rare. As perhaps it should be.

LM: Have you ever thought of using historical material further, bringing your ideas and experiences together with established facts? I think of Werfel's *Forty Days of Musa Dagh* or the book you reviewed for the *New York Times* on the Spanish Civil War [*The Life of Manuel Cortes* by Ronald Fraser].

AM: Yeah, I have. In a different age a lot of adaptation was done by playwrights. Shakespeare ransacked Sir Thomas North; I did it with *The Crucible*. I also wrote a play about Cortez and Montezuma 'way back (never produced). I tried that play again about five or six years ago. Yes, I have thought of it. And I'm sorry that I didn't do more with it, because the great thing about working out of stock material is that the story is there. See, stories can be a waste of time as far as the final work is concerned. Yet you can't proceed without them.

LM: And you're a lover of stories.

AM: Yes, finally it is one of the best ways of putting everything else, one of the most efficient means. Look at what Shakespeare did with Plutarch. It would have saved me a lot of wasted time, all those attempts to create a total story. I don't call it a story: it's a career, the play's career—its trajectory, its path. Find the entry. It's easy to shoot an arrow; its hard to follow it once it gets far away, and it's almost impossible to see it land—you have to imagine that.

LM: So what about the possibility of trying historical ideas now?

AM: Well, I tried it again. I did it again with a book by Studs Terkel dealing with the Thirties. I worked for a whole year on it, and gave it up. I suppose what I'm demanding of myself now is an absolutely intimate connection between the event on stage and my self.

I wrote another play which we did in Washington, and I may do some revision on, called *The Archbishop's Ceiling*, which is about some Czech writers now. I would call it a historical work. I just got fed up with it; I got angry at the material and the production—all wrong.

LM: *Are* you going to revise *The Archbishop's Ceiling*?

AM: I was just this morning for the first time in a year looking through some notes about it. I move in tremendous spurts: I plan and plan, and then do something absolutely different. I've written the first act of another play I had no intention of writing, and now I'll see if I can put the rest of it together.

LM: I'm not going to ask about what's in the mill.

AM: That's what I'm working on, that play. I've written a book about China, a 40,000-word report and speculation, with photographs by Inge Morath, my wife.

LM: I read the essay in the *Atlantic*.

AM: That's about twenty percent of the text. What do you teach?

LM: A little of everything. I'm in comparative literature. I teach our classical literature course, I teach Shakespeare, I have a course called Arthur Miller and Eugene O'Neill.

AM: It's courses like that make people say to me, "Gee, I didn't know you were still alive!" A British director who was staying at my house said, "eighty percent of the people who know you are living say, 'How old is he?' If they were students they studied this, and maybe their children did, so they figure, 'He must be ninety-four'!" I'm sixty-four.

LM: Have you read *The Forty Days of Musa Dagh*?

AM: 'Way back, when it first came out.

LM: For some reason, when I read that I thought, "Here is a great vehicle for Arthur Miller to do an adaptation, either as a screenplay—"

AM: Well, I'll tell you what I just did, which I hope you'll see: I wrote a film which Vanessa Redgrave is going to play, and they're starting to shoot. And I worked from a memoir written by a woman who had been in the Auschwitz women's orchestra. She's a half-Jewish Frenchwoman. She got picked up with the Communist resistance. She was a café singer. They nearly killed her there. It's a chaotic book, but I think it will make a marvelous movie. There's a piece of history; see, I know how to do that. I did that in two and one-half weeks (actually, four). Of course, the movie industry has lived on adaptations. It's just that you are at one remove from what you write—it's inevitable.

LM: I don't want to sound like a Jewish mother giving you advice, but you could probably knock off something about the Spanish Civil War in no time. Is it available to your imagination?

AM: Oh yeah, yeah. I used to know a lot of people who were there; friends of mine died there, in fact, that I went to Michigan with. I have an ongoing memoir that I've been working on, on and off, for years, and one chapter is about a guy named Ralph Neaphus. He came from New Mexico and was a volunteer in the Spanish Civil War. He was nineteen. I drove him from Ann Arbor; he'd never been east of Ann Arbor; his father was a rancher. I drove him to New York, and he stayed at our house waiting for his commission to go. He got killed. And twenty years later I went to Ann Arbor and was amazed at this Socialist club named for him. That was in the Fifties and they were persecuting the club members.

LM: I've always admired the great patience you have during public appearances and interviews, and the very good sense with which you answer the most idiotic questions.

AM: Well, you can't be too selective or there won't be any conversation. Academia harbors a lot of nonsense, but not only academia—the newspapers are worse. What's marvelous is that they interview you as if they are never going to leave, and it all ends up about eight paragraphs.

They made a pretty good movie of me, though; it will be shown in New York in October. Made by a Canadian—Harry Rasky. There is a real inner continuity in that film that surprised me. It was shot in Harlem, in Brooklyn, on the waterfront, and up here.

LM: Did they go to any of your former houses?

AM: Yes. In fact when I was in Brooklyn two old ladies came charging out of their houses, calling me. I said to one of these tottering old gals, "gee, this place looks better than it did when I lived here in the Depression." She said, "we're all like your mother used to be." She hadn't seen my mother for thirty years. "Your mother was *strict*." She wasn't strict at all. That was a dream that they had, that if you were strict your children would turn out OK.

LM: What was your mother like?

AM: She was very warm, very nice, musical. She was a good storyteller. And subject to fits of depression. A Jewish mother.

LM: What was bothering her?

AM: What bothers everybody in this country? Frustration. You are surrounded with what you think is opportunity. But you can't grab on to it. In other countries there's no opportunity, so there's just a general feeling of fatality. Here, no matter what happens to the economy, everybody can think of somebody who made it. Uncle Harry, look at him.

LM: And he didn't make it with any more intelligence—

AM: He's dumber than anybody!

LM: Did that bother her?

AM: Oh yes—we came through a very rough time. I suppose we're going to have it again, now.

III   *The One Thing We've Got*

LM: Can I ask, How do you feel? Where are you at these days?

AM: Quite frankly, all I really care about is what's going on in this room [Miller's studio]. I hear rumors of things outside. I don't look for a helluva lot, for too much change. I've seen too many repetitions of things I never thought I would see again. We don't change very much—a tiny bit—it's almost imperceptible. Fashions change. You can get very skeptical—I am—about people dying for anything except greed. And there's been a lot of that. We've expended a lot of people for no goddam good reason.

LM: That's been weighing on your mind through the years?

AM: Yeah, we get careless of human rights. The older I get the more I feel I'd be at home in Periclean Athens, and I could get along great in Dickens's London. I don't think a helluva lot has changed, with one exception. It's a big exception, and the one I hope we don't lose.

I think there's two ways of looking at life. One is that you hope to fit in completely. It's a feudalistic way; they got it in China, they got it in Russia. In my opinion, socialism in our time is a reversion to an elitist organization of society. Power is at the top and it flows down. The bottom supplies the troops, and the top supplies the direction, the inspiration—and it tries to plan and to be praised. The world awaits a democratic socialism.

This country may be alone in the world in having had no feudalism. The longer I live the more important that becomes to me. It may not ultimately be decisive, but up to this point it is. I think it's the one thing we've got that no other society on the face of the earth can say. And it may be the reason why we have added so much to the world.

It's the whole idea that you can see in the Declaration of Independence, the Constitution, and the Bill of Rights, that the power is in the people—literally, not metaphysically. And that the laws come out of them, and all the order of society. The people at the top are in a literal sense appointed by them.

This sounds so corny and so obvious that it's not even worth discussing except that it doesn't exist anywhere else, including in the "democratic" countries. They had a long-term feudalism which was based on a native aristocracy which swung the country around its head. And we didn't have that. I've just come back from China, and I've spent time in Russia, Poland, Hungary, Czechoslovakia, France, Germany, Austria: this is where the difference begins.

Our cultural or race memory takes for granted that finally the culture represents—and is *supposed* to represent, and *must* represent—the sense of right, or the sense of the world felt by the masses of people. Not in a metaphorical sense: you are supposed to be able really to stand up and tell a Congressman he's full of shit, which happens now and then. It even happens right here in Connecticut. I think that this is the essential difference, and to me it's the only hope there is.

Because if you get integrated into a system heart and soul, belly and head, I despair. I really do, I despair. I don't think that the *invention* comes out. It stultifies people; they find every good reason not to do something. Because it's dangerous to do something. Then you've got to have heroes; then you progress by somebody being crucified. Then you know he was right.

We have done a remarkable amount of killing of fathers in this country—legally. And the invention comes out. Right now, we're suffering from a hardening of the arteries.

LM: Did you say "killing of fathers"?

AM: Yes, this is the essential thing: if you can kill the fathers without the government falling down, you've got a real civilization. There's hope, there's continuity.

A place like Russia, imagine, a leader falls like Stalin, it's like kicking over an anthill—chaos. They're still suffering from it, they still haven't come to terms with that. Now with Mao in China, they're just terrified that he could have been as wrong as he was. They don't even want to hear about it, even though objectively they know they've got to face this or they can't go on. They can't go on repeating errors endlessly in order to defer to the memory of some beloved saint.

See, we don't do that.

LM: So you still have a kind of weary hope.

AM: It's a weary hope in this country because of that history. We have something terrific going for us in the sense that people are ninety-nine percent their history, their cultural history. In their little one percent they have choices to make, but their conditioning by history is formidable. Well, our history is good in this; we're in great shape that way.

The Chinese are conscious now that their fundamental problem is invisible. They have concrete problems which are obvious, but the fundamental problem is inside: they revert to feudal relationships at the slightest stress. Both those who want more freedom and more progressive thinking and those who are innately bureaucratic and don't want anything to change, both sides. The enlightened ones recognize this, and Mao recognized it but was helpless to stop it in himself. We have nothing like that, and they envy us, our capacity to make changes when necessary even though they are root and branch changes. I mean getting rid of a leader like that is something that tears the gut out of these people, including the French. It's a heroic kind of thing which we ought to recognize as such.

LM: There has to be the other pull, opposite to General Electric taking things over.

AM: Exactly, exactly. And that is the saving spirit: the tension makes for civilization. If one takes over completely, it's all over. If you're going to knock off leaders every week, the game is over. If you're going to keep them there no matter what they do, the game is over. And that includes ideas and dominating notions of how life goes.

And no matter where you go, including Cuba, where they are supposed to hate us, they wish to God they had that thing. Because the door is always open. As soon as some monolith starts to form that tries to run the country, there is an innate disgust. *Free—*

that's great!—it's a natural, built-in brake which transcends ideology.

Yeah, that's what *The Price* is about—the tension. I didn't name it, but if the idea gets in to the people then the seed is planted.

LM: It's a little hard to see the openness, the change in *The Price* because both brothers are so fixed.

AM: I never resolved it. I didn't want to let the audience off the hook. They're very comfortable in the second act of that play. They say, "ah, this poor nice policeman: how he was screwed by that rich neurotic jerk." Everybody hates surgeons anyway.

LM: So we're all going to love the policeman.

AM: Oh yes, it's terrific, he's our hero. Well, it turns out at a certain point he had something to do with his fate. It's marvelous once the audience can discover that, and then slowly they get to see—"Oh yes, this is a deeper pond than I've been swimming around in"—and they come at the end to appreciate it. They stand up and bravo at the end. They're happy to be treated like adults—it's quite wonderful! I haven't been to a play were people have done that in years: they're not supposed to care that much. They sure do care.

LM: Why do they applaud?

AM: They are grateful for having been forced to live through this thing. I could have let them off the hook; they sense that. I say, "You're grown-up people. This is the way it really is, isn't it? You need this search."

LM: But isn't there a lack of consummation, satisfaction?

AM: The satisfaction is the perception of the tension. 'Cause it is not solved, and life isn't. It can't be solved. It's a play without any candy.

LM: You don't feel that you've reached a dead end there?

AM: You reach a dead end only if all the energy goes out of the problem, but that surgeon's going to go on being a surgeon, and the cop is going to go on being a cop. But they are bigger for it; neither one will forget this evening. They become aware of what they have to see. The way they behave you know they are denying what they realize is true. Their denial is enormous, and when it gets that big you know it's saying the opposite.

LM: Could you ever write a play in which instead of a negative lesson, you just go out there and present a thorough-going, optimistic, here-it-is solution?

AM: The closest I ever came to that is probably in the last few minutes of *All My Sons*, where the surviving son does lay down the law as to what they should have done. And that happens in life. If the situation is that way then I'll do it, but to twist it around is impossible.

Dostoyevsky in *The Brothers Karamazov* tried to define at the end of that book in Alyosha the Christian way of life, and you believe it's possible, but it detaches itself from the rest of the book. The fundamental impulse of this book was tragic. There is some aesthetic violation that goes on here.

In *Death of a Salesman*, at the end Biff tries to say that this was unnecessary, that Willy never knew himself. But compared to the monstrousness of the whole action, he can't possibly counter that action with some opinion or connection as to what Willy should have been doing all this time. Emotionally, we cannot juggle the two things.

Furthermore, the emotions of people who have been through such events don't admit of it: the emotions occupy the whole space. I mean supposing that somebody you loved and knew well, by virtue of some failure to take precautions, died. Well, you could say, "Jesus, if he or she had only done this. . . ." That lasts only a minute or two, but compared to the grief—the sense of "my God, this can happen"—the other is sort of empty.

The Greeks tried to do that a lot. They made speeches about the right way to live, common sense—

LM: the tragic chorus, especially.

AM: Does anybody remember what the chorus says? You look at Oedipus: when that coal comes down the chute, that's what you hear, not some guy saying you got the wrong basement, deliver it up the street! It's going down the chute, and you can't stop it—that long drag of the past that becomes imperious at a certain moment, knows no bounds, and cannot be stopped.

LM: Can you ever funnel that coal in another direction?

AM: You try to. Look at Carter trying to generate the moral equivalent of a war for the conservation of energy. But who's going to get as excited about the conservation of energy as about the Battle of Stalingrad? Nobody I know. We would have to change our ways.

When you think of it, it's such a waste. It's such a waste—it's appalling!

Notes and References

Preface

1. Tom Driver, "Strength and Weakness in Arthur Miller," *Tulane Drama Review* 4 (May 1960): 48.
2. William Wiegand, "Arthur Miller and the Man Who Knows," *Western Review* 21 (1956): 85–103.
3. Eleanor Clark, *"Death of a Salesman,"* *Partisan Review* 16 (1949): 633.
4. The first line appears in Harold Clurman, "Arthur Miller," *Lies Like Truth* (New York, 1958), p. 71. The second is in Clurman's "Attention," *New Republic* 120 (Feb. 28, 1949): 27.
5. Paul West, "Arthur Miller and the Human Mice," *Hibbert Journal* 61 (Jan. 1963): 84.
6. Henry Popkin, "Arthur Miller: The Strange Encounter," *Sewanee Review* 68 (1960): 34, 59. Of course, there are critics who denounce him for *not* being a moralist. For example, Joseph A. Hynes, "Arthur Miller and the Impasse of Naturalism," *South Atlantic Quarterly* 62 (1963): 327–34, thinks Miller is "a true naturalist" who usually evades the dramatist's obligation to deliver judgment. For other opinions on this question, see the Bibliography (for the most part, critics' views are discussed in notes and in the Bibliography).
7. "Arthur Miller on 'The Nature of Tragedy,'" *New York Herald-Tribune*, March 27, 1949, Sec. V, p. 1.
8. "The Shadows of the Gods," *Harper's* 217 (Aug. 1958): 36, 38. Miller's ideas on "social plays" are treated more fully in Chapter 7.
9. Unless otherwise noted, *Arthur Miller's Collected Plays* (New York, 1957) is the source of all quotations taken from Miller's plays.
10. Quotations are taken from a typescript in the Theatre Collection, New York Public Library. The following remark by Miller is quoted in James Goode, *The Story of "The Misfits"* (Indianapolis, 1963), pp. 76–77: "most of American drama, not only in the Forties and Fifties, but from the Twenties on, revolves around the story of the victimization of the hero by the inhuman forces of society." Willy Loman, he adds, is such a hero.
11. Author's Forward, *After the Fall*, *Saturday Evening Post* 237 (Feb. 1, 1964): 32. Miller's attitude here coincides with that of his drama instructor at the University of Michigan, Professor Kenneth Thorpe Rowe. Rowe, in *Write That Play* (New York, 1939), p. 404, taught that "social drama

deals with evils which can be changed, and energizes the audience to
constructive activity. But there are circumstances beyond human control
and elements of evil and suffering in life beyond change. . . . Man is
capable of no great goodness without the energy of passion, and passion
misguided is proportionately destructive."

Chapter One

1. Author's Introduction, *Arthur Miller's Collected Plays*, pp. 17, 42.
Subsequent references to this essay, a superlative piece of drama criticism,
will be abbreviated as *C.P.*
2. *Situation Normal . . .* (New York, 1944), pp. 156–57.
3. For autobiographical reference in this play, see Chapter 5.
4. Miller reports the last fact in "A Boy Grew in Brooklyn," *Holiday* 17
(March 1955): 124. "I Don't Need You Any More" was published in
Esquire 52 (Dec. 1959): 270–309; a father and two sons appear in this story,
in the plays cited, and in *The Man Who Had All the Luck*, *The Price*, and
The Creation of the World.
5. Daniel E. Schneider, "Play of Dreams," *Theatre Arts* 33 (Oct.
1949):20.
6. Allan Seager, "The Creative Agony of Arthur Miller," *Esquire* 52
(Oct. 1959): 123, reports that Willy Loman developed from "a memory" of
a salesman Miller once knew. Willy Loman's situation, of course, may have
been derived in part from fictional sources. In particular, Eudora Welty's
short story, "Death of a Traveling Salesman" (published in "*A Curtain of
Green" and Other Stories* in 1941), presents (as does *Death of a Salesman*)
an "exhausted" salesman who has confused reveries, suffers an automobile
accident, and dies in pathetic isolation. Even the names of the two
salesmen are similar—Welty's is R. J. Bowman. Apart from these
similarities, however, Miller's treatment differs radically from Welty's.
Robert B. Heilman comments, "Salesmen's Deaths: Documentary and
Myth," *Shenandoah* 20 (Spring 1969): 20, "Miller's drama of death drifts
toward documentary, Miss Welty's toward myth."
7. The two brothers in *The Price* straddle Miller's birthdate: the elder
(Walter) was born about 1913, the younger (Victor), 1918.
8. Arthur Miller in "My Wife Marilyn," *Life* 50 (Dec. 22, 1958): 147.
Two other uneducated but naïvely wise heroines who resemble the late
actress are Maggie (*After the Fall*) and the girl in "Please Don't Kill
Anything," a short story in *Noble Savage* 1 (March 1960): 126–31.
According to Goode, pp. 18–19, several characters in *The Misfits* are
modeled after people the playwright met while residing in Nevada in
1956. Other characters said to resemble people known by Miller include
John Proctor in *The Crucible* (James D. Proctor) and Alfieri in *A View
from the Bridge* (Vincent J. Longhi); Miller (*C.P.*, 50) remarks that *A View
from the Bridge* offers, "in some part, an analogy to situations in my life."

Situations *not* in Miller's life provided the plots for *The Man Who Had All the Luck* (see *C.P.*, 14), *All My Sons* (*C.P.*, 17), *The Crucible, Incident at Vichy,* and *The Creation of the World.*

9. "With respect for her agony—but with love," *Life* 56 (Feb. 7, 1964): 66.

10. Arthur Miller quoted in Stanley J. Kunitz, *Twentieth Century Authors, First Supplement* (New York, 1955), p. 669.

11. Quoted in Jim Cook, "Their Thirteenth Year Was the Most Significant," *Washington Post and Times Herald,* July 10, 1956, p. 24.

12. Joan Miller quoted in Cook. Miller's sister, under a stage name (Joan Copeland), became an actress; Kermit, Miller's elder brother, went into sales work and now is a successful businessman.

13. Quoted in Cook. The playwright continues to pursue carpentry as an avocation. On his property in Roxbury, Connecticut, he built without help—from foundation and plumbing to roof—a one-room cabin, and at last report had also constructed a new guest house.

14. On the psychological impact of his father's bankruptcy, see my discussion of *After the Fall* and *The Price* in Chapters 5 and 6.

15. "The Shadows of the Gods," p. 36.

16. Miller (*C.P.*, 30) states that in *Death of a Salesman* he conceived "the image of a man making something with his hands being a rock to touch and return to."

17. Arthur Miller quoted in Kunitz, p. 669.

18. For Ibsen's influence, see Chapters 2 and 7; for other literary influences, see Chapter 5. The problem of Miller's literary sources has bemused several scholars. William Wiegand detects the influence of Odets ("Arthur Miller and the Man Who Knows"); Alan S. Downer, Saroyan ("Mr. Williams and Mr. Miller"); Vernon Elso Johnson, Chekhov ("Dramatic Influences in the Development of Arthur Miller's Concept of Social Tragedy"); and Seymour L. Flaxman, Strindberg ("The Debt of Williams and Miller to Ibsen and Strindberg"). Louis Broussard, in *American Drama: Contemporary Allegory from Eugene O'Neill to Tennessee Williams,* equitably assigns Miller's indebtedness to Elmer Rice, Robert Sherwood, Tennessee Williams, and Eugene O'Neill. Besides discovering these supposed influences, essayists have made fanciful analogies between Miller and Sinclair Lewis (Gordon W. Couchman, "Arthur Miller's Tragedy of Babbitt"), Shakespeare (Paul N. Siegal, "Willy Loman and King Lear"), and Sophocles (Arthur W. Boggs, "*Oedipus* and *All My Sons*"). Publication data for these works are in the Bibliography.

19. Quoted in *Cross-Section*, ed. Edwin Seaver (New York, 1944), p. 556.

20. Arthur Miller, "University of Michigan," *Holiday* 14 (Dec. 1953): 70, 143.

21. Quoted in Seaver, p. 556.

22. Quoted in Kunitz, p. 669. On the influence of Professor Rowe, see

the Preface, note 11 and Chapter 7, note 19.

23. John Gassner in *A Treasury of the Theatre*, rev. ed. (New York, 1950), p. 1060.

24. Maurice Zolotow, *Marilyn Monroe* (New York, 1961), p. 264. Miller had a son and a daughter with his first wife (a Roman Catholic) and a daughter with his third.

25. *Radio's Best Plays*, ed. Joseph Liss (New York, 1947), p. 306.

26. Quoted in Virginia Stevens, "Seven Young Broadway Artists," *Theatre Arts* 31 (June 1947): 56. He was greatly impressed by two stage organizations—the Group Theatre, whose productions in the 1930s gave him his "sole sense of connection with theater" (*C.P.*, 16), and the Lincoln Center Repertory Theater, with which he was associated for two seasons (1963–64 and 1964–65). However, soon after the premiere of *Incident at Vichy* in December, 1964, Miller—prompted by the resignations of Robert Whitehead and Elia Kazan—announced "that he would not contribute any future plays" to the Lincoln Center Theater (*New York Times*, Dec. 20, 1964, Sec. II, p. 3).

27. Quoted in John P. Shanley, "Miller's 'Focus' on TV Today," *New York Times*, Jan. 21, 1962, Sec. II, p. 19.

28. Miller estimated, in Leslie Hanscom, "'After the Fall': Arthur Miller's Return," *Newsweek* 63 (Feb. 3, 1964): 52, that in any given season about fifty theaters offer productions of his plays in Europe.

29. In 1973 Miller taught dramatic literature at the University of Michigan with the rank of associate professor.

30. Robert Sylvester, "Brooklyn Boy Makes Good," *Saturday Evening Post* 222 (July 16, 1949): 26.

31. Zolotow, pp. 264–67, contends that the love triangles in *The Crucible* and in *A View from the Bridge* reflect "an acute personal crisis" (supposedly Miller's guilty love for Miss Monroe) occurring between 1950 and 1956.

32. "Many Writers: Few Plays," *New York Times*, Aug. 10, 1952, Sec. II, p. 1.

33. Quoted in Seager, p. 124.

34. Richard H. Rovere, "Arthur Miller's Conscience," *New Republic* 136 (June 17, 1957): 13–15, comments on similarities in the ethical problems encountered by the playwright and by the protagonists of *The Crucible* and *A View from the Bridge*. Eric Bentley, "On the Waterfront," *What Is Theatre?* (Boston, 1956), p. 99, claims that in those two plays "Mr. Miller comes to the informer theme because (to put it mildly) it is one of the great issues of the day."

35. *New York Times*, March 31, 1954, p. 16.

36. "A Modest Proposal for Pacification of the Public Temper," *Nation* 179 (July 3, 1954): 5.

37. *New York Times*, Oct. 26, 1955, p. 62. See also *New York Times*, Nov. 30, 1955, p. 38, and Dec. 8, 1955, p. 33. Miller published his

"background notes" for the script under the title, "Bridge to a Savage World," *Esquire* 50 (Oct. 1958): 185–90, and also wrote an article, "The Bored and the Violent," *Harper's* 225 (Nov. 1962): 50–56, explaining the causes of juvenile gang behavior.

38. *New York Times*, June 22, 1956, p. 1. A portion of the testimony recorded at the hearing of June 21, 1956, is reprinted in Sheila Huftel, *Arthur Miller: The Burning Glass* (New York, 1965), pp. 31–49.

39. Reported in *Current Biography*, ed. Anna Rothe (New York, 1947), p. 440.

40. The last three are cited in Zolotow, p. 261.

41. These items are listed in the *New York Times*, June 22, 1956, p. 1.

42. Quoted in *New York Times*, Feb. 19, 1957, p. 1.

43. Ibid.

44. See *New York Times*, June 1, 1957, p. 1, and July 20, 1957, p. 4.

45. Mary McCarthy, "Naming Names: The Arthur Miller Case," *Encounter* 8 (May 1957): 25. Two other intelligent analyses of the case are Harry Kalven, Jr., "A View from the Law," *New Republic* 136 (May 27, 1957): 8–13, and Rovere, "Arthur Miller's Conscience."

46. Quoted in Kenneth Alsop, "A Conversation with Arthur Miller," *Encounter* 13 (July 1959): 59.

47. "Broadway, From O'Neill to Now," *New York Times*, Dec. 21, 1969, Sec. II, pp. 3, 7. See also "A New Era in American Theatre?" *Drama Survey* 3 (1963): 70–71; "Lincoln Repertory Theater—Challenge and Hope," *New York Times*, Jan. 19, 1964, Sec. II, pp. 1, 3; "A Theatre: Heart and Mind," *Theatre: Annual of the Repertory Theater of Lincoln Center* I (1964): 56–61; *New York Times*, Dec. 20, 1964, Sec. II, p. 3; and "Arthur Miller *vs.* Lincoln Center," *New York Times*, April 16, 1972, Sec. II, pp. 1, 5.

48. On one weekend reported by Lydia McClean, "A Weekend with the Arthur Millers," *Vogue* 159 (March 15, 1972): 102–109, Miller, his wife and daughter Rebecca entertained the William Styrons, the Harrison Salisburys, and the Russian poet Andrei Voznesensky.

49. He discusses violence during the 1968 convention in "The Battle of Chicago: From the Delegates' Side," *New York Times Magazine*, Sept. 15, 1968, pp. 29–31, 122–28; explains his support for presidential candidate Senator Eugene McCarthy in "The New Insurgency," *Nation* 206 (June 3, 1968): 717; decries political hypocrisy at the 1972 convention in "Politics as Theater," *New York Times*, Nov. 4, 1972, p. 33; and analyzes the "McGovern phenomenon" (1972) in "Making Crowds," *Esquire* 78 (Nov. 1972): 160–61, 216–28.

50. "Men and Words in Prison," *New York Times*, Oct. 16, 1971, p. 31. Miller's travels have not always been grim. He describes, for example, a delightful visit to a Prince of Thailand in "The Bangkok Prince," *Harper's*, 241 (July 1970): 32–33.

51. This play was presented at the Kennedy Center, Washington, D.C.,

and has not yet been published or released for study.

52. See "Stars Help Arthur Miller Film TV Antiwar Allegory," *New York Times*, Nov. 17, 1969, p. 58.

53. "Arthur Miller Returns to Genesis for First Musical," *New York Times*, April 17, 1974, p. 37.

54. "Every Play Has a Purpose," *Dramatists Guild Quarterly* 15 (Winter 1979): 15.

Chapter Two

1. Miller's phrase in "On Social Plays," an essay prefacing *A View from the Bridge* (New York, 1955), p. 8.

2. In *The Best One-Act Plays of 1944*, ed. Margaret Mayorga (New York, 1945), pp. 45–60. The play was performed by an amateur group in New York during the 1943–44 season.

3. In *One Hundred Non-royalty Radio Plays*, ed. William Kozlenko (New York, 1941), pp. 20–30.

4. *The Man Who Had All the Luck* was published before its stage production in Seaver, pp. 486–552. Miller (*C.P.*, 15) writes that he understood only belatedly the kinship between Amos Beeves, the disenchanted baseball player, and David Frieber—both of whom wish to prove their worth in society. Not until the play was staged did Miller make brothers of the two characters, using "Beeves" as the family name.

Dennis Welland, *Arthur Miller* (New York, 1961), pp. 28–35, comments at length on the similar father-son relationships in *The Man Who Had All the Luck* (Patterson, David, and Amos Beeves), *All My Sons* (Joe, Larry, and Chris Keller), and *Death of a Salesman* (Willy, Biff, and Hap Loman). Helen McMahon, "Arthur Miller's Common Man: The Problem of the Realistic and the Mythic," *Drama and Theatre* 10 (1972): 128, sees Miller treating "the father as primary figure of authority, [and] the conflict between brothers" in a "sub-text of myth" derived from "Judeo-Christian beliefs." Irving Jacobson, "The Child as Guilty Witness," *Literature and Psychology* 24 (1974): 12–23, offers a detailed exposition of Miller's "family themes" in the 1959 short story "I Don't Need You Any More."

5. "The Family in Modern Drama," *Atlantic Monthly* 197 (April 1956): 36.

6. Published by Reynal & Hitchcock in 1945 (publication rights since assumed by Harcourt, Brace & World), the work was dramatized on television in January 1962. Gassner, *Treasury of the Theatre*, p. 1060, points out that Miller "had originally planned [*Focus*] as a three-act play."

7. "Tragedy and the Common Man," *New York Times*, Feb. 27, 1949, Sec. II, p. 1.

8. Another purpose served by Finkelstein, in the two chapters written from his perspective, is to allow relief from the tension associated with the protagonist.

9. Popkin, "Strange Encounter," p. 34, comments, "Arthur Miller's regular practice in his plays is to confront the dead level of banality with the heights and depths of guilt."

10. At one point in *All My Sons*, thirteen of twenty sentences spoken by Joe Keller are questions. "The keynote of the play is its questioning," Dennis Welland notes, p. 39; "dialogue in the theatre is regularly carried on in terms of questions and answers, but in *All my Sons* [*sic*] the questions are in effect dialogue-stoppers. The dramatic power resides in the sort of questions asked and in the inability of the characters to answer them."

11. Similarities between the father-son oppositions in *All My Sons* and in *The Wild Duck* suggest a possible debt to Ibsen. In both plays the owner of a factory has been implicated in a business scandal and then exonerated, his partner disgraced and sent to prison—the matter is alluded to fragmentarily in the early part of the two dramas. Each of the former partners has a son: one young man was shamed by his parent's imprisonment; the other, now heir to the business, counters his wealthy father's materialism with idealistic notions. The two sons, having been out of contact for years despite their common interest in a young lady, stage a reunion at the home of the plant-owner during which they try to cultivate good humor with inconsequential chatter. The reunion, however, is disturbed by intrusive reminders of the unpleasant past. Finally, antagonism generated by the earlier situation ends in a suicide that is announced by the sound of a pistol.

Correspondences exist also at the verbal level, so far as one can judge from a translation of Ibsen (*Three Plays by Ibsen* [New York, 1959]). For instance, Werle, the entrepreneur in *The Wild Duck*, proposes that his boy join the firm, since "we are father and son after all"; Keller makes the same request, insisting "I'm his father and he's my son." Werle's son rejects the offer because, as another character says, "he is suffering from an acute attack of integrity"; in *All My Sons*, a minor character complains that Chris (who also spurns his father's business) "makes people want to be better than it's possible to be."

There are, of course, radical differences between the two plays. Moreover, Miller claims to have gotten the idea for his work while listening to "a pious lady from the Middle West [who] told of a family in her neighborhood which had been destroyed when the daughter turned the father in to the authorities on discovering he had been selling faulty machinery to the Army" (*C.P.*, 17). Still, it may be that Ibsen's influence, which Miller admits was substantial enough in other respects, extended to the theme of father-son conflict. (In response to my inquiry, Miller stated that he could not remember whether Ibsen had influenced him in this connection.)

12. Arvin R. Wells. *"All My Sons," Insight I* (Frankfurt, 1962), p. 169, remarks that "because [Chris] is closely identified with his father, his necessary sense of personal dignity and worthiness depends upon his

belief in the ideal image of his father; consequently, he can only accept the father's exposure as a personal defeat."

13. The abruptness of Keller's conversion has disturbed other critics; for example, see Arthur Ganz, "The Silence of Arthur Miller," *Drama Survey* 3 (1963): 232.

14. Norm Fruchter mentions these conventions in "On the Frontier," *Encore* 9 (Jan. 1962): 19.

Chapter Three

1. Compare Biff's exclamation here with Amos's in *The Man Who Had All the Luck*: "you liar! I'll kill you, you little fake, *you liar!*"

2. John Gassner discusses the father-son antagonism in *The Theatre in Our Times* (New York, 1954), p. 371. So too does William J. Newman in his review of the *Collected Plays*, in *Twentieth Century* 164 (1958): 494; Newman maintains that a "breakdown of the family-world" is the central subject of Miller's plays. In "Play of Dreams," pp. 20–21, Daniel E. Schneider, a neuropsychiatrist, uses Freudian terminology to describe the "inner psychological theme" of *Death of a Salesman*:

Willy Loman is not in the eyes of his sons just a man, but a god in decay. . . . Follow the second act from this point of view, and it is sheer murder of a father by "all his sons"—an irrational Oedipal blood-bath given seeming rationalization by the converging social theme of the worn-out Salesman. . . . Willy reaffirms father-son love. . . . But at the same time it is just this reconciliation between father and first son which must not be tolerated by the basic drive of the play, . . . one of the most concentrated expressions of aggression and pity ever to be put on the stage.

See also W. David Sievers, *Freud on Broadway* (New York, 1955), pp. 376–80, 391–96.

3. But John V. Hagopian, "Arthur Miller: The *Salesman's* Two Cases," *Modern Drama* 6 (1963): 117–25, believes that Biff, who "struggles most for understanding," should be considered the true protagonist; suffering from "a curious dramatic astigmatism," Miller was "in error in seeing the central character of the play in Willy Loman." Error or not, it is probably just as well that the following idea did not occur to Miller until *after* the play was produced: "I am sorry the self-realization of the older son, Biff, is not a weightier counterbalance to Willy's disaster in the audience mind" (*New York Times*, Feb. 5, 1950, Sec. II, p. 3).

4. In Miller's adaptation of Ibsen's *An Enemy of the People* (New York, 1951), the protagonist declares, "nor does one automatically become 'A Man' by having human shape. . . . That name *also* has to be earned."

5. The words "boy" and "kid" together occur almost a hundred times in *Death of a Salesman*; "man" occurs about the same number of times. John V. Hagopian, "*Death of a Salesman*," *Insight I*, p. 185, discusses diminutive titles in the play.

6. Other instances could be cited; and Hap, who has been molded in Willy's image, also displays one or two self-contradictions. Miller (*C.P.*, 23) writes that the play "was conceived half in laughter, for the inside of [Willy's] head was a mass of contradictions."

7. Sister M. Bettina, "Willy Loman's Brother Ben," *Modern Drama* 4 (1962): 410, speaks of the "stylized characterization of Willy's rich brother Ben who, when closely observed, takes shape less as a person external to Willy than as a projection of his personality."

8. Miller, quoted in A. Howard Fuller, "A Salesman Is Everybody," *Fortune* 39 (May 1949): 80, explains that Willy "has taken on a new—a social—personality which is calculated to ensure his material success. In so doing he has lost his essential—his real—nature, which is contradictory to his assumed one, until he is no longer able to know what *he* truly wants, what *he* truly stands for." Gerald Weales, "Arthur Miller: Man and His Image," *Tulane Drama Review* 7 (Sept. 1962): 170, refers to "the conflicting success images that wander through [Willy's] troubled brain." On this subject, see also B. E. Gross, "Peddler and Pioneer in *Death of a Salesman*," *Modern Drama* 7 (1965): 405-10. Stage effects emphasize the conflict in values: a flute melody "telling of grass and trees and the horizon" contrasts with "the hard towers of the apartment buildings."

9. Miller (*C.P.*, 25) writes that Willy Loman "does not gradually imply a deadly conflict with his son, an implication dropped into the midst of serenity and surface calm, he is avowedly grappling with that conflict at the outset." But the playwright overstates the contrast between *All My Sons* and *Death of a Salesman* when he claims, "the ultimate matter with which [*Death of a Salesman*] will close is announced at the outset and is the matter of its every moment from the first. . . . All was assumed as proven to begin with. All I was doing was bringing things to mind" (*C.P.*, 24-25). The conflict between Willy and Biff, while apparent "at the outset" (unlike the conflict in *All My Sons*), does not reach maturity until the subsequent action.

10. Miller (*C.P.*, 26) is quite explicit on this subject: Willy Loman "is literally at that terrible moment when the voice of the past is no longer distant but quite as loud as the voice of the present." On subjectivity in *Death of a Salesman*, see Sievers, p. 391; Gassner, *Theatre in Our Times*, p. 373; Frederick J. Hunter, "The Value of Time in Modern Drama," *Journal of Aesthetics and Art Criticism* 16 (1958): 194-201; and Edward Groff, "Point of View in Modern Drama," *Modern Drama* 2 (1959): 268-82.

11. In *Theatre in Our Times*, p. 347, Gassner comments, "Miller's *ordinary* hero is *extraordinary* in the passionate manner in which he lives and dies for his dream."

12. *A Memory of Two Mondays*, he adds, is his "one exception" to this rule.

13. Willy, Miller writes (*C.P.*, 34), "has achieved a very powerful piece

of knowledge, which is that he is loved by his son and has been embraced by him and forgiven."

14. Newton P. Stallknecht in "Symposium: *Death of a Salesman*," *Folio* (Indiana University) 17 (March 1952): 4.

15. Clurman, "Arthur Miller," p. 70.

16. What Miller calls the "law of success," Erich Fromm, in *Man For Himself* (New York, 1947), p. 72, labels the "marketing orientation": "since modern man experiences himself both as the seller and as the commodity to be sold on the market, his self-esteem depends on conditions beyond his control. If he is 'successful,' he is valuable; if he is not, he is worthless. The degree of insecurity which results from this orientation can hardly be overestimated. . . . If the vicissitudes of the market are the judges of one's value, the sense of dignity and pride is destroyed.'

17. Welland, pp. 51-57, in reviewing (and rejecting) arguments of critics who interpret the work as Marxist propaganda, discusses at some length the short scene in which Willy is discharged by his employer. Gassner, *Theatre in Our Times*, p. 347, concludes that Miller "split his play between *social causation* and *individual responsibility*."

18. Using *Death of a Salesman* as his model, David Bleich, "Psychological Bases of Learning from Literature," *College English* 33 (1971): 32–45, finds that the play represents a learning process on the part of the author (derived from his Depression experience) and on the part of the spectator (derived from the universal experience of the "recovery, under the stimulas of the work of art, of hitherto rejected parental authority." For Miller's views on this subject, see Chapter 6, note 1.

Chapter Four

1. Critics subscribing to this view are Eric Bentley, "The Innocence of Arthur Miller"; Henry Popkin, "Arthur Miller's 'The Crucible'"; Philip Walker, "Arthur Miller's 'The Crucible': Tragedy or Allegory?"; Robert Warshow, "The Liberal Conscience in 'The Crucible'"; and Richard Watts, Jr., Introduction to *The Crucible* (publication details in the Bibliography). James W. Douglass, "Miller's *The Crucible*: Which Witch is Which?" *Renascence* 15 (1963): 145–51, berates Miller for distorting the historical facts of the Salem trials. Huftel, pp. 132–43, discusses the critics' reception of *The Crucible* at some length.

2. Miller's phrase in Henry Brandon, "The State of the Theatre," *Harper's* 221 (1960): 66.

3. Miller originally entitled his play *Those Familiar Spirits*; typescripts of this version are in the Academic Center Library, the University of Texas (which Miller has designated as the depository for his manuscripts and other literary papers), and in the Library of Congress. Although Miller consulted the trial records filed at the Salem courthouse, his primary

source was undoubtedly Charles W. Upham, *Salem Witchcraft* (originally published in 1867). Except for the fact that the playwright attaches greater importance to John Proctor's role, he follows Upham's explanations of factual, psychological, sociological, ethical, and religious matters. Miller may also have read Marion L. Starkey's dramatized narrative, *The Devil in Massachusetts* (New York, 1949). Relatively few plays have dealt with the Salem affair; Miller could have heard a short radio play, *Panic in Salem*, by Wilfred H. Pettitt, published in Kozlenko, pp. 620–28. Welland, p. 74, mentions Florence Stevenson's *Child's Play* and Louis O. Coxe's *The Witchfinders* (both 1952).

4. Miller quoted in Henry Hewes, "Broadway Postscript," *Saturday Review* 36 (Jan. 31, 1953): 24.

5. Similar courtroom histrionics occur in Miller's adaptation of *An Enemy of the People*, produced three years earlier (1950).

6. Miller quoted in Hewes, p. 25.

7. Miller completely restaged the play six months after its premiere and added a short scene to the end of Act Two that develops the love triangle. This scene, omitted in the *Collected Plays*, can be found in the edition published in *Theatre Arts* 37 (Oct. 1953): 35–67.

8. Miller may have been betrayed by following his primary source too closely. Upham's *Salem Witchcraft*, otherwise extremely comprehensive, flags on this point also: "a sudden collapse took place in the machinery, and [the court] met no more. . . . The curtain fell unexpectedly, and the tragedy ended. It is not known precisely what caused this sudden change. . . . It has generally been attributed to the fact, that the girls became over-confident, and struck too high" (Ungar edition, II, 344).

9. This problem was largely solved by an excellent television production (May 4, 1967) that stressed the pathos rather than triumph of the Proctors, and so cultivated a single mood. *The Crucible* lends itself to directorial shaping more than any other play by Miller, including *Death of a Salesman*.

10. This discussion is based upon, and all quotations are taken from, the expanded two-act version presented in London (1956) and published in the *Collected Plays*. The original one-act play, also published by Viking, was produced in New York in 1955; a still earlier version was entitled *From under the Sea*, copies of which are deposited in the Library of Congress and at the University of Texas.

11. According to Popkin, "Strange Encounter," p. 56, "the root and symptom of his heroes' disorders" in *Death of a Salesman* and *The Crucible*, as well as in *A View from the Bridge*, is "illicit sexual activity."

12. Students of Freud will undoubtedly be able to offer a more professional diagnosis, perhaps one involving daughter-surrogates and incest-motives. The details Miller added to the longer London production tend to call attention to the sexual implications. One such detail is puzzling—Eddie's conjugal abstinence. Perhaps guilt associated with a

desire for Catherine, or fear of losing her to a rival, depresses Eddie's sexual potency, although Beatrice rejects the second possibility by testifying that "it's almost three months you don't feel good; [the immigrants are] only here a couple of weeks." In any case, the argument with Beatrice on this matter points up Eddie's sense of lessening authority.

13. Because so much is implied rather than stated here, the scene demands considerable acting skill—a demand satisfied admirably by Van Heflin in the original Broadway production.

14. Miller's phrase describing the tragic hero, in "Tragedy and the Common Man," p. 1.

15. In the original one-act version the dialogue was cast in free verse, presumably to augment esthetic distance.

16. In addition to his narrative, rhetorical, and philosophical duties, Alfieri expedites time and space transitions. For example, during his second appearance the setting changes from inside Eddie's apartment to the street; and a time change accompanies his third entrance ("now, as the weeks passed . . .").

17. Author's Introduction, *A View from the Bridge* (New York, 1960), pp. viii–ix. Miller (*C.P.*, 52) writes that in the London production he employed realistic staging to alleviate Eddie's "oddness" and to show him more directly "as a creature of his environment."

18. In performance this diversion of attention from Catherine and Rodolpho to Alfieri and Marco might well be minimized or even exploited by a skillful director.

19. Quotation from Miller's discussion of *A Memory of Two Mondays* in "On Social Plays" (preface to the original edition of *A View from the Bridge*), p. 15.

20. Quotation taken from a review of an Italian film by Stanley Kauffmann, *New Republic* 150 (Feb. 15, 1964): 35.

21. The screenplay was published by Viking in 1961; an earlier version appeared as a short story in *Esquire* 48 (Oct. 1957): 158–66. Goode, *Story of "The Misfits"*, presents a minutely detailed account of how the movie was made in 1960.

22. Similar criticisms are delivered by Fruchter, p. 26, and by Henry Popkin, "Arthur Miller Out West," *Commentary* 31 (May 1961): 433–36.

Chapter Five

1. Except where otherwise noted, quotations are from the second edition of *After the Fall* (Viking). Several months after the play was first published in February 1964, Miller published a "revised final stage version" incorporating extensive deletion, rephrasing, and rearrangement. The *Saturday Evening Post* edition, cited earlier, includes the author's Foreword but otherwise differs only slightly from the first Viking edition; the Bantam edition (1965) is a reissue of the revised version.

2. Each of Quentin's three women has a dream that reveals her insecurity. Louise "was standing beside a high mountain. With my legs cut off" (first edition); Maggie becomes engulfed by smoke pouring from a closet; and Holga futilely runs from a "horrible" idiot baby. Quentin's responses when told the dreams are consistent with his attitude toward each woman: he disregards Louise, reassures Maggie, and profits from Holga, whose dream is the only one that suggests an antidote for its terror.

3. Miller's phrase describing *Death of a Salesman* (*C.P.*, 23). In *After the Fall* the scenery is non-representational ("there are no walls or substantial boundaries") except for a "blasted stone tower of a German concentration camp" overhanging the stage.

4. In the first edition, reminded of the "treacherous" Elsie, he asks a third question: "if I see a sin why is it in some part mine?"

5. "The Miller's Tale" (anon.), *Time* 83 (Jan. 31, 1964): 54.

6. Ganz, "Silence of Arthur Miller," and Leslie Epstein, "The Unhappiness of Arthur Miller," *Tri-Quarterly* (Spring 1965): 165–73, are also disturbed by the lack of correlation between the Nazis' guilt and Quentin's.

7. The original edition of the play contained far more verbiage than the shorter revised version.

8. In the first edition the word "love" occurs over a hundred times; "truth" and "death", in various forms, around fifty times each. About fifty of the lines deleted in the revision refer to pointlessness, fraud, destruction, grief, guilt, and death; perhaps Miller thought Quentin's negative reactions were overemphasized in the original production (although he also eliminated about a dozen references to love and truth).

9. Robert Brustein, "Arthur Miller's Mea Culpa," *New Republic* 150 (Feb. 8, 1964): 28, claims that "dishonesty remains the worst flaw in the play"; Quentin does not "recognize how much self-justification is hidden in his apparent remorse."

10. These observations are taken from letters to the Drama Editor, *New York Times*, Feb. 2, 1964, Sec. II, p. 3, and Feb. 23, 1964, Sec. II, p. 7.

11. Hanscom, p. 50.

12. Brustein, p. 27.

13. "The Miller's Tale," p. 54.

14. Quoted in Hanscom, p. 51.

15. "With respect for her agony," p. 66.

16. When asked whether his mother had been the model for Quentin's mother, Miller answered only that his too had been "very dramatic" (quoted in Hanscom, p. 52).

17. But Miller writes, in "With respect for her agony," that he never knew "anyone who committed suicide [as Lou does] as a result of action by a Congressional committee." The individual analogous to Mickey, the informer, is Elia Kazan. Kazan directed both *All My Sons* (the original edition was dedicated to him) and *Death of a Salesman*, and in 1950

worked with Miller on an unproduced screenplay entitled *The Hook*, dealing with waterfront labor extortion in New York City. According to Morgan Y. Himelstein, in *Drama Was a Weapon: The Left-Wing Theatre in New York, 1929-1941* (New Brunswick, N.J., 1963), pp. 159–60, 252, Kazan in 1952 testified to the House Committee on Un-American Activities that he had joined the Communist party in 1934; he also named eight other actors as members of a communist cell within the Group Theatre from 1934 to 1936. This admission led to an estrangement between Kazan and Miller (who refused to "name names" at his own hearing in 1956). However, the two men were later reconciled, and Kazan directed the production of *After the Fall*.

18. In Miller's story, "Monte Saint Angelo," *Harper's* 202 (March 1951): 39–47, an American Jew of Austrian parentage (as is Miller) discovers a sense of continuity with his people, "as though he had been newly joined with something very old and work-worn and honorable." A later short story, 'I Don't Need You Any More" (1959) contains a similar theme. In an essay, "A Boy Grew in Brooklyn," Miller tells anecdotes about his upbringing in a Jewish neighborhood.

On the subject of Miller as a Jewish writer, some interesting opinions have been advanced. Henry Adler, "To Hell with Society," *Tulane Drama Review* 4 (May 1960): 62, decries Miller's "Jewish humanitarian sympathy for passive suffering." On the other hand, West, p. 84, praises Miller's works as "Christian plays."

19. George Ross, "*Death of a Salesman* in the Original", *Commentary* 11 (Feb. 1951): 184–85, asserts that the production of *Death of a Salesman* in Yiddish translation "reveals the real Willy Loman" to be a Jew, a conclusion similar to one reached by Mary McCarthy, *Sights and Spectacles 1937–1956* (New York, 1956), pp. xiv–xvi.

20. In "My Wife Marilyn," Miller praised Miss Monroe's "innocence," "cunning," and "sweet wit." The source for most of the facts cited here concerning Marilyn Monroe is Zolotow's book.

21. "Like a little stubborn boy," she adds (first edition).

22. In addition to the references to Genesis, Quentin's complaint, "I can't find myself in this vanity," may be an allusion to Ecclesiastes.

23. Translation by Justin O'Brien (New York, 1957). (I assume that Miller would have consulted the translation.) Miller acknowledged, in a letter, that *After the Fall* "is probably linked to the work of Camus, especially *The Fall* . . .—my play takes up where that leaves off." I am indebted to Professor Carrol Coates of Harpur College for pointing out this connection.

On correspondences between Miller's play and Camus's novel, see also Allen J. Koppenhaver, "*The Fall* and After: Albert Camus and Arthur Miller," *Modern Drama* 9 (1966): 206–209; C. W. E. Bigsby, "The Fall and After: Arthur Miller's Confession," *Modern Drama* 10 (1967): 124–36; and Alfred Cismaru, "Before and *After the Fall*," *Forum* (University of

Houston) 11, no. 2 (1973): 67–71. On correspondences between *Death of a Salesman* and Camus's *Exile and the Kingdom*, see O. Thomas Miles, "Three Authors in Search of a Character," *Personalist* 46 (1965): 65–72.

24. Translation by Stuart Gilbert (New York, 1948), pp. 79, 82.

25. Translation by Anthony Bower (New York, 1956), p. 4.

26. A friend advises Quentin to enhance his marriage to Louise by "imagining" her "as a stranger." The motif is present in other plays also: "what am I, a stranger?" Joe Keller asks; and Roslyn in *The Misfits* announces, "I couldn't ever stay with a stranger."

27. Miller advances this opinion in "Our Guilt for the World's Evil," *New York Times*, Jan. 3, 1965, Sec. VI, pp. 10–11, 48. The quotations attributed to Miller in the following paragraph are taken from this source.

28. In "With respect for her agony," Miller alludes to Hannah Arendt's *Eichmann in Jerusalem* (New York, 1963). Arendt's conclusion on the "banality of evil," p. 253, is similar to Miller's: "the trouble with Eichmann was precisely that so many were like him, and that the many were neither perverted nor sadistic, that they were, and still are, terribly and terrifyingly normal."

29. Quotations are taken from the Viking edition (1965).

30. Compare with Lawrence Newman's discovery in *Focus* that "the evil nature of the Jews and their numberless deceits . . . were the reflections of his own desires with which he had invested them."

31. The words "again and again forever" occur as a refrain in Miller's writing of this period, suggesting here the persistence of violence, but in "Our Guilt" and in *After the Fall* referring to a rebirth of the ability to "forgive."

32. Epstein, p. 172, comments that "characterization is replaced by attitude and type," as in a "medieval Morality Play." For an account of Miller's changing artistic strategies, see Chapter 7.

Chapter Six

1. Miller has made several significant references to the autobiographical content of this subject. After writing *The Price* he said, in "On Creativity," *Playboy* 15 (Dec. 1968): 139; "a remarkable number of writers of talent have had in common the experience of a parent's destruction, either at puberty or before. Destruction by physical death or spiritual overthrow. The matrix of the artist, his quest for form, consists of his need to reconstitute the lost or debilitated authority. . . . In other words, a case can be made for art as a response to the death or spiritual bankruptcy of the father." In his introduction to *Kesey's Garage Sale* (New York, 1973), p. xiv, he adds that after his father's bankruptcy during the Great Depression, "I was listening only for what I wanted to know—how to restore my family. How to be their benefactor. How to bring the good times back. How to fix it so my father would again stand there as the leader, instead of

coming home at night exhausted, guilty." Finally, In "Arthur Miller Says the Time Is Right for *The Price*," *New York Times*, June 17, 1979, Sec. II, p. 6., Miller states that he has finished exploring this father-son situation: "there is exorcising going on for me [in *The Price*]. . . . The father is dead. The sons have to deal with their own characters."

2. Quotations are from *The Price* (New York: Viking, 1968).

3. David Higgins observes, "Arthur Miller's *The Price*: the Wisdom of Solomon," *Itinerary 3: Criticism* (Bowling Green, Ohio, 1977), pp. 90, 92, "though their masks become more and more naked as a result of their relentless probing, they are unable, finally, to come together, because they are unable to sufficiently escape their own points of view. . . . They need, in other words, to retain their separate identities, with the values which accrue to them. Like all of Miller's major characters, they are worried about their 'names'; they need acceptable images for their lives."

4. "In terms of theme," Miller writes in "Arthur Miller Ponders *The Price*," *New York Times*, Jan. 28, 1968, Sec. II, p. 5, "I think this play is an outgrowth of *Death of a Salesman*."

5. *A View from the Bridge* approximates this scheme if Eddie is seen as a father-surrogate to his niece and the two immigrant brothers.

6. Miller likes Solomon. In "Arthur Miller Says the Time Is Right for *The Price*," p. 6, he writes that Solomon "expresses the welcoming of life, the overwhelming of fear." In "The Creative Experience of Arthur Miller," *Educational Theatre Journal* 21 (1969): 315, he explains how the dealer's outlook relates to his religion: "Gregory Solomon in *The Price* has to be Jewish, for one thing because the theme of survival, of a kind of acceptance of life, seemed to me to point directly to the Jewish experience through centuries of oppression."

7. In "A Million Sales for Willy Loman," *New York Times*, March 8, 1968, p. 36, Miller comments that Victor Franz is "about the most direct antithesis of Willy Loman that could exist. He is devoted to a rational existence as opposed to an existence of dreams and irrationality [and] is in a way a descendant of John Proctor, the hero in *The Crucible*."

8. "Classic tragedy, like a religious ceremony," Miller observes in *Writers at Work: The "Paris Review" Interviews*, Third Series (New York, 1967), p. 203, "has to do with the community sacrificing some man whom [it] both adores and despises in order to reach its basic and fundamental laws and, therefore, justify its existence and feel safe."

9. The work was produced in 1972. Quotations are from *The Creation of the World and Other Business* (New York: Viking, 1973).

10. Insofar as Lucifer's notion (promoted also by Walter Franz, Leduc, and Quentin) of the individual freely willing engagement with others, *The Creation of the World*, like all Miller's late plays, shows an affinity with certain "existentialist" works. A prominent spokesman for this idea, for example, is Orestes in Sartre's *The Flies* (1943, translated in 1946); he sounds like Lucifer, moreover, on the point that traditional religions

exploit guilt as an instrument of oppressive power. See my earlier comparisons between *Incident at Vichy* and Sartre's *The Victors* and between *After the Fall* and Camus's *The Fall*; on the affinity between Miller and Sartre, see also Chapter 7, note 8.

Ronald Hayman claims in "Arthur Miller: Between Sartre and Society," *Encounter* 37 (Nov. 1971): 73, that "a good case could be made for calling Miller the most Sartrean of living dramatists." Lawrence D. Lowenthal, in "Arthur Miller's *Incident at Vichy*: A Sartrean Interpretation," *Modern Drama* 18 (1975): 29, sees *Incident at Vichy* as "an explicit dramatic rendition of Sartre's treatise on Jews [*Anti-Semite and Jew*], as well as a clear structural example of Sartre's definition of the existential 'theatre of situation.'" Miller himself, in "Arthur Miller on *The Crucible*," *Audience* 2 (July 1972): 46–47, felt that Sartre's "overly Marxist" screenplay of *The Crucible* "weakened" his play.

Chapter Seven

1. As previously noted, "the one exception among [Miller's] plays is *A Memory of Two Mondays*" (*C.P.*, 8): its characters establish their identities in acts of ego-subordination.

2. This classification is necessarily somewhat arbitrary. Joe Keller is grouped with the unreformed because he resigns his egocentric position in word only, not in spirit. Quentin, on the other hand, has been placed in the category of the reformed because his contrition, though questionable, directs the movement of the play. While both modes of conduct occur in almost every work, sometimes the morally rigid are only minor characters who act as a foil to the protagonist. Thus, the dogmatic Shory disagrees with an impressionable David Frieber; the inflexible Carlson, with an awakened Newman; the unregenerate Guido, with Gay Langland; Lebeau and his benighted associates, with Leduc and Von Berg.

3. Arthur Miller in "With respect for her agony."

4. Arthur Miller quoted in "American Playwrights Self-Appraised," ed. Henry Hewes, *Saturday Review* 38 (Sept. 3, 1955): 19.

5. Quoted in Stevens, p. 56.

6. This last style, well exemplified in the works of George Bernard Shaw, has also been called "discursive" and "classical"; it is described under the latter classification, in *The Reader's Companion to World Literature*, ed. L. H. Hornstein et al. (New York, 1956), as "social, formal, intellectual, and static."

7. The expressionistic techniques in *Death of a Salesman* are reminiscent more of Strindberg's late plays (*A Dream Play*, for example), than of "German expressionism." Strindberg (like Miller) projects the irrational inner life of characters through abrupt transitions and juxtapositions in time, place, mood, and theme; through hallucination, nightmare, and fantasy; and through generalized characters and symbolic images. See

Seymour L. Flaxman, "The Debt of Williams and Miller to Ibsen and
Strindberg," *Comparative Literature Studies* (Special Advance Issue,
1963): 51–59.

8. Miller's rationale here is almost identical with that expressed by
Jean-Paul Sartre in remarks on the post-war theater in France, "Forgers of
Myths" (1946), trans. Rosamond Gilder, in *The Modern Theatre*, ed.
Robert W. Corrigan (New York, 1964), pp. 782, 784:

> . . . we are not greatly concerned with psychology. . . . For us psychology is the
> most abstract of the sciences because it studies the workings of our passions without
> plunging them back into their true human surroundings, without their background
> of religious and moral values, the taboos and commandments of society, the
> conflicts of nations and classes, of rights, of wills, of actions. . . . We do not take
> time out for learned research, we feel no need of registering the imperceptible
> evolution of a character or a plot. . . . To us a play should not seem too *familiar*. Its
> greatness derives from its social and, in a certain sense, religious functions: it must
> remain a rite. . . .

9. Arthur Miller, "Lincoln Repertory Theater—Challenge and Hope,"
New York Times, Jan. 19, 1964, Sec. II, p. 3.

10. Arthur Miller quoted in Barry Hyams, "A Theatre: Heart and
Mind," *Theatre: Annual of the Repertory Theatre of Lincoln Center* 1
(1964): 61. Miller's American audience has not always been receptive to
discursive analysis in drama, a fact that has greatly annoyed the author:
"for a variety of reasons I think that the Anglo-Saxon audience cannot
believe the reality of characters who live by principles and know very
much about their own characters and situations, and who say what they
know. Our drama . . . is condemned, so to speak, to the emotions of
subjectivism, which, as they approach knowledge and self-awareness,
become less and less actual and real to us" (*C.P.*, 44–45). Europeans, Miller
states in "The Playwright and the Atomic World," *Colorado Quarterly* 5
(1956): 117–37, are more philosophical and therefore maintain a higher
regard for professional thinkers, particularly artists who arise "to articulate if not to immortalize their age." But Americans distrust ideas. They do
not lack awareness; they simply do not care "to rationalize how [they]
feel" (122). This pragmatic tendency, Miller warns, can be a great
disadvantage in international politics, for if Americans "are content to
apppear solely as businessmen, technicians, and money-makers, [they]
are handing to the Russian, who appears to make so much of culture, an
advantage of regiments" (127).

11. Miller's phrase, quoted in Huftel, p. 196.

12. Interestingly (though coincidentally), the two plays have much in
common in respect to theme, character, and technique. *Long Day's
Journey into Night*, completed in 1940, was not published and produced
until 1956; in that year Miller called the work, in "Concerning the Boom,"
International Theatre Annual 1 (1956): 88, "the most enthralling dramatic

experience I have had since I first read Ibsen." For another expression of Miller's admiration for O'Neill, see "Eugene O'Neill: An Evaluation by Fellow Playwrights," ed. Edward T. Herbert, *Modern Drama* 6 (1963): 239-240.

13. Referring to *All My Sons*, *Death of Salesman*, and *The Misfits*, Popkin in "Arthur Miller Out West," p. 434, comments that Miller "likes to play with symbolic vocations."

14. The importance of the "legal metaphor" in *After the Fall* was brought to my attention by Mr. Paul Klamer.

15. As Henry Popkin writes, in "Arthur Miller's 'The Crucible,'" *College English* 26 (1964): 142, "like other works by Miller, *The Crucible* has something of the quality of a trial, of a court case, even before the formal hearings begin."

16. Quotations are taken from the Viking edition (1951). Besides simplifying Ibsen's polarity between a defiant individual and an oppressive community, Miller "modernized" the dialogue, shortened some speeches, and de-emphasized Ibsen's poisoned water symbolism (in his Preface to the Viking edition, 1951, he stated that his major change was simply to expedite continuity by reducing the number of scene and act divisions).

Miller's modifications have been variously interpreted. Robert Brustein, *The Theatre of Revolt* (Boston, 1964), p. 72, claimed that Miller "watered down" Ibsen's aristocratic bias. In the same vein, Alan Thompson, "Professor's Debauch," *Theatre Arts* 35 (March 1951): 27, found the protagonist of the adaptation "a Hollywoodish-heroical Champion of Democracy, too serious and wise to descend to horseplay or to delight in making a rumpus." However, Welland, p. 47, saw the adapter "increasing the element of humour."

According to Benjamin Nelson, *Arthur Miller* (London, 1970), pp. 142-44, Miller mistakenly glorified an "ambivalent" protagonist, who in Ibsen's work is "both heroic rebel and fool," unable to separate a noble cause "from his inflated and bruised ego." And according to Martin Dworkin, in "Miller and Ibsen," *Humanist* 11 (June 1951): 110-15, Ibsen and Miller are both attacking irrationality, whether it be found in a democratic majority, an aristocratic elite, or an idiosyncratic individual. See also Arthur Miller, "Ibsen's Message for Today's World," *New York Timers*, Dec. 24, 1950, Sec. II, pp. 3, 4; and David Bronson, "An Enemy of the People: A Key to Arthur Miller's Art and Ethics," *Comparative Drama* 2 (1968): 229-47.

17. Miller has protested against injustice in the United States and abroad in many essays and interviews (see the Selected Bibliography). Most recently, as he reports in his long essay, "In China," *Atlantic* 243 (March 1979): 97, 98, he found a striking absence of legal principles in Communist China. "The law [is] a subject in which no one in China seems to have the least interest. . . . Certain things have surely been learned,

among them that under socialism, no less than capitalism, the human being is unsafe without the protection of his rights by law, and a law that the state is obliged to obey." Robert A. Martin, in his introduction to *The Theater Essays of Arthur Miller* (New York, 1978), p. xxxiii, points out the recurrence in Miller's writing of "law, lawyers, a policeman, courtrooms, or judges as representatives of truth, justice, and morality. . . . *After the Fall*, although very different thematically and structurally, also places the protagonist on trial in much the same way that Joe Keller in *All My Sons*, Willy Loman in *Death of a Salesman*, John Proctor in *The Crucible*, and Eddie Carbone in *A View from the Bridge* had also undergone moral and legal litigation."

18. The confrontation between Victor and Walter in *The Price* composes a simpler structure.

19. His structural principles reflect the teaching, as presented in *Write That Play*, of his instructor in playwriting at the University of Michigan, Kenneth Thorpe Rowe, who is probably the source of his interest in Ibsen. Some apparently influential observations made by Professor Rowe are the following: "Complications may also be interwoven by the introduction of a new complication while an earlier complication is still in suspense. The answer to each minor dramatic question points toward an answer to the major dramatic question" (58). In *A Doll's House*, "the antecedent material is no longer introductory, but the center of the immediate conflict, the past coming to life in the present and creating drama" (203). "Expressionism, although it has the appearance of fantasy, is an extension of realism inward to the areas of psychological experience and of abstract ideas. . . . Expressionism is an attempt to lift the skullcap and look inside at the brain and see how it works [Miller, *C.P.*, 23: "we would see the inside of a man's head"], or to X-ray human life in society and see the forces at work underneath the external phenomena" (358–59). "Man is capable of no great goodness without the energy of passion, and passion misguided is proportionately destructive" (404). "The exaltation of tragedy, whether Greek, Shakespearean, or modern, is a response to the spectacle of man's power to maintain the integrity of his own mind and will in the face of the utmost life can inflict" (406).

To point out Rowe's influence is not to denigrate in any way Miller's inventiveness; indeed, Rowe himself referred (in 1939) to a "brilliant young man" (presumably Miller) who came to him with "a new method for revision": "his last rewriting was for the purpose of eliminating every superfluous word, and especially to eliminate expository analysis for direct revelation of the character" (343–45). Miller recognized his central problem quite early.

20. "The speeches in *All My Sons*," John Prudhoe writes in "Arthur Miller and the Tradition of Tragedy," *English Studies* 43 (1962): 436, "frequently remind me of Elizabethan and Jacobean patterned language in their balance of phrases and conscious repetition of words and ideas."

21. A similar exchange takes place later in the play. "But sometimes, Willy, it's better for a man just to walk away," Bernard says. Willy responds, "but if you can't walk away?"

22. Albert Hunt, "Realism and Intelligence," *Encore* 7 (May 1960): 12–17, makes the same point. But Weales, p. 179, believes that "the lines are as awkward and as stagily false as those in John Drinkwater's *Oliver Cromwell*." It is true that the language of *The Crucible*, supposedly patterned after the dialect spoken by Salemites at the end of the seventeenth century, is often anachronistic, especially insofar as the frequent use of the subjunctive ("it were sport"; "there be no blush"; "he have his goodness now"). The actual testimony recorded at the Salem trials, reprinted in *What Happened in Salem?*, ed. David Levin (New York, 1960), is far less archaic.

Selected Bibliography

PRIMARY SOURCES

1. Chief Works (exclusive of foreign, book club, and anthology editions)

After the Fall. New York: Viking, 1964.
(periodical edition). *Saturday Evening Post* 237 (Feb. 1, 1964): 32–59.
(revised stage version). New York: Viking, 1964, 1965.
(paperback edition, revised stage version). New York: Bantam, 1965.
(acting edition, revised stage version). New York: Dramatists Play Service, 1965.
(paperback edition, revised stage version). New York: Compass, 1968.
(paperback edition, television adaptation). New York: Bantam, 1974.
(paperback edition, revised stage version). New York: Penguin, 1978.
All My Sons. New York: Reynal & Hitchcock, 1947.
(acting edition). New York: Dramatists Play Service, 1947.
Arthur Miller's Collected Plays. New York: Viking, 1957. Contains *All My Sons, Death of a Salesman, The Crucible, A Memory of Two Mondays,* and *A View from the Bridge* (two-act version).
The Creation of the World and Other Business. New York: Viking, 1973.
(acting edition). New York: Dramatists Play Service, 1973.
The Crucible. New York: Viking, 1953.
(periodical edition). *Theatre Arts* 37 (Oct. 1953): 35–67. Contains additional dialogue (Act II, Scene 2).
(acting edition). New York: Dramatists Play Service, 1954 (includes II, 2).
(paperback edition). New York: Bantam, 1959 (includes II, 2).
(paperback edition). New York: Compass, 1964 (includes II, 2).
(text and criticism), Gerald Weales, ed. New York: Viking, 1971 (includes II, 2).
(paperback edition). New York: Penguin, 1976 (includes II, 2).
Death of a Salesman. New York: Viking, 1949.
(periodical edition). *Theatre Arts* 35 (March 1951): 49–91.
(paperback edition). New York: Bantam, 1951, 1955.
(acting edition). New York: Dramatists Play Service, 1952.
(paperback edition). New York: Compass, 1958.
(text and criticism), Gerald Weales, ed. New York: Viking, 1967.

Focus (novel). New York: Reynal & Hitchcock, 1945.
    (paperback edition). New York: Dell, 1959.
    (paperback edition). New York: Penguin, 1978.
Incident at Vichy. New York: Viking, 1965.
    (acting edition). New York: Dramatists Play Service, 1966.
    (paperback edition). New York: Bantam, 1967.
    (paperback edition). New York: Penguin, 1978.
The Man Who Had All the Luck. In Edwin Seaver, ed. *Cross-Section: A Collection of New American Writing*, pp. 486–552. New York: Fischer, 1944.
A Memory of Two Mondays. In *A View from the Bridge: Two One-Act Plays.* New York: Viking, 1955 (with *A View from the Bridge*).
    (acting edition). *New York: Dramatists Play Service*, 1956.
    (periodical edition). *Theatre Arts* 40 (Sept. 1956): 33–68.
The Misfits (screenplay). New York: Viking, 1961.
    (paperback edition). New York: Dell, 1961.
    (paperback edition, final shooting script). In George P. Garrett, et al., eds. *Film Scripts Three*, pp. 202–382. New York: Appleton-Century-Crofts, 1972.
The Portable Arthur Miller, Harold Clurman, ed. New York: Penguin, 1977. Contains *Death of a Salesman, The Crucible, Incident at Vichy, The Price*, and shorter works.
The Price. New York: Viking, 1968.
    (periodical edition, condensed version). *Saturday Evening Post* 241 (Feb. 10, 1968): 40–59.
    (acting edition). New York: Dramatists Play Service, 1968.
    (paperback edition). New York: Bantam, 1969.
    (paperback edition). New York: Penguin, 1978.
A View from the Bridge (one-act play). In *A View from the Bridge: Two One-Act Plays.* New York: Viking, 1955 (with *A Memory of Two Mondays*).
    (periodical edition). *Theatre Arts* 40 (Sept. 1956): 33–68.
    (acting edition, two-act version). New York: Dramatists Play Service, 1957.
    (paperback edition, two-act version). New York: Compass, 1960.
    (paperback edition, two-act version). New York: Bantam, 1961.
    (paperback edition, two-act version). New York: Penguin, 1977.

2. Essays, Short Stories, Minor Plays, Journals, Speeches, and Letters (a chronological listing)

"In Memorium" [*sic*] (unpublished short story), c. 1932. Typescript in the Academic Center Library, University of Texas (listed as the "story which became *Death of a Salesman*").
Various titles, *Michigan Daily* (student newspaper, University of Michi-

gan), Feb. 2, 1936, p. 6; March 1, 1936, p. 1; Jan. 26, 1937, p. 4; March 6, 1937, p. 1; March 31, 1937, p. 4; Jan. 18, 1938, p. 4. Selected news reports and letters written by Miller as a student journalist.

No Villain (unpublished play), 1936. Typescript in the Hopwood Room, University of Michigan.

They Too Arise (unpublished revision of *No Villain*), 1936. Typescript in the Theatre Collection, New York Public Library.

Honors at Dawn (unpublished play), 1937. Typescript in the Hopwood Room, University of Michigan.

The Grass Still Grows (unpublished revision of *They Too Arise*), 1938. Typescript in the Academic Center Library, University of Texas.

The Great Disobedience (unpublished play), 1938. Typescript in the Hatcher Library, University of Michigan.

Listen My Children (unpublished "comedy satire with music"), with Norman Rosten, 1939. Typescript in the Library of Congress.

The Golden Years (unpublished play), 1939–40. Typescript in the Academic Center Library, University of Texas.

The Half-Bridge (unpublished play), 1941–43. Typescript in the Academic Center Library, University of Texas.

The Pussycat and the Expert Plumber Who Was a Man (radio play). In William Kozlenko, ed., *One Hundred Non-royalty Radio Plays*, pp. 20–30. New York: Greenberg, 1941. A clever but unscrupulous cat discovers an honest man.

William Ireland's Confession (radio play). In Kozlenko, *Radio Plays*, pp. 512–21. An anecdote about a poetic forger of Shakespeare's manuscripts.

The Four Freedoms (unpublished radio play), 1942. Typescript in the Library of Congress.

Autobiographical statement (untitled) in Seaver, *Cross-Section*, p. 556. On writing plays at the University of Michigan.

Situation Normal . . . (journal). New York: Reynal & Hitchcock, 1944. Excerpt reprinted in condensed form, "Their First Look at Live Bullets," *Science Digest* 17 (April 1945): 73–76. Miller's observations after visiting army camps during World War II: he found a "unity of feeling" among the soldiers.

That They May Win (one-act play). In Margaret Mayorga, ed., *The Best One-Act Plays of 1944*, pp. 45–60. New York: Dodd, Mead, 1945. A "message" play making the point that responsible civilians should take an active interest in politics.

Grandpa and the Statue (radio play). In Erik Barnouw, ed., *Radio Drama in Action*, pp. 267–81. New York: Farrar & Rinehart, 1945. Reprinted in A. H. Lass et. al., eds., *Plays from Radio*. Boston: Houghton Mifflin, 1948. A patriotic exercise lauding the Statue of Liberty ("this statue kinda looks like what we believe").

"The Plaster Masks" (short story). *Encore: A Continuing Anthology* 9

(April 1946): 424-32. Probably Miller's first nationally circulated short story: a writer tries to understand the impact of terrible war injuries on World War II veterans.

"It Takes A Thief" (short story). *Collier's* 119 (Feb. 8, 1947): 23, 75-76. A light study of a racketeer's conscience, somewhat similar in theme to *All My Sons.*

"Subsidized Theatre" (essay). *New York Times*, June 22, 1947, Sec. II, p. 1. The only way to raise artistic standards and to break the businessman's control of the Broadway stage is to establish permanent theater companies supported by private or public subsidy.

The Guardsman, by Ferenc Molnar (adaptation for radio). In H. William Fitelson, ed., *Theatre Guild on the Air*, pp. 69-97. New York: Rinehart, 1947. Preface, pp. 67-68: Miller explains his changes and additions.

The Story of Gus (radio play). In Joseph Liss, ed., *Radio's Best Plays*, pp. 303-20. New York: Greenberg, 1947. On the necessity for all Americans to pitch in and win the war.

Three Men on a Horse, by George Abbott and John Cecil Holm (adaptation for radio). In Fitelson, *Theatre Guild on the Air*, pp. 207-38. Preface, pp. 205-206: "really fine radio drama . . . is an impossibility."

"Tragedy and the Common Man" (essay). *New York Times*, Feb. 27, 1949, Sec. II, pp. 1, 3. Reprinted in *Theatre Arts* 35 (March 1951): 48-50. Harlow O. Waite and Benjamin P. Atkinson, eds., *Literature for Our Time*. New York: Holt, 1953. Richard Levin, ed., *Tragedy: Plays, Theory, and Criticism*. New York: Harcourt, Brace, 1960. John D. Hurrell, ed., *Two Modern American Tragedies*. New York: Scribner's, 1961. Sylvan Barnet et al., eds., *Aspects of Drama*. New York: Little, Brown, 1962. Robert W. Corrigan, ed., *The Modern Theatre*. New York: Macmillan, 1964. Horst Frenz, ed. *American Playwrights on Drama*. New York: Hill & Wang, 1965. Weales, *Death of a Salesman*. Martin, *Theater Essays*. Miller's controversial thesis that the "common man" may suitably symbolize an individual in tragic displacement from his "'rightful' position in his society."

"Arthur Miller on 'The Nature of Tragedy'" (essay). *New York Herald-Tribune*, March 27, 1949, Sec. V, pp. 1, 2. Reprinted in Martin, *Theater Essays*. Tragedy should demonstrate the possibility of good as well as the power of evil.

"The 'Salesman' Has a Birthday" (essay). *New York Times*, Feb. 5, 1950, Sec. II, pp. 1, 3. Reprinted in Weales, *Death of a Salesman*. Martin, *Theater Essays*. On the exhilarating experience of writing *Death of a Salesman.*

"Ibsen's Message for Today's World" (essay). *New York Times*, Dec. 24, 1950, Sec. II, pp. 3, 4. In his adaptation of *An Enemy of the People*, Miller proposes "the question of whether the democratic guarantees

protecting political minorities ought to be set aside in time of crisis."
"Monte Saint Angelo" (short story). *Harper's* 202 (March 1951): 39–47.
Reprinted in Herschel Brickell, ed. *Prize Stories of 1951*. New York:
Doubleday, 1951. Miller, *I Don't Need You Any More*. An American
Jew becomes aware of his racial identity.
"An American Reaction" (short essay). *World Theatre* 1 no. 3 (1951): 21–
22. Reply to article in same issue byWalter Prichard Eaton, "Can the
Craft of Playwriting Be Learned?" Miller's answer: "a man is born
with a sense of play structure," but college writing courses can
develop that sense.
The Hook (unpublished screenplay), 1951. Typescript in the Academic
Center Library, University of Texas. Deals with waterfront rackets
in New York City.
An Enemy of the People, by Henrik Ibsen (adaptation). New York: Viking, 1951. New York: Dramatists Play Service, 1951. New York: Penguin, 1977. Dr. Stockmann resists public pressures in order to fight for
the public welfare. Miller's preface, pp. 7–12. Reprinted in Martin, *Theater Essays*. A theater of ideas, like Ibsen's, must discuss "the
complexities of life" and "man's fate."
"Many Writers: Few Plays" (short essay). *New York Times*, Aug. 10, 1952,
Sec. II, p. 1. Reprinted in Weales, *The Crucible*. Martin, *Theater Essays*. The contemporary theater lacks vitality because dramatists are
too timid, security-minded, and "practical"; without moral conviction, they are merely entertainers.
"Journey to 'The Crucible'" (short essay). *New York Times*, Feb. 8, 1953,
Sec. II, p. 3. Reprinted in Martin, *Theater Essays*. On the experience
of checking the 1692 courthouse records in Salem as preparation for
writing the play.
"University of Michigan" (essay). *Holiday* 14 (Dec. 1953): 68–71, 128–43.
Reprinted in A. J. Carr and W. R. Steinhoff, eds. *Points of Departure*.
New York: Harper, 1960. Miller's recollection of his student years at
the university: today it is much larger in size, but the students lack
the intensity they had in the 1930s.
"A Modest Proposal for Pacification of the Public Temper" (essay). *Na-
tion* 179 (July 3, 1954): 5–8. A Swiftian satire on the obsession in
America to prove one's patriotism.
"The American Theater" (essay). *Holiday* 17 (Jan. 1955), 90–104. Re-
printed in Nathan Comfort Starr, ed. *The Pursuit of Learning*. New
York: Harcourt, Brace, 1956. George Oppenheimer, ed. *Passionate
Playgoer*. New York: Viking, 1958. Harry William Rudman and
Irving Rosenthal, eds. *A Contemporary Reader*. New York: Ronald,
1961. Weales, *Death of a Salesman*. Martin, *Theater Essays*. On the
"glamour" and problems of theater people.
"A Boy Grew in Brooklyn" (essay). *Holiday* 17 (March 1955): 54–55, 117–
24. Anecdotes about the Brooklyn of Miller's youth.

"Picking a Cast" (short essay). *New York Times*, Aug. 21, 1955, Sec. II, p. 1. Choosing actors for *A View from the Bridge*.

"American Playwrights Self-Appraised" (short answers to a questionnaire, ed. Henry Hewes). *Saturday Review* 38 (Sept. 3, 1955): 18–19. General statements by Miller on his techniques and aims.

Short reply (untitled) to article in same issue by John Gassner, "Modern Drama and Society." *World Theater* 4 (Autumn 1955): 40–41. "Social drama is only another way of saying Whole Drama."

Autobiographical statement (untitled) in Stanley J. Kunitz, *Twentieth Century Authors, First Supplement*, pp. 669–70. New York: Wilson, 1955. Remarks confined mainly to the earlier years.

"On Social Plays," preface to the original edition of *A View from the Bridge*, pp. 1–18. New York: Viking, 1955. Reprinted as "A View of One-Actors," *New York Times*, Sept. 25, 1955, Sec. II, pp. 1, 3. Reprinted also in Hurrell, *Two Tragedies*. Martin, *Theater Essays*. Excerpts reprinted as "Viewing *A View from the Bridge*," *Theatre Arts* 40 (Sept. 1956): 31–32. An important statement on the social relevance of drama: the tragic protagonist must be attuned to the values of his society if only to question them intelligibly. Specific comments on *A View from the Bridge* and *A Memory of Two Mondays*.

"Red and Anti-Red Curbs on Art Denounced by U.S. Playwright" (letter). *New York Times*, Feb. 13, 1956, p. 9. On the seventy-fifth anniversary of Dostoyevsky's death, Miller protests the suppression of writers in both the U.S. and Russia.

"The Family in Modern Drama" (essay). *Atlantic Monthly* 197 (April 1956): 35–41. Reprinted in Travis Bogard and William I. Oliver, eds. *Modern Drama*. New York: Oxford University Press, 1965. Martin, *Theater Essays*. The crucial question for serious drama is this: "how may a man make of the outside world a home?"

"The Testimony of Arthur Miller, accompanied by Counsel, Joseph L. Rauh, Jr." In *Investigation of the Unauthorized Use of United States Passports, 84th Congress, Congressional Record*, Part IV, June 21, 1956, pp. 4660–90. See also "Proceedings Against Arthur Miller," *Congressional Record*, CII, Part II, June 25, 1956, pp. 14519–38. Transcripts of Miller's testimony before the House Committee on Un-American Activities, June 1956.

"Arthur Miller Speaking on and Reading from *The Crucible* and *Death of a Salesman*" (recording). Spoken Arts, No. 704, 1956. Miller's focus has alternated between "social causation" and "psychological or what we call private causes."

"Concerning the Boom" (essay). *International Theatre Annual* 1 (1956): 85–88. A skeptical glance at plays produced during the 1956 New York season: "in a word, it is the usual trendless jumble."

"The Playwright and the Atomic World" (essay). *Colorado Quarterly* 5 (1956): 117–37. Reprinted in *Tulane Drama Review* 5 (June 1961):

3–20. Robert W. Corrigan, ed. *Theatre in the Twentieth Century.* New York: Grove, 1963. Reprinted as "1956 and All This" in Martin, *Theater Essays.* On the connection between American attitudes to culture and strategy in the Cold War.

"The Writer in America" (speech). *Mainstream* 10 (July 1957): 43–46. Reprinted as "The Writer's Position in America" in *Coastlines* 2 (Autumn 1957): 38–40. Excerpts reprinted in *New York Times*, May 8, 1957, p. 5. Miller insists on freedom of expression and denounces the State Department for interference with news media, writers, and artists.

"Global Dramatist" (short essay). *New York Times*, July 21, 1957, Sec. II, p. 1. Miller discusses the foreign reception of his plays.

"The Misfits" (short story). *Esquire* 48 (Oct. 1957): 158–66. Reprinted in Miller, *I Don't Need You Any More.* Clurman, *Portable Arthur Miller.* This story, from which the screenplay was developed, celebrates the "custom of men" uncomplicated by the presence of a heroine.

Introduction to *Arthur Miller's Collected Plays*, pp. 3–55. New York: Viking, 1957. Reprinted in Weales, *Death of a Salesman.* Weales, *The Crucible.* Martin, *Theater Essays. Playwrights on Playwriting.* New York: Hill & Wang, 1960. Miller's most extensive analysis of his own plays and drama in general. "I have stood squarely in conventional realism; I have tried to expand it with an imposition of various forms in order to speak more directly . . . of what has moved me behind the visible façades of life."

"Brewed in 'The Crucible'" (short essay). *New York Times*, March 9, 1958, Sec. II, p. 3. Reprinted in Weales, *The Crucible.* Martin, *Theater Essays. The Crucible* is not political polemic but rather an examination of "what happens" when one's conscience "is handed over" to others.

"The Shadows of the Gods" (essay). *Harper's* 217 (Aug. 1958): 35–43. Reprinted in Frenz, *American Playwrights.* Martin, *Theater Essays.* Character is unintelligible when viewed apart from its social context, which shapes it more significantly than does the family.

"Bridge to a Savage World" (essay). *Esquire* 50 (Oct. 1958): 185–90. Preliminary observations for a film on juvenile delinquency. For many young toughs, "fighting represents . . . an opportunity for courage against an enemy that can be seen and felt and hurt."

"My Wife Marilyn" (short essay). *Life* 50 (Dec. 22, 1958): 146–47. An appreciation of Miss Monroe. Like the most famous actresses of the 1930s, she transmits "sweet wit," "ebullience," "sauciness," an "exact combination of innocence and cunning," "full-blown daintiness and dignity in tights," "a rather elegant sentimentalism," "world-weary intensity," "spontaneous joy," "quick sympathy," and "a miraculous sense of sheer play."

"Arthur Miller on Adaptations" (letter). *New York Times*, Nov. 29, 1959,

Sec. II, p. 13. Reprinted in Martin, *Theater Essays*. Condensing serious literature for television production is a disservice to literature and to the audience.

"I Don't Need You Any More" (short story). *Esquire* 52 (Dec. 1959): 270–309. Reprinted in Miller, *I Don't Need You Any More*. The private, confused world of a five-year-old Jewish boy.

"Please Don't Kill Anything" (short story). *Noble Savage* 1 (March 1960): 126–31. Reprinted in *Redbook* 117 (Oct. 1961): 48–49. Miller, *I Don't Need You Any More*. Sketch of an innocent, wonder-full woman cast in the Roslyn-Marilyn mold.

"Art and Commitment" (short essay). *Anvil and Student Partisan* 11 (Winter 1960): 5. A writer must reveal, not mask reality.

Preface, *A View from the Bridge* (two-act version), pp. v–x. New York: Compass, 1960. Reprinted in Corrigan, *Modern Theatre*. Martin, *Theater Essays*. Miller's reasons for revising and expanding the play in 1956.

"The Prophecy" (short story). *Esquire* 56 (Dec., 1961), 140, 268–87. Reprinted in Miller, *I Don't Need You Any More*. On the need for love rather than "sexual advantage."

"Glimpse at a Jockey" (short story). *Noble Savage* 5 (Oct. 1962): 138–40. Reprinted in Miller, *I Don't Need You Any More*. Brief humorous monologue spoken in racetrack cant by a philosophical jockey who loves life, women, and his new-found father.

"The Bored and the Violent" (essay). *Harper's* 225 (Nov. 1962): 50–56. Reprinted in Herbert Gold (ed.), *First Person Singular*. New York: Dial, 1963. Miller explains juvenile gang behavior as a "flight from self in any defined form," a "violent manifestation of social nihilism."

"A New Era in American Theater?" (short essay). *Drama Survey* 3 (1963): 70–71. The Broadway theater has been damaged by "commercial considerations"; new hope rests with repertory organizations such as the Tyrone Guthrie Theatre in Minneapolis (which opened its first season in 1963 with *Death of a Salesman*) and the Lincoln Center Theater in New York (which opened its first season in 1964 with *After the Fall*).

"Eugene O'Neill: An Evaluation by Fellow Playwrights" (short answers to a questionnaire, ed. Edward T. Herbert). *Modern Drama* 6 (1963): 239–40. American dramatists today are less "fanatic" and less challenging than was O'Neill.

Jane's Blanket (children's story for ages 4–6; illustrated by Al Parker). New York: Crowell-Collier, 1963. Reprinted with illustrations by Emily A. McCully. New York: Viking, 1972. Simple tale about the process of weaning a girl from her comforter blanket.

"On Recognition" (speech). *Michigan Quarterly Review* 2 (1963): 213–20. Reprinted in Arno L. Bader, ed. *To the Young Writer* (Hopwood Lectures, 2nd series). Ann Arbor: University of Michigan Press, 1965.

Martin, *Theater Essays*. The 1963 Hopwood Lecture at the University of Michigan. Young writers should speak for and to their society.

"Lincoln Repertory Theater—Challenge and Hope" (essay). *New York Times*, Jan. 19, 1964, Sec. II, pp. 1, 3. Free from the pressures of the commercial theater, Miller hoped to "speak openly to the heart" with *After the Fall*.

Foreword, *After the Fall*. *Saturday Evening Post* 237 (Feb. 1, 1964): 32. Reprinted in Martin, *Theater Essays*. *After the Fall* shows the unwisdom of "Cain's alternative"—the will to destroy.

"With respect for her agony—but with love" (short essay). *Life* 56 (Feb. 7, 1964): 66. Contrary to the public's opinion, *After the Fall* is not a biographical play. It is "about" man's unwillingness to confront his own evil.

"Our Guilt for the World's Evil" (essay). *New York Times*, Jan. 3, 1965, Sec. VI, pp. 10–11, 48. Miller's account of the genesis and meaning of *Incident at Vichy*. Guilt is "the soul's remorse for its own hostility."

"Miller Sees P.E.N. Growing Mightier" (excerpts of speech). *New York Times*, July 6, 1965, p. 30. Complete speech reprinted as "Literature and Mass Communications," *World Theatre* 15 (1966): 164–67. "Mass communications, in a very great part, do not exist to communicate anything [of value], but to go on blackening white space."

"What Makes Plays Endure?" (essay). *New York Times*, Aug. 15, 1965, Sec. II, pp. 1, 3. Reprinted in Martin, *Theater Essays*. *A Memory of Two Mondays* and *A View from the Bridge* "are at the bottom reassertions of the existence of the community."

"The Role of P.E.N." (speech). *Saturday Review* 49 (June 4, 1966): 16–17. Excerpts reprinted as "P.E.N., Politics and Literature," *Publisher's Weekly* 190 (July 18, 1966): 32–33. Miller's presidential address: "literature is probably the only 'discipline' in which it can be emotionally proven that without moral vision the people must truly perish."

"The Recognitions" (short story). *Esquire* 66 (July 1966): 76, 118. Reprinted as "Fame" in Miller, *I Don't Need You Any More*. Clurman, *Portable Arthur Miller*. Revised as one-act play, "Fame," *Yale Literary Magazine* 140 (March 1971): 32–40. Revised and produced on television, Nov. 30, 1978. An amusing sketch about the patina with which fame covers a celebrity.

"Search for a Future" (short story). *Saturday Evening Post* 239 (Aug. 13, 1966): 64–68, 70. Reprinted in Martha Foley and David Burnett, eds. *Best American Short Stories, 1967*. Boston: Houghton Mifflin, 1967. Miller, *I Don't Need You Any More*. An aging actor regrets his career and admires his ailing father.

"It Could Happen Here—And Did" (essay). *New York Times*, April 30, 1967, Sec. II, p. 17. Reprinted in Martin, *Theater Essays*. A reasoned analysis of "paranoid politics"—the target of *The Crucible*.

"The Age of Abdication" (essay). *New York Times*, Dec. 23, 1967, p. 22.

Americans have failed to assume responsibility for the Vietnam war.

"Arthur Miller Talks." *Michigan Quarterly Review* 6 (1967): 153-84. Contains three items: (1) "Arthur Miller Talks: The Contemporary Theater" (speech), pp. 153-63. Reprinted in Martin, *Theater Essays*. In America the state of the theater (playwrights, producers, audience) is poor—only commercially viable "shows" succeed. (2) "Arthur Miller Talks: Freedom in the Mass Media" (panel discussion), pp. 163-78. On journalism and censorship in the media: news as reported in journals like *Time* is "all a fiction." (3) "Arthur Miller Talks Again:A Chat with a Class in Stage Directing" (speech), pp. 178-84. Miller discusses writing and directing plays.

I Don't Need You Any More. New York: Viking, 1967. New York: Bantam, 1968. Contains nine short stories, 1951-67: "I Don't Need You Any More," "Monte Sant' Angelo," "Please Don't Kill Anything," "The Misfits," "Glimpse at a Jockey," "The Prophecy," "Fame," "Fitter's Night," and "A Search for a Future." Foreword, "About Distances," pp. ix-xii: on differences between the short-story form and the play. "Fitter's Night," a previously unpublished story, reprinted in Clurman, *Portable Arthur Miller:* in a world that has disappointed every hope, a shipfitter experiences a moment of grace through his skill and courage at work.

"The New Insurgency" (excerpts of speech). *Nation* 206 (June 3, 1968): 717. Miller explains his support for Sen. Eugene McCarthy's presidential campaign.

"On the Shooting of Robert Kennedy" (letter). *New York Times,* June 8, 1968, p. 30. Miller challenges Americans to avoid violence and to develop "a common consciousness of social responsibility."

"Writers in Prison" (essay). *Encounter* 30 (June 1968): 60-61. On Soviet repression of liberal writers: "I protest . . . not in order to make matters worse between the Soviet Union and the rest of the world, but to make them better."

"The Battle of Chicago: From the Delegates' Side" (essay). *New York Times Magazine,* Sept. 15, 1968, pp. 29-31, 122-28. Reprinted as "Eyewitness" in Donald Myrus, ed. *Law and Disorder,* ACLU, 1968. On the violence during the Democratic presidential nominating convention in 1968: it was "the result of this mockery of a vast majority who had so little representation."

"On Creativity" (short essay). *Playboy* 15 (Dec. 1968): 139. "A case can be made for art as a response to the death or spiritual bankruptcy of the father."

"Kidnapped?" (essay). *Saturday Evening Post* 242 (Jan. 25, 1969): 40-42, 78-82. During a trip to Rome in the 1960s, Miller recalls an encounter with Lucky Luciano in Palermo just after World War II.

"Lines from California" (poem). *Harper's* 238 (May 1969): 97. Reprinted

154 ARTHUR MILLER

in Clurman, *Portable Arthur Miller.* Witty prose epigrams on many subjects.

"Are We Interested in Stopping the Killing?" (essay). *New York Times,* June 8, 1969, Sec. II, p. 21. On American politicians' lack of desire to end the war in Vietnam.

"Some Would Forge Ahead in Space, Others Would Turn to Earth's Affairs" (short essay). *New York Times,* July 21, 1969, p. 7. After the first manned landing on the moon, Miller hoped that someday Congress would authorize expeditions to needy places on the earth.

In Russia (journal, with photos by Inge Morath). New York: Viking, 1969. *Harper's* 239 (Sept. 1969): 37–78. Excerpts reprinted in Martin, *Theater Essays.* Miller's impressions, during his trip to the Soviet Union with his wife Inge, of ordinary people, officials, and celebrities (mainly writers and theater people).

"Broadway, From O'Neill to Now" (essay). *New York Times,* Dec. 21, 1969, Sec. II, pp. 3, 7. Reprinted in Martin, *Theater Essays.* "Marketplace laws . . . will by themselves destroy what remains of the New York theater. The only interference imaginable is public subsidy of some kind."

Brief remarks (untitled) in Rosamond Gilder, ed. *Theater 1,* pp. 4, 7. New York: International Theatre Institute, 1969. "We have never recognized that perhaps in this art a society does create an image of itself."

"The Bangkok Prince" (essay). *Harper's* 241 (July 1970): 32–33. Miller's interview with a charming Prince of Thailand.

"The War between Young and Old" (essay). *McCall's* 97 (July 1970): 32. "What the young are threatening is the very existence, psychologically and spiritually speaking, of the old. The very idea of self-deprivation for the sake of the hallowed upward climb to success—the most fundamental tenet of America—they deny."

"Banned in Russia" (essay). *New York Times,* Dec. 10, 1970, p. 47. Miller was shocked on learning that his plays were banned from production in the Soviet Union.

"When Life Had at Least a Form" (essay). *New York Times,* Jan. 24, 1971, Sec. II, p. 17. *A Memory of Two Mondays,* meant to evoke Depression years in the United States, fell on deaf ears during the "glamourtime" of 1955.

"Men and Words in Prison" (essay). *New York Times,* Oct. 16, 1971, p. 31. Through P.E.N., Miller has protested (with some results) the unjust imprisonment of writers around the world.

"Arthur Miller *vs.* Lincoln Center" (essay). *New York Times,* April 16, 1972, Sec. II, pp. 1, 5. Reprinted in *Dramatists Guild Quarterly* 8 (Winter 1972): 6–11. Otis L. Guernsey, Jr., ed. *Playwrights, Lyricists, Composers on Theater.* New York: Dodd, Mead, 1974. Martin, *Theater Essays.* On problems involved in the attempt to establish a repertory company at the Lincoln Center in New York.

"In Hiding" (review of *The Life of Manuel Cortes*, by Ronald Fraser). *New York Times*, July 9, 1972, Sec. VII, p. 1. For Miller this book about a Spaniard's passive resistance to Franco shows "what the Spanish Civil War was really about," and why that war "was the watershed of our age."

"Arthur Miller on *The Crucible*" (essay). *Audience* 2 (July 1972): 46–47. In the French movie version, *The Crucible* "was weakened and made less actual, rather than more pointed, by Sartre's overly Marxist screenplay."

"Politics as Theater" (essay). *New York Times*, Nov. 4, 1972, p. 33. After attending the Democractic national convention in Florida: "an election campaign is like theater. . . . What we want now is the theatrical impression of a man successfully impersonating integrity."

"Making Crowds" (essay). *Esquire* 78 (Nov. 1972): 160–61, 216–28. On the Democratic convention of 1972, crowd psychology, and the "McGovern phenomenon."

"The Measure of Things Is Man" (essay). *Theatre 4*, pp. 96–97. New York: International Theatre Institute, 1972. "I wondered whether the measure of things is man anymore or the reigning artistic style in which man sees himself."

"Symposium: Playwriting in America" (essay). *Yale/Theatre* 4 (Winter 1973): 19–21. In the last decade, dramatists retreated from their traditional role of pointing out "some overall significance to behavior and events; . . . theatre became a sort of celebration of the chaos itself."

Introduction to *Kesey's Garage Sale*, by Ken Kesey, pp. xiii–xviii. New York: Viking, 1973. Reprinted in revised form as "Miracles," *Esquire* 53 (Sept. 1973): 112–15, 203–204. Comparisons between the cultural "revolutions" in the United States during the 1930s and the 1960s.

"What's Wrong with This Picture?" (essay). *Esquire* 82 (July 1974): 124–25, 170. On Soviet repression of artistic and intellectual talent in Czechoslovakia.

"The Limited Hang-out" (essay). *Harper's* 249 (Sept. 1974): 13–20. On the immorality of President Nixon and his advisers during the Watergate scandal.

"Rain in a Strange City" ("prose poem"). *Travel and Leisure* 4 (Sept. 1974): 8.

"Soliloquys" (essay). In Guernsey, *Playwrights, Lyricists, Composers*, pp. 217–18. Miller remembers writing radio scripts early in his career.

Up From Paradise (unpublished musical version of *The Creation of the World and Other Business*). Produced in Ann Arbor, Michigan, 1974.

"On True Identity" (essay). *New York Times Magazine*, April 13, 1975, p. 111. On the stupidity of new governmental efforts to control passports in the United States.

"The Prague Winter" (essay). *New York Times*, July 16, 1975, p. 37. On the oppression of liberal writers in Czechoslovakia.

"Toward a New Foreign Policy" (essay). *Society* 13 (March 1976): 10, 15–16. For the U.S. government, "the real problem . . . is how to place our weight on the side of human rights and the sanctity of the individual."

The Archbishop's Ceiling (unpublished play). Produced in New Haven, Connecticut, 1976, and in Washington, D.C., 1977.

"Ham Sandwich" (fragment of a short story). *Boston University Quarterly* 24, no. 2 (1976): 5–6

"The Poosidin's Resignation" (fragment of a play). *Boston University Quarterly* 24, no. 2 (1976): 7–13. About mindless sacrifice of self to country and religion.

In the Country (journal, with photos by Inge Morath). New York: Viking, 1977. Miller reflects on local people and their tales after twenty-five years' residence in rural Connecticut.

"Our Most Widespread Dramatic Art Is Our Most Unfree" (essay). *New York Times*, Nov. 26, 1978, Sec. II, pp. 1, 33. On the occasion of Miller's first television play, "Fame": television has "ceded almost always to control and almost never to creation."

The Theater Essays of Arthur Miller, Robert A. Martin, ed. New York: Viking, 1978. New York: Penguin, 1978. A well-edited collection of Miller's commentaries (1949 to 1972) on his plays and on the theater. Miller's forword, pp. xli-xliv: in modern tragedy, "instead of grief we have come to substitute irony and even comedy, black or otherwise."

"A Playwright's Choice of 'Perfect' Plays" (short essay), Robert Anderson, ed. *New York Times*, Jan. 14, 1979, Sec. II, p. 10. Miller chooses *Oedipus Rex* because "it is a play about political tyranny and at the same time an implacable confrontation with the processes of personal guilt, innocence and the human claim to justification."

"Every Play Has a Purpose" (essay). *Dramatists Guild Quarterly* 15 (Winter 1979): 13–20. "Dissident works somehow confront the audience's or the critics' presumptions about life and society and imply that something might be terribly hollow or tragically wrong about them."

"In China" (journal, with photos by Inge Morath). *Atlantic* 243 (March 1979): 90–117. Published in expanded form as *Chinese Encounters*. New York: Farrar, Straus and Giroux, 1979. Sensitive impressions of China after Mao's death.

3. Interviews

HUTCHENS, JOHN K. "Mr. Miller Has a Change of Luck." *New York Times*, Feb. 23, 1947, Sec. II, pp. 1, 3. After the favorable reception of *All My Sons*: Miller "is a young man on his way."

STEVENS, VIRGINIA. "Seven Young Broadway Artists." *Theatre Arts* 31 June 1947): 56. Autobiographical comments after *All My Sons*.

Selected Bibliography

SCHUMACH, MURRAY. "Arthur Miller Grew in Brooklyn." *New York Times,*
Feb. 6, 1949, Sec. II, pp. 1, 3. General observations on life, the theater,
and *Death of a Salesman.*

WOLFERT, IRA. "Arthur Miller, Playwright In Search of His Identity." *New
York Herald-Tribune,* Jan. 25, 1953, Sec. IV, p. 3. Miller recalls his
earliest years as a writer.

HEWES, HENRY. "Broadway Postscript: Arthur Miller and How He Went
to the Devil." *Saturday Review 36* (Jan. 31, 1953): 24–26. *The Crucible*
is not so much concerned with a "historical" phenomenon (the Mc-
Carthy investigations) as with "Proctor's sense of personal inviolabil-
ity."

GRIFFEN, JOHN and ALICE. "Arthur Miller Discusses *The Crucible.*" *Theater Arts* 37 (Oct. 1953): 33–34. Discussion of the restaged, revised
version of the play presented in July 1953.

SAMACHSON, DOROTHY and JOSEPH. "Why Write a Play?" *Let's Meet the
Theatre,* pp. 15–20. New York: Abelard-Schuman, 1955. Comments
on playwriting directed to young people.

GELB, PHILLIP. "Morality and Modern Drama." *Educational Theatre Journal* 10 (1958): 190–202. Reprinted in Weales, *Death of a Salesman.*
Martin, *Theater Essays.* On the relation between modern drama and
society: Willy Loman cultivates his "selfhood" despite the pressures
of a "machine civilization."

ALLSOP, KENNETH. "A Conversation with Arthur Miller." *Encounter* 13
(July 1959): 58–60. General discussion of Miller's dramaturgic problems and intentions.

BRANDON, HENRY. "The State of the Theatre: A Conversation with Arthur
Miller." London *Sunday Times,* March 20, 1960. Reprinted in *Har-
per's* 221 (Nov. 1960): 63–69. Henry Brandon, *As We Are.* New York:
Doubleday, 1961. *World Theatre* 11 (1962): 229–40. Martin, *Theater
Essays.* "So, I would say, our main tradition from O'Neill to the
present revolves around the question of integrity."

SHANLEY, JOHN P. "Miller's 'Focus' on TV Today." *New York Times,* Jan.
21, 1962, Sec. II, p. 19. Miller remains unenthusiastic about the commercial entertainment media.

GOYEN, WILLIAM. "Arthur Miller's Quest for Truth." *New York Herald-
Tribune Magazine,* Jan. 19, 1964, p. 35. In *After the Fall* "the Garden
of Eden theme combined with the Cain and Abel theme."

ANON. "Arthur Miller Ad-Libs on Elia Kazan." *Show* 2 (Jan. 1964): 55–56,
97–98. Miller praises the director of *After the Fall,* who developed
the author's intent while working in his own distinctive, intense style.

GELB, BARBARA. "Question: 'Am I My Brother's Keeper?'" *New York
Times,* Nov. 29, 1964, Sec. II, pp. 1, 3. *Incident at Vichy* "concerns the
question of insight—of seeing in oneself the capacity for collabor-
ation with the evil one condemns."

HYAMS, BARRY. "A Theatre: Heart and Mind." *Theatre: Annual of the*

Repertory Theater of Lincoln Center 1 (1964): 56–61. On the potentials of a repertory theater.

FERON, JAMES. "Miller in London to See 'Crucible.'" *New York Times*, Jan. 24, 1965, p. 82. Miscellaneous comments.

MORLEY, SHERIDAN. "Miller on Miller." *Theater World* (London) 61 (March 1965): 4, 8. Miller comments on the 1965 production of *The Crucible* in London (he approved) and on a variety of other topics.

FALLACI, ORIANA. "*A Propos* of *After the Fall*." *World Theatre* 14 (1965): 79–81. "In my opinion, this is the best play I have ever written."

CARLISLE, OLGA and STYRON, ROSE. "Arthur Miller." *Paris Review* 10 (Summer 1966): 61–98. Reprinted in George Plimpton, ed. *Writers at Work: The "Paris Review" Interviews*, Third Series. New York: Viking, 1967. Miller reflects on his drama and his society: "I'm in deadly fear of people with too much power. I don't trust people that much any more. I used to think that if people had the right idea they could make things move accordingly."

FUNKE, LEWIS. "A Zestful Miller Starts Rehearsal." *New York Times*, Dec. 6, 1967, p. 40. Miller's hopeful comments during the production of *The Price*.

WAGER, WALTER. "Arthur Miller." In Walter Wager, ed. *The Playwrights Speak*, pp. 1–24. New York: Dell, 1967. Observations about his plays, their origins and reception. "Dramatic conflict of significance always . . . deals with the way men live together."

BARTHEL, JOAN. "Arthur Miller Ponders 'The Price.'" *New York Times*, Jan. 28, 1968, Sec. II, pp. 1, 5. "Responsibility is a kind of love. It's the only thing that prevents total slaughter, violence and nihilism."

CALTA, LOUIS. "Miller Defends Theme of 'Price.'" *New York Times*, March 5, 1968, p. 32. Miller defends himself against the accusation that he is insulated from the "events of his time."

GILROY, HARRY. "A Million Sales for Willy Loman." *New York Times*, March 8, 1968, p. 36. The paperback edition of *Death of a Salesman* has sold a million copies, more than any other contemporary play in the past ten years.

GRUEN, JOHN. "Arthur Miller." *Close-Up*, pp. 58–63. New York: Viking, 1968. Miller's activities in 1965 against the war in Vietnam. "We [Americans] really *do* revolution and *talk* reaction, they [Communists] do reaction and talk revolution!"

RAYMONT, HENRY. "Miller Refuses Greek Book Plan." *New York Times*, July 3, 1969, p. 29. Miller refuses to allow publication in Greece of his most recent works as a protest to its repressive military regime.

FUNKE, LEWIS. "Stars Help Arthur Miller Film TV Antiwar Allegory." *New York Times*, Nov. 17, 1969, p. 58. During the noncommercial production of a one-act script he wrote entitled "The Reason Why," Miller ponders the "impulses of the human animal toward war, violence, and murder."

EVANS, RICHARD I. *Psychology and Arthur Miller.* New York: Dutton, 1969. In dialogue with a psychologist, Miller offers sensible replies concerning the writing process; as usual, he is obliging, consistent, and thoughtful in dealing with both sensitive and outlandish queries. "To think that a work of art is going to overthrow ignorance, for example, or the absence of charity or something else, that's a pretty impossible dream. But it can help unveil reality, the present in history."

MARTIN, ROBERT A. "Arthur Miller—Tragedy and Commitment." *Michigan Quarterly Review* 8 (1969): 176–78. "I am fully aware of the impermanence of all arrangements and I choose to commit myself, nevertheless."

MARTIN, ROBERT A. "The Creative Experience of Arthur Miller." *Educational Theatre Journal* 21 (1969): 310–17. Miller speculates on his intentions and accomplishments.

HAYMAN, RONALD. "Interview." *Arthur Miller,* pp. 1–14. London: Heinemann, 1970. In *The Price,* "the policeman has refused to adopt the sex and success motives of the society."

MARTIN, ROBERT A. "Arthur Miller and the Meaning of Tragedy." *Modern Drama* 13 (1970): 34–39. In *After the Fall,* Quentin "is betrayed by his illusion that . . . the real nature of people is to be consistent. . . . Implicit in that play is the idea of a primeval unity of people, a community, a family which is all for one and one for all."

HILLS, RUST. "Conversation: Arthur Miller and William Styron." *Audience* 1 (Nov. 1971): 6–21. On critics (intolerable), teachers of playwriting (supportive), and young playwrights (amoral).

GREENFELD, JOSH. "'Writing Plays Is Absolutely Senseless,' Arthur Miller Says, 'But I Love It. I Just Love It.'" *New York Times Magazine,* Feb. 13, 1972, pp. 16–17, 34–39. Miller's daily life and working habits at his country house in Roxbury, Connecticut. "My plays are getting more and more mythological; the people are getting less and less psychological."

BUCKLEY, TOM. "Miller Takes His Comedy Seriously." *New York Times,* Aug. 29, 1972, p. 22. Miller wrote *The Creation of the World* in six weeks. "There is no religion that is closer to a man than the one he invents."

SELIGSOHN, LEO. "Arthur Miller on the Eve of 'Creation.'" *Newsday,* Nov. 26, 1972, Sec. II, pp. 4–5, 28. "Without the belief that man has a choice and without his willingness to take responsibility for that choice, you are unable to rely on conscientious objection to anything. I've been writing about it for a long time."

MAAS, WILLARD. "Poetry and the Film: A Symposium." New York: Gotham Book Mart, 1972. A discussion with Dylan Thomas and others in 1953 on methods of conveying meaning in film.

CARR, JAY. "Arthur Miller Sheds Light on 'Salesman.'" *Detroit News,*

Nov. 25, 1973. Reprinted in Barbara Nykoruk, ed. *Authors in the News*, Vol. I., p. 341. Detroit: Gale, 1976. Comments on dialogue ("I believe in mimicry. I do accents well"), *All My Sons* ("no one will take any responsibility"), and *Death of a Salesman* ("I'm criticizing these values in society which drive people crazy").

HAYMAN, RONALD. "Arthur Miller." *Playback*, pp. 111–26. New York: Horizon, 1973. Miller dislikes most recent experimental styles in drama, especially the new "naturalism" and the "absurdist" mode.

GUSSOW, MEL. "Arthur Miller Returns to Genesis for First Musical." *New York Times*, April 17, 1974, p. 37. For a musical version of *The Creation of the World*, Miller wrote twenty-three song lyrics, directed, and narrated in the production at Ann Arbor, Michigan.

CORRIGAN, ROBERT W. "Interview." *Michigan Quarterly Review* 13 (1974): 401–405. Dramatic form may reflect a playwright's involvement with his society.

SCHUMACH, MURRAY. "Miller Still a 'Salesman' for a Changing Theater." *New York Times*, June 26, 1975, p. 32. On various political and theatrical subjects.

MARTIN, ROBERT A., and MEYER, RICHARD D. "Arthur Miller on Plays and Playwriting." *Modern Drama* 19 (1976): 375–84. "A play teaches, not by proposing solutions but by defining problems."

MCGINNISS, JOE. Untitled. *Heroes*, pp. 120–21. New York: Viking, 1976. Miller's experience during the Great Depression of the 1930s: "there was no place for a hero in a world of self-contempt."

GOLLUB, CHRISTIAN-ALBRECHT. "Interview with Arthur Miller." *Michigan Quarterly Review* 16 (1977): 121–41. Among American playwrights, Miller likes O'Neill best; among recent writers in Europe, Pinter.

TYLER, RALPH. "Arthur Miller Says the Time Is Right for *The Price*." *New York Times*, June 17, 1979, Sec. II, pp. 1, 6. Miller discusses the successful revival of *The Price*.

SECONDARY SOURCES

1. Bibliographies

EISSENSTAT, MARTHA TURNQUIST. "Arthur Miller: A Bibliography," *Modern Drama* 5 (1962): 93–106. A useful listing (to its date), but omits some important items and includes much peripheral material (e.g., reviews, abbreviated treatments in books and encyclopedias, and short news announcements). Lists foreign contributions. Not annotated.

HAYASHI, TETSUMARO. *Arthur Miller Criticism (1930–1967)*. Metuchen, New Jersey: Scarecrow, 1969. An exhaustive bibliographic chaos. 2nd ed., *An Index to Arthur Miller Criticism*. Metuchen, New Jersey: Scarecrow, 1976. Many errors are corrected, many retained; much peripheral material and duplication remains, as well as omissions. Organization is simpler though still confused. The title still misleads: listings include works by Miller and noncritical items about him. Not annotated.

JENSEN, GEORGE. H. *Arthur Miller: A Bibliographical Checklist.* Columbia, S.C.: Faust, 1976. A careful, reliable descriptive bibliography (editions, printings, states, and issues) of Miller's major works, together with a simpler enumerative listing of the minor works. Some annotations on publication data.

MARTIN, ROBERT A. "Bibliography of Works (1936–1977) by Arthur Miller," *The Theater Essays of Arthur Miller,* pp. 379–92. New York: Viking, 1978. A reliable list of primary sources; includes recordings of plays and manuscript collections. Not annotated.

UNGAR, HARRIET. "The Writings of and about Arthur Miller: A Check List 1936–1967," *Bulletin of the New York Public Library* 74 (1970): 107–34. Helpful, but secondary source listings are both incomplete and cluttered with peripheral items (reviews, etc.). Lists anthology reprintings of major plays, foreign translations, motion pictures, and biographical material. Most entries are not annotated.

2. Critical Books and Articles: General Appraisals

ADLER, HENRY. "To Hell with Society," *Tulane Drama Review* 4 (May 1960): 53–76. Reprinted in Corrigan, *Theatre in the Twentieth Century.* On Miller and others as poor sociologists.

AYLEN, LEO. "Miller," *Greek Tragedy and the Modern World,* pp. 248–57. London: Methuen, 1964. Superficial accounts of *Death of a Salesman* and *A View from the Bridge.*

BARKSDALE, RICHARD K. "Social Background in the Plays of Miller and Williams," *College Language Association Journal* 6 (March 1963): 161–69. Miller's plays reflect current social problems.

BERMEL, ALBERT. "Right, Wrong and Mr. Miller," *New York Times,* April 14, 1968, Sec. II, pp. 1, 7. Miller's concern for "rational behavior" is misplaced; "it is to irrational behavior that attention must be paid."

BIGSBY, C. W. E. "Arthur Miller," *Confrontation and Commitment: A Study of Contemporary American Drama, 1959–66,* pp. 26–49. Columbia: University of Missouri Press, 1967. Sees Miller as a playwright of "metaphysical" problems and ideas.

BLUMBERG, PAUL. "Sociology and Social Literature: Work Alienation in the Plays of Arthur Miller," *American Quarterly* 21 (1969): 291–310. Miller's work shows "alienation as a perversion or misuse of the products of one's own labor."

BRASHEAR, WILLIAM R. "The Empty Bench: Morality, Tragedy, and Arthur Miller," *Michigan Quarterly Review* 5 (1966): 270–78. An excellent comparison between Miller and Nietzsche: Miller usually backs away from Nietzschean ideas of cosmic irrationality and individual solitude; like Quentin in *After the Fall,* he seeks security in concepts of social or personal morality, such as mutual responsibility.

BRIEN, ALAN. "There Was a Jolly Miller," *Spectator* 201 (Aug. 8, 1958): 191–92. "I was struck again by the enormous, naive high spirits and good humour woven into even the most tragic themes" in Miller's writing.

BROUSSARD, LOUIS. *American Drama: Contemporary Allegory from Eugene O'Neill to Tennessee Williams,* pp. 116–21. Norman, Okla.: University of Oklahoma Press, 1962. Proposes some tenuous connections between Miller and several other American dramatists.

CASSELL, RICHARD A. "Arthur Miller's 'Rage of Conscience,'" *Ball State Teachers College Forum* 1 (Winter 1960): 31–36. Miller's social justice message is verbal, not carried by the action.

CLURMAN, HAROLD. "Arthur Miller: Theme and Variations," *Theatre* (Lincoln Center) 1 (1964): 13–24. Reprinted in Corrigan, *Arthur Miller.* An oversimplified biographical and critical inventory.

———. Editor's Introduction, *The Portable Arthur Miller,* pp. xi–xxv. New York: Viking, 1971. On Miller's themes of "connection with others" and mutual responsibility.

———. "The Merits of Mr. Miller," *New York Times,* April 21, 1968, Sec. II, pp. 1, 7. Reprinted in Corrigan, *Arthur Miller.* Rebuts Albert Bermel (q.v.): Miller's concern for "traditional morality" is valuable.

COHN, RUBY. "The Articulate Victims of Arthur Miller," *Dialogue in American Drama,* pp. 68–96. Bloomington: Indiana University Press, 1971. On Miller's language and its "Jewish inflections."

CORRIGAN, ROBERT W., ed. *Arthur Miller: A Collection of Critical Essays.* Englewood Cliffs, N.J.: Prentice-Hall, 1969. Contains ten previously published articles. Editor's introduction, "The Achievement of Arthur Miller," pp. 1–22, reprinted from *Comparative Drama* 2 (1968): 141–60. Excerpts reprinted as "Arthur Miller" in James Vinson, ed. *Contemporary Dramatists,* 2nd ed. New York: St. Martin's, 1977. Studies Miller's plays in terms of a "crisis of Identity" (the early writing) and a "crisis of Generativity" (after *The Misfits*).

DILLINGHAM, WILLIAM B. "Arthur Miller and the Loss of Conscience," *Emory University Quarterly* 16 (1960): 40–50. Reprinted in Weales, *Death of a Salesman.* Miller's tragedies depict the failure of men to fulfill meaningful social roles because of anti-social crimes.

DOWNER, ALAN S. "Mr. Williams and Mr. Miller," *Furioso* 4 (Summer 1949): 66–70. States the obvious fact that expectations have been aroused by the two foremost living American playwrights.

———. *Recent American Drama* (pamphlet), pp. 33–39. Minneapolis: University of Minnesota Press, 1961. Sketch of Miller's work.

DRIVER, TOM. "Strength and Weakness in Arthur Miller," *Tulane Drama*

Review 4 (May 1960): 45–52. Reprinted in Corrigan, *Arthur Miller*. Driver, along with others such as Warshow, Popkin, Wiegand, and Clark (q.v.,), commits the sin he finds in Miller—distorting facts in the light of some radical preconception. His condemnation of Miller as a Marxist entirely disregards the plays' esthetic integrity; his main source, in fact, seems to be the playwright's introductory essay in the *Collected Plays*.

EDWARDS, JOHN. "Arthur Miller: An Appraisal," *Time and Tide* 42 (May 4, 1961): 740–41. Brief discussion, focusing on *The Misfits*.

FINDLATER, RICHARD. "No Time for Tragedy?" *Twentieth Century* 161 (Jan. 1957): 56–66. Both Miller and Brecht break Aristotle's "rules" in their tragedies.

FLAXMAN, SEYMOUR L. "The Debt of Williams and Miller to Ibsen and Strindberg," *Comparative Literature Studies*, Special Advance Issue (1963): 51–59. Correspondences among the four dramatists.

FREEDMAN, MORRIS. "Bertolt Brecht and American Social Drama," *The Moral Impulse: Modern Drama from Ibsen to the Present*, pp. 99–114. Carbondale: Southern Illinois University Press, 1967. "The characters of Hellman, Miller, and often of Odets are out of some small formula for making propaganda plays."

———. "The Jewishness of Arthur Miller; His Family Epic," *American Drama in Social Context*, pp. 43–58. Carbondale: Southern Illinois University Press, 1971. Miller's plays reflect a "phase of the Jewish experience in America."

FRUCHTER, NORM. "On the Frontier," *Encore* 9 (Jan. 1962): 17–27. Criticizes Welland (q.v.) for "refusing to offer any critical evaluation of most of Miller's work," and criticizes Miller for not centering his drama, after *The Crucible*, "within any context we can meaningfully identify as American society."

GANZ, ARTHUR. "The Silence of Arthur Miller," *Drama Survey* 3 (1963): 224–37. Miller's plays reveal a naïve "faith in the efficacy of self-knowledge."

GASCOIGNE, BAMBER. "Arthur Miller," *Twentieth-Century Drama*, pp. 174–83. London: Hutchinson University, 1962. Summaries of Miller's plots; weak in evaluation.

GOLDEN, JOSEPH. "The Modern Medievalists," *The Death of Tinker Bell: the American Theatre in the 20th Century*, pp. 131–37. Syracuse: Syracuse University Press, 1967. "So it's not society he blames [in *All My Sons*] but rather . . . the deadly middle-class ethic that unconsciously distorts a man's values."

HAYMAN, RONALD. *Arthur Miller*. London: Heinemann, 1970. Hayman makes some relevant comments on Miller's language, but pays too little attention to other aspects.

———. "Arthur Miller: Between Sartre and Society," *Encounter* 37 (Nov.

1971): 73–79. In both Sartre and Miller, the vital individual opts for freedom in society.

HEILMAN, ROBERT BECHTOLD. "Arthur Miller," *The Iceman, the Arsonist, and the Troubled Agent: Tragedy and Melodrama on the Modern Stage.* pp. 142–64. Seattle: University of Washington Press, 1973. This critic finds Miller's plays incomplete as tragedies because they fail to satisfy his formulas.

HUFTEL, SHEILA. *Arthur Miller: The Burning Glass.* New York: Citadel, 1965. Ms. Huftel admires Miller intensely, but she generates little illumination.

HUGHES, CATHARINE. "Arthur Miller," *American Playwrights 1945–75,* pp. 32–43. London: Pitman, 1976. A simple survey.

HUNT, ALBERT. "Realism and Intelligence," *Encore* 7 (May 1960): 12–17, 41. Reprinted in Weales, *The Crucible.* "Miller uses a heightened naturalism."

HYNES, JOSEPH A. "Arthur Miller and the Impasse of Naturalism," *South Atlantic Quarterly* 62 (1963): 327–34. "To speak mildly," Miller suffers from "a deficient aethetic awareness and a stunted moral imagination" because he fails to see that his subhuman characters are only pathetic, not tragic.

KITCHIN, LAURENCE. "The Potent Intruder," *Mid-Century Drama,* 2nd ed., pp. 56–63. London: Faber & Faber, 1962. Random comments on productions of Miller's plays in England.

LEWIS, ALLAN. "Arthur Miller—Return to the Self," *American Plays and Playwrights of the Contemporary Theatre,* rev. ed., pp. 35–52. New York: Crown, 1970. In *After the Fall* and elsewhere, "Miller is baffled by the mystery of sex."

———. *The Contemporary Theatre,* pp. 282–302. New York: Crown, 1962. Another journalistic survey.

MARTIN, ROBERT A. "Editor's Introduction," *The Theater Essays of Arthur Miller,* pp. xv–xxxix. New York: Viking, 1978. A chronological survey that relates ideas in the essays to themes in the plays.

MCANANY, EMILE G. "The Tragic Commitment: Some Notes on Arthur Miller," *Modern Drama* 5 (1962): 11–20. Approaches Miller through his essays, primarily the introduction to the *Collected Plays.*

MCCARTHY, MARY. "'Realism' in the American Theatre," *Harper's* 223 (July 1961): 45–52. Reprinted as "Americans, Realists, Playwrights" in *Encounter* 17 (July 1961): 24–31. "Realism is a depreciation of the real."

MCMAHON, HELEN. "Arthur Miller's Common Man: The Problem of the Realistic and the Mythic," *Drama and Theatre* 10 (1972): 128–33. In Miller's writing a "sub-text of myth includes certain archetypal patterns and characters primarily as they appear to be related to the Bible and to Judeo-Christian beliefs."

MOSS, LEONARD. "Arthur Miller and the Common Man's Language,"

Modern Drama 7 (1964): 52–59. Reprinted in Meserve, *Merrill Studies*. Miller's colloquial dialogue artfully implies concealed feelings but awkwardly expounds moral generalizations.

MOTTRAM, ERIC. "Arthur Miller: The Development of a Political Dramatist in America," In John Russell Brown and Bernard Harris, eds. *American Theatre*, pp. 126–61. New York: St. Martin's, 1967. Reprinted in Corrigan, *Arthur Miller*. "Miller's restless social conscience moves toward the logical nihilism of *Incident at Vichy*.

MURRAY, EDWARD. *Arthur Miller, Dramatist*. New York: Ungar, 1967. Murray lists "themes," summarizes plots, and counts the "traits" of Miller's characters.

NELSON, BENJAMIN. *Arthur Miller*. London: Owen, 1970. Nelson lacks interpretive depth and viewpoint, but he offers sensible plot analyses, and his detailed biographical coverage makes good use of published interviews.

NEWMAN, WILLIAM J. Review of *Arthur Miller's Collected Plays*, *Twentieth Century* 164 (1958): 491–96. Reprinted in Hurrell, *Two Tragedies*. In all Miller's plays except *The Crucible*, a father-child-conflict is the "central situation"; even in *A Memory of Two Mondays* "the warehouse gang acts as the family to Bert," but fails him.

O'CONNOR, FRANK. "The Most American Playwright," *Holiday* 19 (Feb. 1956): 35, 68, 70. "An inarticulate character cannot be either classical or tragic, . . . he can only be dumb."

ÖVERLAND, ORM. "The Action and Its Significance: Arthur Miller's Struggle with Dramatic Form," *Modern Drama* 18 (1975): 1–14. Miller's career attests to the difficulty of reconciling a psychological with a sociological viewpoint.

POPKIN, HENRY. "Arthur Miller: The Strange Encounter," *Sewanee Review* 68 (1960): 34–60. Miller assigns the blame for the misfortunes of his "little people" (whose banality is appropriately revealed by their drab speech and values) to their socio-economic "System," their parents, and sex. Popkin subscribes to the opinion that Miller's plays are instruments for social criticism.

PRUDHOE, JOHN. "Arthur Miller and the Tradition of Tragedy," *English Studies* 43 (1962): 430–39. Deals pertinently with the language of the major plays. The inarticulateness of Miller's characters reflects the failure of modern society to clarify its values.

RENO, RAYMOND H. "Arthur Miller and the Death of God," *Texas Studies in Literature and Language* 11 (1969): 1069–87. "In a world emptied of theology, there is nothing left but a kind of sociology, the doctrine of man's responsibility for man."

SCANLAN, TOM. "Reactions I: Family and Society in Arthur Miller," *Family, Drama, and American Dreams*, pp. 126–55. Westport, Conn.: Greenwood, 1978. "Miller has had difficulty in dramatizing sub-

jects other than the individual consciousness concerned for its own
integrity and adjustment to family."

SHEPHERD, ALLEN. "'What Comes Easier—': The Short Stories of Arthur
Miller," *Illinois Quarterly* 34 (Feb. 1972): 37–49. Plot summaries.

SIEVERS, W. DAVID. *Freud on Broadway: A History of Psychoanalysis and
the American Drama*, pp. 376–80 et passim. New York: Hermitage,
1955. An extensive outline of Freud's influence on Broadway dramatists. Miller's plays (to 1955) are variations on the Freudian theme of
a maturing son discovering his father's fallibility, which leads to hatred and disillusionment in the son and fear of abandonment in the
father.

STAMBUSKY, ALAN A. "Arthur Miller: Aristotelian Canons in the Twentieth Century Drama," In William E. Taylor, ed. *Modern American
Drama*, pp. 91–116. DeLand, Fla.: Everett-Edwards, 1968. On balance, Miller's plays do not fulfill the "Aristotelian canons" of tragedy.

STEINBERG, M. W. "Arthur Miller and the Idea of Modern Tragedy," *Dal-
housie Review* 40 (1961): 329–40. Reprinted in Corrigan, *Arthur Miller*. Excerpts reprinted in Ferres, *The Crucible*. Miller's work points
to an antithesis between the two basic "ideas" of Western tragedy—
the Greek concept of external (e.g., fatal) conflict and the "modern"
or Christian concept of internal conflict.

TYNAN, KENNETH. *Curtains*. New York: Atheneum, 1961. Contains three
items. Review of "On Social Plays, pp. 123–24: tragedy does *not*
have to be a "social" drama in Miller's sense; *Hamlet*, e.g., is a "tragedy of private life." Review of *The Crucible*, pp. 253–54. Essay,
"American Blues," pp. 257–66, reprinted from *Encounter* 2 (May
1954): 13–19: both Miller and Tennessee Williams take up a subject
prevalent in the drama of the 1930s (and in all great drama)—the
suffering martyr.

WEALES, GERALD. "Arthur Miller," in Alan S. Downer, ed. *The American
Theater*, pp. 95–108. Washington, D.C.: Voice of America, 1967.
Reprinted as "Arthur Miller's Shifting Image of Man," in Alan S.
Downer, ed. *The American Theater Today*. New York: Basic Books,
1967. Reprinted as "Williams and Miller" in Gerald Weales, *The
Jumping-Off Place: American Drama in the 1960s*. London: Mac-
millan, 1969. Also in Corrigan, *Arthur Miller*. Comments on the plays
up to *Incident at Vichy*.

———. "Arthur Miller: Man and His Image," *Tulane Drama Review* 7
(Sept. 1962): 165–80. Reprinted in Gerald Weales, *American Drama
Since World War II*. New York: Harcourt, 1962. Weales, *Death of a
Salesman*. Weales, *The Crucible*. Miller's social critique is built upon
the conflict each protagonist experiences between his native "identity
and the image that society demands of him."

WELLAND, DENNIS. *Arthur Miller*. Edinburgh, Scotland: Oliver & Boyd,
1961; New York: Grove, 1961. Welland's book, a British contribution,

emphasizes character analysis, and attempts to relate Miller to other recent authors.

WEST, PAUL. "Arthur Miller and the Human Mice," *Hibbert Journal* 61 (Jan. 1963): 84–86. "Miller's plays are meant to alert us to the facts of community, pride and spiritual sanctity."

WHITLEY, ALVIN. "Arthur Miller: An Attempt at Modern Tragedy," *Transactions of the Wisconsin Academy of Sciences, Arts & Letters* 42 (1953): 257–62. This perfunctory study finds that *All My Sons* and *Death of a Salesman* fail to measure up to Aristotelian standards of tragedy.

WIEGAND, WILLIAM. "Arthur Miller and the Man Who Knows," *Western Review* 21 (1956): 85–103. Reprinted in Weales, *Death of a Salesman*. Weales, *The Crucible*. Miller's martyr-heroes tune in on and die for an evasive "truth" (Marxist truth, in the playwright's early career) that alone ensures salvation in a corrupt society. Wiegand belongs to the school that sees Miller as a practical social preacher and reformer.

WILLETT, RALPH W. "The Ideas of Miller and Williams," *Theatre Annual 1965–66* 22 (1966): 31–40. Though not brilliant, "their ideas are important for a study of American cultural history."

WILLIAMS, RAYMOND. "The Realism of Arthur Miller," *Critical Quarterly* 1 (1959): 140–49. Reprinted in *Universities & Left Review* 7 (Autumn 1959): 34–37. Weales, *Death of a Salesman*. Corrigan, *Arthur Miller*. Miller "has restored active social criticism to the drama, and has written on such contemporary themes as the social accountability of business, the forms of the success-ethic, intolerance and thought-control, the nature of modern work-relations."

WINEGARTEN, RENEE. "The World of Arthur Miller," *Jewish Quarterly* (London) 17 (Summer 1969): 48–53. Comments on the plays through *The Price*.

3. Critical Books and Articles: *Death of a Salesman*

ADAMCZEWSKI, ZYGMUNT. "The Tragic Loss—Loman the Salesman," *The Tragic Protest*, pp. 172–92. The Hague: Nizhoff, 1963. Prolix statement on Willy Loman's loss of identity.

ATKINSON, BROOKS, et al. *New York Theatre Critics' Reviews* 10 (1949): 358–61. Reviews in seven New York City newspapers.

BATES, BARCLAY W. "The Lost Past in *Death of a Salesman*," *Modern Drama* 11 (1968): 164–72. "Willy is four anachronisms": pastoral lover, artisan, outlaw frontiersman, and patriarch.

BENEDEK, LASLO. "Play into Picture," *Sight and Sound* 22 (Oct. 1952): 82–84, 96. The film director of *Death of a Salesman* explains how he transformed stage values into motion picture techniques.

BENTLEY, ERIC. "Back to Broadway," *Theatre Arts* 33 (Nov. 1949): 10–19.

The play presents the "little man as victim," the social drama blurring the tragedy.

BETTINA, SISTER M. "Willy Loman's Brother Ben: Tragic Insight in *Death of a Salesman*," *Modern Drama* 4 (1962): 409–12. Reprinted in Meserve, *Merrill Studies*. Ben plays an important role as the personification of "his brother's dream of easy wealth."

BLEICH, DAVID. "Psychological Bases of Learning from Literature," *College English* 33 (1971): 32–45. On the basis of his students' and his own responses, the author analyzes the "psychoanalytic circumstances" that allow spectators to learn from the play.

BLIQUEZ, GUERIN. "Linda's Role in *Death of a Salesman*," *Modern Drama* 10 (1968): 383–86. Reprinted in Meserve, *Merrill Studies*. "Linda's facility for prodding Willy to his doom is what gives the play its direction and its impetus."

BROOKS, CHARLES. "The Multiple Set in American Drama," *Tulane Drama Review* 3 (Dec. 1958): 30–41. This play "best realizes the potentialities of a multiple set."

BROWN, IVOR. "As London Sees Willy Loman," *New York Times Magazine*, Aug. 28, 1949, pp. 11, 59. Reprinted in Weales, *Death of a Salesman*. "There are many points of psychological detail in which Loman is a stranger to British playgoers. But now the little man is everywhere the center of attention and sympathy."

CLARK, ELEANOR. Review, *Partisan Review* 16 (1949): 631–35. Reprinted in Hurrell, *Two Tragedies*. Weales, *Death of a Salesman*. The play is a crude Marxist attack on the brutal capitalist "system" in America. This essay represents one extreme in the wide range of opinion among critics writing about Miller.

CLURMAN, HAROLD. "Arthur Miller," *Lies Like Truth*, pp. 64–72. New York: Grove, 1958. Reprinted in Weales, *Death of a Salesman*. Excerpts reprinted in Hurrell, *Two Tragedies*. Moralistic interpretations of *Death of a Salesman* and *All My Sons*.

COUCHMAN, GORDON W. "Arthur Miller's Tragedy of Babbitt," *Educational Theatre Journal* 7 (1955): 206–11. Reprinted in Meserve, *Merrill Studies*. On parallels between Lewis's protagonist and the Salesman.

DUSENBURG, WINIFRED L. *The Theme of Loneliness in Modern American Drama*, pp. 12–26. Gainesville, Fla.: University of Florida Press, 1960. *Death of a Salesman* illustrates a theme of loneliness since each member of Willy's family feels isolated.

EISINGER, CHESTER E. "Focus on Arthur Miller's *Death of a Salesman*: The Wrong Dreams," in David Madden, ed. *American Dreams, American Nightmares*, pp. 165–74. Carbondale: Southern Illinois University Press, 1970. Miller "romanticizes the rural-agrarian dream."

FIELD, B. S., JR. "Hamartia in *Death of a Salesman*," *Twentieth Century Literature* 18 (1972): 19–24. "Willy's crime is that he has tried to mould his sons in his own image."

FOSTER, RICHARD J. "Confusion and Tragedy: The Failure of Miller's *Sales-man*," in Hurrell, *Two Tragedies*, pp. 82–88. Analyzes Willy Loman's
 inadequate values as the vehicle for Miller's comment on contem-
porary society.

FULLER, A. HOWARD. "A Salesman is Everybody," *Fortune* 39 (May 1949):
 79–80. Reprinted in Weales, *Death of a Salesman*. The play properly
 shows the failures and strength of "the hero of American society"—
the salesman.

GASSNER, JOHN. *Form and Idea in Modern Theatre*, pp. 109–49 et passim.
New York: Dryden, 1956. *Salesman* alternates between naturalistic
and symbolic styles; though grounded in the former, it synthesizes
techniques employed by the expressionists, futurists, constructi-
vists, and surrealists of the 1920s and 1930s.

————. *The Theatre in Our Times*, pp. 342–55 et passim. New York:
Crown, 1954. Reprinted in Weales, *Death of a Salesman*. The play
concentrates on a personal destiny, not some propagandistic theory
of "social causation." Gassner's observations, here and elsewhere,
are perceptive and balanced.

GELB, PHILLIP, et al. "A Matter of Hopelessness in *Death of a Salesman*,"
Tulane Drama Review 2 (May 1958): 63–69. Reprinted in Hurrell,
Two Tragedies. Condensation of a series of radio discussions; a
complete transcript of the part of the series that involved Miller has
been published as "Morality and Modern Drama" (q.v.).

GORDON, LOIS. "*Death of a Salesman*: An Appreciation," in Warren French,
ed. *The Forties: Fiction, Drama, Poetry*, pp. 273–83. Deland, Fla.:
Everett-Edwards, 1969. The play combines psychological and social points of view.

GROFF, EDWARD. "Point of View in Modern Drama," *Modern Drama* 2
(1959): 268–82. Places *Death of a Salesman* in a subjectivist tradition in twentieth-century literature.

GROSS, BARRY EDWARD. "Peddler and Pioneer in *Death of a Salesman*,"
Modern Drama 7 (1965): 405–10. Reprinted in Meserve, *Merrill
Studies*. "One source of Willy's failure is his inability to apply the
values of his father's world to his own."

HAGOPIAN, JOHN V. "*Death of a Salesman*," *Insight I*, pp. 174–86. Frank-
furt: Hirschgraben, 1962. Reprinted in shorter form as "Arthur Miller:
The *Salesman's* Two Cases" in *Modern Drama* 6 (1963): 117–25.
Also in Meserve, *Merrill Studies*. Miller did not perceive that Biff
Loman, who "achieves the most transforming insight," is the real
protagonist.

HAYS, PETER L. "Arthur Miller and Tennessee Williams," *Essays in Literature* 4 (1977): 239–49. The influence of *The Glass Managerie* on
Death of a Salesman may be seen "in a number of parallels."

HEILMAN, ROBERT B. "Salesmen's Deaths: Documentary and Myth," *Shenandoah* 20 (Spring 1969): 20–28. On Miller's play and Eudora Welty's

first short story, "The Death of a Traveling Salesman" (1936): they are too unlike to be compared.

HUNTER, FREDERICK J. "The Value of Time in Modern Drama," *Journal of Aesthetics & Art Criticism* 16 (1958): 194–201. The play's "double time" (past and present) allows the simultaneous development of both a "lengthy story" and an intense climactic moment.

HURRELL, JOHN D., ed. *Two Modern American Tragedies: Reviews and Criticism of "Death of a Salesman" and "A Streetcar Named Desire."* New York: Scribner's, 1961. A student casebook collection reprinting two essays by Miller, eight reviews of *Salesman*, and other relevant articles.

HYNES, JOSEPH A. "'Attention Must Be Paid . . . ,'" *College English* 23 (1962): 574–78. Reprinted in Weales, *Death of a Salesman*. The play is seriously marred by three faults: the probabilities of motivation are violated, the protagonist lacks tragic self-awareness, and the social criticism is confused because of Miller's ambivalent feeling toward Willy.

INSERILLO, CHARLES R. "Wish and Desire: Two Poles of the Imagination in the Drama of Arthur Miller and T. S. Eliot," *Xavier University Studies* 1 (1962): 247–58. On the imaginative goals of Willy Loman and characters in Eliot's plays.

JACKSON, ESTHER M. "*Death of a Salesman*: Tragic Myth in the Modern Theatre," *College Language Association Journal* 7 (Sept. 1963): 63–76. Reprinted in Meserve, *Merrill Studies*. The play represents "perhaps the most nearly mature myth about human suffering in an industrial age."

JACOBSON, IRVING. "Family Dreams in *Death of a Salesman*," *American Literature* 47 (1975): 247–58. "A man's frenetic attempt to make the world a home can defeat the viability of his private home."

JAMES, STUART B. "Pastoral Dreamer in an Urban World," *University of Denver Quarterly* 1, no. 3 (1966): 45–57. "The play speaks to us of those Americans who cannot make their peace with change and who live out their lives in a starkly urban world longing backward toward an older American past."

KAZAN, ELIA. Excerpts from Kazan's notebooks for *Death of a Salesman* (untitled), in Kenneth Thorpe Rowe, *A Theater in Your Head*, pp. 44–59. New York: Funk & Wagnalls, 1960. Interesting comments that Kazan wrote preparatory to directing the original production.

KENNEDY, SIGHLE. "Who Killed the Salesman?" *Catholic World* 171 (May 1950): 110–16. Miller presents only a negative view of man's potentials.

KERNODLE, GEORGE R. "The Death of the Little Man," *Tulane Drama Review* 1 (Jan. 1956): 47–60. The play teaches that "the death of a little man is a thing of dignity and importance."

LAWRENCE, STEPHAN A. "The Right Dream in Miller's *Death of a Sales-*

man," *College English* 25 (1964): 547–49. Willy Loman's "delusion is that he thinks men can be magnificent because they love." Though impractical, this "dream" commands a certain respect.

LEASKA, MITCHELL A. "Miller," *The Voice of Tragedy*, pp. 273–78. New York: Speller, 1963. Conventional summary.

MANDER, JOHN. "Arthur Miller's *Death of a Salesman*," *The Writer and Commitment*, pp. 138–52. Philadelphia: Dufour, 1962. Willy Loman serves as an index to the "quality of life conceivable" in "modern capitalistic society."

MESERVE, WALTER, J., ed. *The Merrill Studies in "Death of a Salesman."* Columbus, Ohio: Merrill, 1972. Contains six reviews and ten longer essays, most previously published.

MIELZINER, Jo. "Designing a Play: *Death of a Salesman*," *Designing for the Theatre*. New York: Atheneum, 1965. Reprinted in Weales, *Death of a Salesman*. Mielziner's design for a fluid stage set affected the direction, performance, and rewriting.

MILES, O. THOMAS. "Three Authors in Search of a Character," *Personalist* 46 (1965): 65–72. In Huxley's *Brave New World*, Camus's *Exile and the Kingdom*, and *Death of a Salesman*, "the end result is that a human being is not certain what to believe or whom to believe."

MURRAY, EDWARD. "Arthur Miller—*Death of a Salesman, The Misfits,* and *After the Fall*," *The Cinematic Imagination*, pp. 69–85. New York: Ungar, 1972. Compares *Death of a Salesman* as a stage play with the movie version: "a theatrical approach clashes with a realistic and cinematic one—thus ensuring the failure of the film."

OBERG, ARTHUR K. "*Death of a Salesman* and Arthur Miller's Search for Style," *Criticism* 9 (1967): 303–11. Reprinted in Meserve, *Merrill Studies*. "Miller relentlessly pins down by means of New York dialect, and with a talent akin to Pinter's, the shrinkage and simplification of living made possible by cliché."

OTTEN, CHARLOTTE F. "Who Am I? A Re-investigation of Arthur Miller's *Death of a Salesman*," *Cresset* 26 (Feb. 1963): 11–13. The play explores the problem of self-knowledge.

PARKER, BRIAN. "Point of View in Arthur Miller's *Death of a Salesman*," *University of Toronto Quarterly* 35 (1966): 144–57. Reprinted in Corrigan, *Arthur Miller*. "Miller is not using expressionistic techniques in the way they are used by the German writers of the 1920's, to dramatize abstract forces in politics or economics or history. He is using the techniques solely as a means of revealing the character of Willy Loman."

PAUL, RAJINDER. "*Death of a Salesman* in India," in Meserve, *Merrill Studies*, pp. 23–27. "Of all American dramatists, modern or not, Miller is the best known in India, and his *Death of a Salesman* the most popular play."

PORTER, THOMAS E. "Acres of Diamonds: *Death of a Salesman*," *Myth and Modern American Drama*, pp. 127–52. Detroit: Wayne State University Press, 1969. "*Salesman* deals with the Horatio Alger ideal, the rags-to-riches romance of the American dream."

Ross, George. "*Death of a Salesman* in the Original," *Commentary* 11 (1951): 184–86. Reprinted in Weales, *Death of a Salesman*. The Yiddish performance reveals, through Willy Loman's speech cadences and fatherly concern, that the protagonist was conceived as a Jew.

Schneider, Daniel E. "Play of Dreams," *Theatre Arts* 33 (Oct. 1949): 18–21. Reprinted, with an additional note on *All My Sons*, as "A Modern Playwright—Study of Two Plays by Arthur Miller" in *The Psychoanalyst and the Artist*. New York: Farrar, Straus, 1950. Also in Weales, *Death of a Salesman*. A neuropsychiatrist's interesting analysis of the "Oedipal" father-son relationship.

de Schweinitz, George. "*Death of a Salesman*: A Note on Epic and Tragedy," *Western Humanities Review* 14 (1960): 91–96. Reprinted in Weales, *Death of a Salesman*. Meserve, *Merrill Studies*. The work involves traditional "structures of value" radically rearranged in a modern mode.

Shatzky, Joel. "Arthur Miller's 'Jewish' Salesman," *Studies in American Jewish Literature* 2, no. 2 (1976): 1–9. On Yiddish language and experience in the play: "Miller felt that his future lay in expressing the inhumanity of society to all Americans, not just to those who identify themselves with American Jews."

———. "The 'Reactive Image' and Miller's *Death of a Salesman*," *Players* 48 (1973): 104–10. The play illustrates a "reactive pattern" of entrapment and the struggle to escape.

Siegel, Paul N. "Willy Loman and King Lear," *College English* 17 (1956): 341–45. Parallels and differences between the two figures.

Stallknecht, Newton P. et al. "Symposium: *Death of a Salesman*," *Folio* (Indiana University) 17 (March 1952): 3–26. Four essays by faculty and students at Indiana University.

Vogel, Dan. "Willy Tyrannos," *The Three Masks of American Tragedy*, pp. 91–102. Baton Rouge: Louisiana State University Press, 1974. Willy Loman as a tragic figure in the tradition established by Aristotle and Sophocles.

Weales, Gerald, ed. *Arthur Miller: Death of a Salesman*. New York: Viking, 1967. In addition to the text of the play, this edition reprints five essays by Miller, seven reviews, thirteen critical essays, and other material.

Welland, Dennis. "*Death of a Salesman* in England," in Meserve, *Merrill Studies*, pp. 8–17. "For all the differences of opinion, Miller has become a respected and honored dramatist in England, largely because of the impact of this play."

4. Critical Books and Articles: Other Individual Plays

ATKINSON, BROOKS, et al. *New York Theatre Critics' Reviews* 5 (1944):
73–74 (*The Man Who Had All the Luck*); 8 (1947), 475–78 (*All My Sons*); 11 (1950), 154–56 (*An Enemy of the People*); 14 (1953), 383–86 (*The Crucible*); 16 (1955), 272–75 (*A View from the Bridge*); 25 (1964), 374–78 (*After the Fall*).

BAXANDELL, LEE. "Arthur Miller: Still the Innocent," *Encore* 11 (May 1964): 16–19. Reprinted in Weales, *The Crucible*. *After the Fall* does not project a coherent, socially relevant view of damnation and salvation.

BENTLEY, ERIC. "On the Waterfront," *What Is Theatre?*, pp. 98–102, 222–25. New York: Beacon, 1956. The "informer theme" is important not only in *A View from the Bridge* but also in *All My Sons* and *The Crucible*.

———. "The Innocence of Arthur Miller." *The Dramatic Event*, pp. 90–94. New York: Horizon, 1954. Reprinted in Weales, *The Crucible*. John Proctor is unreal because he has no faults, only weaknesses. All Miller's plays, indeed, are melodramatic in that their battles are fought by "the wholly guilty and the wholly innocent."

BERGERON, DAVID M. "Arthur Miller's *The Crucible* and Nathaniel Hawthorne: Some Parallels," *English Journal* 58 (1969): 47–55. This affinity study shows parallels between Miller's play and *The Scarlet Letter*, regarding setting, characters, themes, and language.

BERGMAN, HERBERT. "'The Interview of a Heart': *The Crucible* and *The Scarlet Letter*," *University College Quarterly* 15 (May 1970): 27–32. Another comparative study of themes and characters (cf. David M. Bergeron).

BIGSBY, C. W. E. "The Fall and After: Arthur Miller's Confession," *Modern Drama* 10 (1967): 124–36. A comparison of *After the Fall* with Camus's *The Fall*: "they both underline the failure of success to serve anything but the ego."

———. "What Price Arthur Miller? An Analysis of *The Price*," *Twentieth Century Literature* 16 (1970): 16–25. "*The Price* could scarcely have been written before *After the Fall* had successfully laid some of Miller's more persistent personal ghosts."

BLAU, HERBERT. "Counterforce I: The Social Drama," *The Impossible Theater*, pp. 188–92. New York: Macmillan, 1964. Reprinted in part in Corrigan, *Arthur Miller*. Ferres, *The Crucible*. Weales, *The Crucible*. "This absence of doubt [in Proctor] reduced the import of *The Crucible* for those who thought about it, while increasing the impact for those who didn't."

BOGGS, ARTHUR W. "*Oedipus* and *All My Sons*," *Personalist* 42 (1961): 555–60. Oedipus recognizes his guilt; Keller does not.

BRONSON, DAVID. "*An Enemy of the People*: A Key to Arthur Miller's Art

and Ethics," *Comparative Drama* 2 (1968): 229-47. On changes in
the Ibsen play and "Miller's recoil from complexity."

BRUSTEIN, ROBERT. "Arthur Miller's Mea Culpa," *New Republic* 150
(Feb. 8, 1964): 26-30. *After the Fall* is vulgar, dishonest, and static.

BUITENHUIS, PETER. "Arthur Miller: The Fall from the Bridge," Canadian
Association for American Studies *Bulletin* 3 (1967): 55-71. After
After the Fall: "the fortress of unrelatedness that he lay siege to down
the years since *All My Sons* still stands."

CALARCO, N. JOSEPH. "Production as Criticism: Miller's *The Crucible*,"
Educational Theatre Journal 29 (1977): 354-61. A very interesting
interpretation by a director who during his production found unsuspected structural and emotional complexities in the play.

CASTY, ALAN. "Post-Loverly Love: A Comparative Report," *Antioch Review* 26 (1966): 399-411. On "the difficulty of living with love" in
After the Fall, Bellow's *Herzog*, and Fellini's 8½.

CISMARU, ALFRED. "Before and *After the Fall*," *Forum* (University of
Houston) 11, no. 2 (1973): 67-71. Correspondences between Miller's
play and Camus's novel *The Fall*.

CLURMAN, HAROLD. "Director's Notes: *Incident at Vichy*," *Tulane Drama
Review* 9 (Summer 1965): 77-90. Reprinted in Corrigan, *Arthur
Miller*. Production notes on the plot, characterization and stage busi-
ness.

CURTIS, PENELOPE. "The Crucible," *Critical Review* (University of Syd-
ney) 8 (1965): 45-58. Reprinted in Weales, *The Crucible*. Excerpts
reprinted in Ferres, *The Crucible*. "Miller has not merely borrowed
an idiom; he has given it considerable range, using it to distinguish
different voices, different qualities of emotion, as well as to suggest the
common sources of their lives."

DOUGLASS, JAMES W. "Miller's *The Crucible*: Which Witch Is Which?" *Renascence* 15 (1963): 145-51. Excerpts reprinted in Ferres, *The Crucible*. Miller finds the Salem judges guilty of injustice, but this verdict
is unjust to the historical facts.

DWORKIN, MARTIN. "Miller and Ibsen," *Humanist* 11 (June 1951): 110-15.
A perceptive critique of Ibsen's and Miller's condemnation of majority rule in *An Enemy of the People*.

EPSTEIN, ARTHUR D. "A Look at *A View from the Bridge*," *Texas Studies
in Literature and Language* 7 (1965): 109-22. A careful reading of
the play.

EPSTEIN, LESLIE. "The Unhappiness of Arthur Miller," *Tri-Quarterly*
(Spring 1965): pp. 165-73. In *After the Fall* "Miller's desire to understand and judge himself is matched only by his desire to deceive and
forgive himself."

FENDER, STEPHEN. "Precision and Pseudo Precision in *The Crucible*," *Journal of American Studies* 1 (April 1967): 87-98. Reprinted in Weales,
The Crucible. "John Proctor acts not as a rebel but as the restorer of
what the audience takes to be normal human values."

FERRES, JOHN H., ed. *Twentieth Century Interpretations of "The Crucible"*
Englewood Cliffs, N.J.: Prentice-Hall, 1972. Contains eighteen essays and a short scene (II, 2) Miller added to his revised version.
Editor's introduction: "the play seems less concerned now with a
social condition than with a moral dilemma that continues to be part
of the human condition."

GANZ, ARTHUR. "Arthur Miller: After the Silence," *Drama Survey* 3 (1964):
520–30. In *After the Fall*, Miller "remains . . . committed to the Great
Romantic postulate that in truth to the self lies virtue."

GIANAKARIS, C. J. "Theatre of the Mind in Miller, Osborne and Shaffer,"
Renascence 30 (1977): 33–42. "In *After the Fall, Inadmissable Evidence*, and *Equus*, [the protagonists] perceive themselves as the
accused on trial for errors of their lives."

GOODE, JAMES. *The Story of "The Misfits."* Indianapolis: Bobbs-Merrill,
1963. A step-by-step, day-to-day diary about organizing and shooting
the motion picture, complete with interviews of the principals.

GORELIK, MORDECAI. "The Factor of Design," *Tulane Drama Review* 5
(March 1961): 85–94. On designing the original set of *All My Sons*:
its informing metaphor was a "New England church."

GROSS, BARRY. *"All My Sons* and the Larger Context," *Modern Drama*
18 (1975): 15–27. In this work Miller "is not guilty of presuming to
teach . . . but of not doing it with sufficient force and directness."

HANSCOM, LESLIE. "'After the Fall': Arthur Miller's Return," *Newsweek* 63
(Feb. 3, 1964): 49–52. On the play and circumstances attending its
production.

HANSEN, CHADWICK. "The Metamorphosis of Tituba, Or Why American
Intellectuals Can't Tell an Indian Witch from a Negro," *New England
Quarterly* 47 (1974): 3–12. Literary and scholarly accounts of Salem
witchcraft, including Miller's *The Crucible*, have followed a racist
bias in changing the race of Tituba from Carib Indian to Negro.

HIGGINS, DAVID. "Arthur Miller's *The Price*: The Wisdom of Solomon," in
Frank Baldanza, ed. *Itinerary 3: Criticism*, pp. 85–94. Bowling Green,
Ohio: Bowling Green University Press, 1977. An intelligent reading:
Solomon symbolizes "moderation"; the brothers, "extremism."

HILL, PHILIP G. *"The Crucible*: A Structural View," *Modern Drama* 10
(1967): 312–17. Reprinted in Ferres, *The Crucible*. "In a competent
performance" tension can be sustained; there is no anticlimax at
the end.

HUGHES, CATHARINE. *"The Crucible," Plays, Politics, and Polemics*, pp. 15–
26. New York: Drama Book, 1973. A plot summary.

JACOBSON, IRVING. "The Child as Guilty Witness," *Literature and Psychology* 24 (1974): 12–23. A competent psychological interpretation of
the short story "I Don't Need You Any More," which illuminates Miller's "family themes," especially a boy's relation to his parents.

———. "Christ, Pygmalion, and Hitler in *After the Fall*," *Essays in Literature* 2 (Aug. 1974): 12–27. Incisive analysis of three behavior pat-

terns in Quentin's consciousness: a shaper and manipulator of others (Pygmalion), a murderer (Hitler), and a martyr (Christ).

———. "The Vestigial Jews on Monte Sant' Angelo," *Studies in Short Fiction* 13 (1976): 507–12. Miller's short story shows an "adult [who] comes to feel himself at home in the larger world outside the family."

KAZAN, ELIA. "Look, There's the American Theatre," *Tulane Drama Review* 9 (Winter 1964): 61–83. Kazan, who directed *After the Fall*, admires the play, its author, and New York's Lincoln Center, where it was produced.

KOPPENHAVER, ALLEN J. "*The Fall* and After: Albert Camus and Arthur Miller," *Modern Drama* 9 (1966): 206–209. Plot and theme similarities between *The Fall* and *After the Fall*.

LEVIN, DAVID. "Salem Witchcraft in Recent Fiction and Drama," *New England Quarterly* 28 (1955): 537–46. Reprinted in Weales, *The Crucible*. In *The Crucible* Miller distorts and simplifies the historical facts; this "damages his play as 'essential' history, as moral instruction and as art."

LEWIS, ALLAN. "Arthur Miller—Return to the Self," *American Plays and Playwrights of the Contemporary Theatre*, pp. 35–52. New York: Crown, 1965. A rambling discussion, mainly on *After the Fall*.

LOUGHLIN, RICHARD L. "Tradition and Tragedy in *All My Sons*," *English Record* 14 (Feb. 1964): 23–27. This critic definitely admires this play.

LOWENTHAL, LAWRENCE D. "Arthur Miller's *Incident at Vichy*: A Sartrean Interpretation," *Modern Drama* 18 (1975): 29–41. "If Miller now seems pessimistic about Mankind, he is still optimistic about individual man."

MANN, PAUL. "Theory and Practice," *Tulane Drama Review* 9 (Winter 1961): 84–96. Mann discusses his portrayal of the father in *After the Fall*.

MARTIN, ROBERT A. "Arthur Miller's *The Crucible*: Background and Sources," *Modern Drama* 20 (1977):279–92. Miller's manipulation of historical facts makes the play "dramatically coherent."

McINTYRE, ALICE T. "Making *The Misfits* or Waiting for Monroe or Notes from Olympus," *Esquire* 45 (March 1961): 74–81. Making the movie of *The Misfits*, with Miller, Marilyn Monroe, Clark Gable, and others.

MEYER, RICHARD D. and NANCY. "'After the Fall': A View from the Director's Notebook," *Theatre* (Lincoln Center) 2 (1965): 43–73. Lengthy excerpts from and comments on Elia Kazan's notes interpreting *After the Fall*.

———. "Setting the Stage for Lincoln Center," *Theatre Arts* 48 (Jan. 1964): 12–16. Report on the exertions of the Lincoln Center Repertory Company in preparing *After the Fall* for the stage.

MILLER, JEANNE-MARIE A. "Odets, Miller, and Communism," *CLA Journal* 19 (1976): 484–93. On *The Crucible* as "veiled allegory."

MOSS, LEONARD. "Biographical and Literary Allusion in *After the Fall*,"

Educational Theatre Journal 18 (March 1966): 34–40. An account of Miller's allusions to his own experiences, to his previous works, to the Bible, and to Albert Camus's *The Fall*.

MURRAY, EDWARD. "Point of View in *After the Fall*," *CLA Journal* 10 (1966): 135–42. The play confuses objective and subjective viewpoints, which makes it "static and repetitious."

POPKIN, HENRY. "Arthur Miller out West," *Commentary* 31 (1961): 433–36. The central theme in *The Misfits* is the difficulty of communicating, a difficulty compounded by the absence of anything intelligible to communicate (the characters are mindless as well as inarticulate).

———. "Arthur Miller's 'The Crucible,'" *College English* 26 (1964): 139–46. Excerpts reprinted in Ferres, *The Crucible*. *The Crucible* "falls short as a play of ideas" because the historical parallel between witch-baiting and Red-baiting is imperfect and because Proctor is too obviously innocent.

PORTER, THOMAS E. "The Long Shadow of the Law: *The Crucible*," *Myth and Modern American Drama*, pp. 177–99. Detroit: Wayne State University Press, 1969. "The [trial] ritual fails, and the hero is isolated with his guilt."

ROTHENBERG, ALBERT, and SHAPIRO, EUGENE D. "The Defense of Psychoanalysis in Literature: *Long Day's Journey into Night* and *A View from the Bridge*," *Comparative Drama* 7 (1973):51–67. Psychological mechanisms in the two works.

STINSON, JOHN J. "Structure in *After the Fall*: The Relevance of the Maggie Episodes to the Main Themes and the Christian Symbolism," *Modern Drama* 10 (1967): 233–40. Stinson admits that he "does not really explain in artistic terms whether or not the second act of the play is good from a structural point of view."

THOMPSON, ALAN. "Professor's Debauch," *Theatre Arts* 35 (March 1951): 25–27. Miller's adaptation of *An Enemy of the People*, with its grim intolerance of tyranny, obliterates Ibsen's comic vision of social injustice.

TROWBRIDGE, CLINTON W. "Arthur Miller: Between Pathos and Tragedy," *Modern Drama* 10 (1967): 221–32. *After the Fall* is Miller's most balanced play.

WALKER, PHILIP. "Arthur Miller's 'The Crucible': Tragedy or Allegory?" *Western Speech* 20 (1956): 222–24. The play is an unsuccessful fusion of a Puritan family tragedy and a modern anti-McCarthy allegory.

WARSHOW, ROBERT. "The Liberal Conscience in 'The Crucible'" *Commentary* 15 (1953): 265–71. Reprinted in Charles Brossard, ed. *The Scene Before You*. New York: Rinehart, 1955. Robert Warshow, *The Immediate Experience*. New York: Doubleday, 1962. Corrigan, *Arthur Miller*. Corrigan, *The Crucible*. *Crucible's* liberal message is without real force because of the evasive historical disguise that covers it.

178   ARTHUR MILLER

WATTS, RICHARD, JR. "Introduction," *The Crucible*, pp. ix–xiv. New
    York: Bantam, 1959. Miller oversimplifies his moral issue: "the charac-
    ters are intended to be dramatized symbols of good and evil."
WEALES, GERALD. "All About Talk: Arthur Miller's *The Price*," *Ohio Re-
    view* 13, no. 2 (1972): 74–84. "Miller is using and questioning the
    dramatic, social, and therapeutic uses of talk."
———, ed. *Arthur Miller: The Crucible*. New York: Viking, 1971. In addi-
    tion to the text of the play, this edition reprints three essays by Miller,
    twelve reviews, eight critical articles, and other material.
WELLS, ARVIN R. "*All My Sons*," *Insight I*, pp. 165–74. Reprinted in revised
    form as "The Living and the Dead in *All My Sons*," *Modern Drama*
    7 (1964): 46–51. *All My Sons* is not a simple thesis play—it is a com-
    plex one, showing Chris's limitations and Keller's strength.
WILLETT, RALPH. "A Note on Arthur Miller's *The Price*," *Journal of Ameri-
    can Studies* 5 (1971): 307–10. Miller proposes "a postulate of ubiqui-
    tous absurdity."
WILLIS, ROBERT J. "Arthur Miller's *The Crucible*: Relevant for All Time,"
    Faculty Journal 1 (1970): 5–14. On Proctor's crisis of conscience and
    the power of evil.
YORKS, SAMUEL A. "Joe Keller and His Sons," *Western Humanities Review*
    13 (1959): 401–407. *All My Sons* realizes a conflict within the play-
    wright, a struggle between "abstract claims" and "private loyalties,"
    the latter enlisting his real, though covert, support.

5. Biographical Articles

ANON. "Arthur Miller," in Charles Moritz, ed. *Current Biography Year-
    book*, 1973, pp. 296–99. New York: Wilson, 1974. Reprinted from
    Current Biography, Feb. 1973, pp. 29–33. Supersedes *Current Biogra-
    phy*, 1947, pp. 438–40. Quotes and synthesizes various sources on
    Miller's career.
COOK, JIM. "Their Thirteenth Year Was the Most Significant," *Washington
    Post & Times Herald*, July 10, 1956, p. 24. Follows Miller through his
    entrance into college; some recollections by Miller quoted.
DEKLE, BERNARD. "Arthur Miller, Spokesman of the 'Little Man,'" *Profiles
    of Modern American Authors*, pp. 147–53. Rutland, Vt.: Tuttle,
    1969. A simplified account of Miller's career.
GOULD, JEAN. "Arthur Miller," *Modern American Playwrights*, pp. 247–
    63. New York: Dodd, Mead, 1966. Miller's life summarized.
KALVEN, HARRY, JR. "A View from the Law," *New Republic* 136 (May 27,
    1957): 8–13. A careful pro-Miller survey of the "principal legal issues"
    and precedents involved in the HUAC hearing and in the trial for
    contempt of Congress.
McCARTHY, MARY. "Naming Names: The Arthur Miller Case," *Encounter*

8 (May 1957): 23–25. Reprinted in Mary McCarthy, *On the Contrary.* New York, Farrar, 1961. Discusses the hearing and indictment; concludes that "the whole purport of such hearings is to reduce the private conscience to a niggling absurdity."

McLEAN, LYDIA. "A View from the Country: A Weekend with the Arthur Millers." *Vogue* 159 (March 15, 1972): 102–109, 114. Miller's family, neighbors, visitors.

New York Times, March 31, 1954, p. 16; Oct. 26, 1955, pp. 1, 62; Nov. 30, 1955, p. 38; Dec. 8, 1955, p. 33; June 22, 1956, p. 1; Feb. 19, 1957, p. 1; June 1, 1957, p. 1; July 20, 1957, p. 4; Aug. 8, 1958, pp. 1, 7. Key news reports on Miller's troubles with the State Department, the New York City Youth Board, and the House Un-American Activities Committee.

ROVERE, RICHARD H. "Arthur Miller's Conscience," *New Republic* 136 (June 17, 1957): 13–15. Reprinted in Richard H. Rovere, *The American Establishment.* New York: Harcourt, 1962. Harry K. Girvetz, ed. *Contemporary Moral Issues.* Belmont, California: Wadsworth, 1963. Corrigan, *The Crucible.* Examining speeches in the plays as well as statements made before the House Committee on Un-American Activities, Rovere is generally sympathetic to Miller but finds confusion both in the hearing procedures and in the author's moral attitudes.

SEAGER, ALLAN. "The Creative Agony of Arthur Miller," *Esquire* 52 (Oct. 1959): 123–26. Reprinted in *Lilliput* 46 (Jan. 1960): 30–33. Weales, *Death of a Salesman.* On Miller's writing habits and problems; quotes the playwright in this connection.

SEYMOUR, JIM. "Couples," *People* 7 (April 4, 1977): 60–62. On the doings of Miller and his wife, Inge, in Roxbury, Connecticut.

STEINBECK, JOHN. "The Trial of Arthur Miller," *Esquire* 47 (June 1957): 86. Reprinted in Girvetz, *Contemporary Moral Issues.* Steinbeck supports Miller's refusal to "name names" at the congressional hearing in 1956.

SYLVESTER, ROBERT. "Brooklyn Boy Makes Good," *Saturday Evening Post* 222 (July 16, 1949): 26–27, 97–100. Biographical sketch written after *Death of a Salesman.*

ZOLOTOW, MAURICE, *Marilyn Monroe,* pp. 260–70 et passim. New York: Bantam, 1961. Touches on Miller in connection with his courtship of and marriage to the actress; advances the intriguing thesis that, contrary to popular opinion, Monroe was the intellectual, Miller the innocent.

Index

180